WHY EVERYONE
HATES
WHITE LIBERALS

(INCLUDING WHITE LIBERALS)

WHY EVERYONE
HATES
WHITE
LIBERALS
(INCLUDING
WHITE LIBERALS)

A History

KEVIN M. SCHULTZ

The University of Chicago Press   CHICAGO AND LONDON

Publication of this book has been aided by the Meijer Foundation Publication Fund, which supports books of enduring interest in the disciplines of American political history, political science, and related areas.

The University of Chicago Press, Chicago 60637
The University of Chicago Press, Ltd., London
© 2025 by Kevin M. Schultz

Published 2025
Printed in the United States of America

34 33 32 31 30 29 28 27 26 25   1 2 3 4 5

ISBN-13: 978-0-226-82436-9 (cloth)
ISBN-13: 978-0-226-82435-2 (e-book)
DOI: https://doi.org/10.7208/chicago/9780226824352.001.0001

Library of Congress Cataloging-in-Publication Data

Names: Schultz, Kevin M., author.
Title: Why everyone hates White liberals (including White liberals) : a history / Kevin M. Schultz.
Description: Chicago : The University of Chicago Press, 2025. | Includes bibliographical references and index.
Identifiers: LCCN 2024043615 | ISBN 9780226824369 (cloth) | ISBN 9780226824352 (e-book)
Subjects: LCSH: Liberals—United States—History. | Liberalism— United States—History. | White people—Political activity—United States.
Classification: LCC JC574.2.U6 S38 2025 | DDC 320.510973—dc23/eng/20241205
LC record available at https://lccn.loc.gov/2024043615

♾ This paper meets the requirements of ANSI/NISO Z39.48-1992 (Permanence of Paper).

CONTENTS

IT'S JUST A WORD

It was an unseasonably warm February when Bill Attwood, a young journalist for the *New York Herald Tribune*, took to the streets of New York to quell a nagging query. The year was 1949 and a single word seemed to be on everyone's lips. The Second World War had ended (Attwood had been a paratrooper), the Cold War was heating up, and lots of people in America seemed to be talking about how great it was to be "liberal." The "liberal" form of government was the sweet spot between communism and fascism, a vital center. "Liberals" were defending "the American way of life," protecting the virtues of "the common man." "Liberals" were using the government to enact reforms that were improving the lives of many Americans. "Be liberal." "He's a liberal." "The liberal form of government is best." Etcetera, etcetera. The trouble was, no one seemed to know what the word *liberal* meant.

Attwood walked the streets in search of an answer.

"One sure way to have an interview start with a long awkward silence is to ask people who regularly use the word 'liberal' to explain just what they mean," he wrote a few days later.

After nineteen interviews with people who identified themselves in a variety of ways—"Republicans, Democrats, Liberals,
Progressives, Communists and non-partisans"—Attwood found
no fixed definition. He invited readers to submit their own definitions. Again, no single answer won out. For a widow living in a
cold-water tenement with ten children, a liberal was "a man who
doesn't just talk about helping people like us but does something
about it." A member of the New York Young Republican Club
suggested, "A liberal has the welfare of all the people at heart."
A man from the tony suburb of Greenwich, Connecticut, was a
bit more dismissive, saying "liberal" was just "a sweet word for an
American Socialist." So far as we know, Attwood did not ask the
man to define "socialist."

When Attwood published his lighthearted piece on Valentine's
Day 1949, he wasn't terribly surprised to locate no single answer.
Most words with such a long and contested history have no settled
meaning. Still, despite all the variety, he felt comfortable saying that,
in 1949 at least, "just about everybody thought that a liberal was a
pretty good thing to be."[1]

———————

Fast-forward sixty years. In 2009, two researchers from East Coast
universities came to the exact opposite conclusion.

James A. Stimson, a political scientist, and his onetime student
Christopher Ellis were surprised by a phenomenon they couldn't
explain: "why the American public, in the aggregate, supports 'liberal'
public policies of redistribution, intervention in the economy, and
aggressive governmental action to solve social problems, *while at the
same time* identifies with the symbols—and ideological label—that
rejects these policies." Why, in short, did Americans prefer "conservative symbols and liberal policy"? Why did Americans now refuse to
say they were liberal?[2] This was more than just another way to ask the
classic question, *What's the matter with Kansas?*—which focuses on

why working-class people in places like Kansas vote against their own economic best interest. Instead, this was a question about why people of all economic classes were so hesitant to call themselves liberal.[3]

Ellis and Stimson surveyed nearly a century's worth of polling data. They went back to when polling first began, the 1930s, a time when Franklin D. Roosevelt portrayed his New Deal as "liberal" and his opponents as "conservative." The politically savvy FDR was suggesting it was the backward-looking policies of "conservatives" that had provoked the Great Depression and that his "liberalism" was the only way forward. It worked. Roughly half of Americans surveyed from the 1930s to the early 1960s claimed to be "liberal." Then, from the mid-1960s onward, those numbers plummeted. John F. Kennedy, they wrote, "would not be the last liberal president. But he would be the last who would call himself a liberal."[4]

This was not exactly true: Lyndon B. Johnson was in fact the last president to call himself a liberal.[5] But Ellis and Stimson's point stands: since the mid-1960s, the number of Americans calling themselves liberal has been on a near perpetual decline. And as more and more Americans stopped defending liberalism, its fate grew worse and worse. One group, then another, then another, hated on liberals. First the right, then the left, then Black leaders of the civil rights movement, which provoked many Americans to narrow their ire to just "white liberals." For many Americans, liberals no longer worked on behalf of the common American. They no longer defended the rights of all people. They no longer successfully occupied the vital center between communism and fascism. Ellis and Stimson called this "a spiral in which 'liberal' not only is unpopular, but *becomes* ever more so."[6]

How did this happen? Why have so many people come to hate white liberals, including, perhaps, even white liberals themselves?

———————

This book answers that question. Tracing the hundred-year history of the white liberal in America (both in reality and as imagined), from the time Franklin Roosevelt first adopted the term to the first quarter of the twenty-first century, this book details a fraught tale of trying hard and failing over and over again, of highlights and low-lights, and of near-constant abuse by conniving actors who realized the best way to defeat liberalism in America was not to tackle it head-on but to destroy the image of its most ardent adherents, white liberals—even if the image they were abusing was largely a fiction of their own creation.

The short answer, then, as to why so many people hate white liberals is that it was an assassination. It was coldhearted, deliberate, and designed to transfer power in America. In a democracy like America's, power does not transfer with the assassination of an individual, whose party will remain in charge. Instead, to truly win power, what needs assassinating is the prevailing ideology, a philosophy of life and politics—in this case, liberalism itself. And the way many people recognized they could defeat liberalism in America was not by attacking its politics or policies, which generally remained popular, but instead to affix idiosyncratic definitions to the term, giving it meanings no self-respecting liberal would accept but from which they couldn't successfully escape. As we will see, there was wave after wave of attacks against American liberals, even often holding them accountable for the variety of reactions against liberalism. Although often done with brazen humor and denigrating mocking, seizing control of the term *liberal* was a deadly serious cultural and political project designed to win power in America. The story that unfolds in this book is how several groups of Americans, either out of frustration, or to enhance their own power, or to actually defeat American liberalism, recognized that attacking the philosophy directly wouldn't work, so instead, they mocked the people who upheld that philosophy, the white liberals. And in doing so, they weaponized the word *liberal*, altering its meaning and giving it so much baggage it became all but impossible to defend. And without defenders, American liberalism grew limp, its haters empowered.

And, in perhaps a surprising turn of events, it turns out there wasn't just a single shooter in this assassination. Instead, there were multiple gunmen, firing from different angles. The left, the right, people of color, and other minoritized groups all learned the advantage of venting their frustrations on someone called the white liberal. The fault for almost every conceivable wrong in American life could be placed on white liberals, maybe even all of modern life itself. When I began researching this book in the early 2020s, I set up a Google Alert for the phrase "white liberal." The daily hits were entirely abusive (and sometimes even self-abusive). White liberals were "the most insufferable people on the planet," wrote one right-winger.[7] A Black columnist for the *Detroit News* bluntly stated, "White liberal politicians don't see through promises made during elections."[8] A left-wing trans singer named Anjimile released a song called "Animal" with the lyrics, "Is this growing old? / Another day, another grief to hold. / And I heard blue lives matter / from a white liberal. / Piece of shit I couldn't stand at all."[9] A white liberal herself wondered "how white liberal people can find [an] alternative basis for knowing so we can stop being an impediment to the change that's necessary to save our humanity, to protect our mother the earth and the people who depend on Her."[10] White liberals were safe from no one, not even from themselves.

Perhaps, just maybe, there is something inherent in the philosophy of liberalism that has invited so many people to pile on. After all, liberalism is a philosophy premised on protecting individual freedom from those who might try to steal it (its origins derive from the Latin word *liber*, meaning "freedom") while also recognizing that some level of equality is required to ensure freedom can be broadly distributed. The battle between freedom and equality has been liberalism's central tension: How much freedom? How much equality? Liberalism doesn't give concrete answers. Sometimes liberals have appeared to be protecting rich people's property too much, downplaying calls for greater equality. Sometimes liberals have appeared to be favoring egalitarian policies like affirmative action, which challenge what people see as a fair-minded meritocracy. Perhaps because of this squishy boundary between freedom and equality liberals have traditionally favored slow change over radical change, a preference that has made them appear weak or only half invested in correcting whatever wrong supposedly needs fixing. And perhaps because those who held power have changed over time (from kings and popes to capitalists and bureaucrats), liberalism's focus has changed, making it seem that liberals lack deep roots. Compared with people who have a concrete foundation in religious faith or utopian certainty or die-hard nationalism, liberals, in their attempts to balance freedom with equality amid changing circumstances, have been led to consider all people's opinions and therefore appear indecisive, uncommitted, and unmoored. Human beings generally favor firm ground, and liberalism's great strength, which is also its weakness, has been its flexibility. There are good reasons not to like liberals, and most people who have called themselves liberals are well aware of them.

But the liberal's ability to change their mind turns out *not* to be the key to our story. More pertinent in understanding why so many people hate white liberals is that from the 1950s onward, several particularly potent political and intellectual actors realized that the best way to attack liberalism as it was defined in the 1930s and 1940s was not to debate its philosophical or political merits, which remained generally popular. Instead it was to craft an image of the white liberal as a foundationless weakling who nonetheless held tremendous power and advantages. To kill liberalism, they created an image of the white liberal and then attacked it mercilessly. The portrait of the white liberal would sometimes venture into the ridiculous, designed to stoke fear of and annoyance at, for example, the "libtards" who are supposedly destroying the country. It sometimes relied on gendered prejudices, as when enemies feminized liberals of all sexes to make them appear weak. It sometimes relied on antisemitic stereotypes, as when liberals were imagined to be "coastal elites" and "global financiers." Sometimes racism was key, as when liberals were imagined to be in bed with civil rights leaders (sometimes literally), and later, when they were deemed foolish proponents of diversity, equity, and inclusion (DEI) efforts. And it sometimes played on class prejudices, as when people portrayed liberals as elitists looking down on "average" Americans. In the 1970s, liberals were even forced to take responsibility for the supposed excesses of the 1960s, a revolt begun, ironically enough, to challenge postwar liberalism. And then more recently (and with equal irony), liberal elites have been forced to take responsibility for the corrective to those 1960s excesses, a business-friendly ethos often called neoliberalism. The politics of resentment are capacious; liberals seem guilty of everything. And—no surprise—it turns out it is much easier to form social and political solidarities (tribal identities, if you will) when you have an amorphous enemy bringing together your fractious group. Hence, the power of the white liberal for much of the twentieth and twenty-first centuries was as much their role as progenitor of ideas as their role as a specter, designed to terrorize people until they saw no option other than joining the war against them, even if the enemy of your enemy sometimes holds pretty terrible opinions.

This book describes one of the most important and understudied scapegoats in American history. We know a lot about racism and antisemitism and "white trash" and anti-Catholicism and "radical feminism" and anti-intellectualism, but not a whole lot about antiliberalism and why the hatred of white liberals is so widespread. And, as this book shows, antiliberalism has served as a specter for a long time, an agent of verbal terrorization in many different hands. The unraveling of liberalism over the second half of the twentieth century is due in no small part to the concerted effort to discredit the term *liberal* and those who most ardently believe in its premises: white liberals.

———————

At the risk of giving away my ending, the story that unfolds in these pages leads to several fascinating findings. First, it might shock some readers to realize that there is no single agreed-upon understanding of who a white liberal is. Instead, it quickly became clear as I did my research that how one defines a white liberal is really just a Rorschach test of one's own political allegiances. In today's schema, if you think white liberals are quasi communists, elitists eager to indoctrinate your children in predatory sex schemes and turn social services into mechanisms of perpetual dependency, then you're likely a conservative who respects Tucker Carlson and watches Fox News or One America News Network. If you think white liberals are mostly beards for the corporate order, too wimpy to advocate real change, NIMBYs cloaked in progressive verbiage, then you're likely a progressive who thinks Alexandria Ocasio-Cortez has some good points and David Graeber was one of America's great thinkers. If you think white liberals are fake friends who fail to show up in times of need, who use nice words but don't recognize microaggressions or the power of structural racism, then you likely sympathize with minoritized communities and may even be a civil rights activist, looking up to people like Lorraine Hansberry, James Baldwin, and Ibram X. Kendi. That these perceptions hardly have anything to do with liberals themselves is irrelevant. What is true is that how you define a white liberal says as much about you as it does about them, and maybe more. Because the white liberal has endured almost a century worth of abuse, their image has become a bucket filled with countless meanings, almost to the point of absurdity. It turns out it's a useful thing to have an amorphous enemy.

Ah, but what would white liberals say to all this? Don't they exist for real?

This question leads to yet another surprising finding: that during the past hundred years, real white liberals have in fact listened to many of these critiques and have adjusted their behaviors accordingly. This is actually quite remarkable. For all the hatred of white liberals, for all the attempts to redefine without their permission what they stand for, it's worth pondering how often the group in power has willingly given up power to accommodate a critique. But time and time again, white liberals have done just that. They take their philosophy of evolutionary change seriously. There have been many moments of introspection. On matters of foreign policy, for example, Cold War liberals were criticized for being anticommunist neocolonialist war hawks. But that critique led many liberals to change their perspective on foreign policy to the point that in the 1970s and 1980s they generally opposed most US interventions abroad. Similarly, when white liberals were deemed wishy-washy

on matters of race, they moved to the forefront in advocating affirmative action, diversity programs, and tax breaks for minority-
owned businesses. Cynics might claim that white liberals were only
making concessions to hold on to whatever power they may have
still had. But white liberals would argue that they take rational
thinking, slow adjustment, and compromise to heart, and have,
time and again, willingly given up their power to accommodate an
injustice revealed.

After all these efforts, though, these modifications haven't en-
deared them to their enemies nor remedied their public relations
problem. The word *liberal* remains sullied and "white liberal" remains a label of abuse leveled, often as a harsh joke, at your enemies
or your frenemies. That's because the white liberal has proven too
valuable as a scapegoat. People from all sides—left, right, civil rights
activists, and more—have used the image of the white liberal, fairly
or unfairly, to unify the various groups within their midsts, often
amplifying the more extreme elements and pushing them away
from the center.

And this leads to my final finding: after reviewing my research
and examining the history, the nearly inescapable conclusion is that
ultimately the country would be better off turning in another direction. Whither the white liberal. Rest in peace. They had a good run.
Now it's time to imagine a future without them.

This book thus ends with a call: it is time for Americans to stop
trying to revitalize the image of the liberal. Many have tried, all have
failed.[11] *Liberal* is, after all, just a word FDR used to market his New
Deal, as we'll see in Chapter 1. Words having meanings, of course,
and FDR heaped a lot of meaning onto it, using it to signify a shift
in the balance between freedom and equality, the use of state action
to advocate more forthrightly on behalf of the public good, and a
widespread "generosity of spirit" when pulling the levers of power.
But ever since then, others have heaped meaning onto it, too. Some
have seen it as the beginning of a slippery slope to communism, while
others have seen it as elitist and dismissive of ordinary Americans,

while still others have seen liberals as defending an indefensible bureaucracy that no longer works (if it ever did). Nearly a hundred years after FDR redefined the word, it is time to recognize that the image of the white liberal has become, at best, little more than compromising cement for a broken two-party system seemingly destined for collapse, and, at worst, a specter solely fueling its enemies. By perpetually defending something they call "the liberal tradition" (which historians have determined was a Cold War invention), liberalism's advocates have held on to a word that has run its course. And, by staying in the fight to save a debased word, liberalism's defenders have left the country's primary centrist philosophy undefended. Without anyone defending the center, the extremes have taken over. Liberalism's rhetorical demise has had consequences.

Although this is a book of history and not one of prognostication, in the conclusion I venture some possibilities for the future. One possible solution to the conundrum of having a broken centrist philosophy would be for the United States to transition to a multiparty parliamentary system whereby the poles of opinion can be marginalized to the fringes of the bell curve and the country won't need a single catchall centrist philosophy (although, as we have seen in other countries, a parliamentary system is no guarantee against polarization). But this kind of systemic change seems highly unlikely considering the deep reach (and pockets) of the two political parties in America's two-party system. Without that or any similar radical reform, Americans simply need a new way to imagine American political and cultural life, a new word to describe the country's amorphous tradition. Some have tried "progressive." Some have tried "the third way." Others have tried the "unity party." None have worked. But the efforts have merit. It's worth remembering that hardly anyone in the United States referred to themselves as a liberal before the 1930s. Nearly a hundred years later, it's time to start imagining what might come next.

But first, to the invention of a tradition, its hundred year history, and a romp through all the baggage heaped upon it in the perpetual play for power in America.

ONE

THE BIRTH OF THE WHITE LIBERAL

1932 to 1960

Franklin Delano Roosevelt was the first white liberal.

Or at least whatever one imagines when one thinks of white liberals today it wouldn't look that way without FDR, and the people who drive so many of us mad certainly wouldn't be called "liberals" without him. It was FDR who first breathed life into its modern iteration.

And we can actually say with a fair amount of certainty exactly when the term took on the meaning it would generally possess for the next century. It was summer 1932 and Roosevelt was deep into his first run for president. The country was in the throes of the Great Depression. The unemployment rate was 25 percent nationally and as high as 50 percent in industry-heavy cities like Detroit. Soup kitchens drew long lines, major cities (Minneapolis, Seattle) experienced food riots with women leading the charge, and Americans roamed the country in search of work to support their families. President Herbert Hoover understood the depth of the economic decline but, more vitally, didn't understand the way it had siphoned off the very spirit of the nation. Hoover hoped businesses and workers would make voluntary concessions to get the economy back on track after what he assumed would be a temporary blip in the economy. He

made gestures toward public works, some of which, like the Hoover
Dam, were quite large. And he engaged in a handful of regulatory
actions and even some agricultural price stabilization efforts. But
because he failed to recognize the deep structural roots of the Great
Depression, Hoover failed to imagine the role government might
play in building a modern industrial economy. To Hoover, too much
government stank of socialism, and, in an avowedly capitalist society, that was anathema. He couldn't imagine a form of capitalism
that was regulated and insured by the state in the ways necessary to
alleviate the Great Depression. What would such a concoction be
called, anyway?

Roosevelt suffered no such misgivings. The upstart Democrat
filled his 1932 presidential campaign with soaring rhetoric and promises of "a New Deal" in which a new hand of cards would be dealt
to all Americans, allowing them another chance in the game of life.
Roosevelt vowed to regulate capitalism, use the government to put
people back to work, and try to force industries to act on behalf of
the good of the country. Critics pointed out that his promises were
vague and untested. They were mostly right. But with hindsight we
know his triumph was not only in easing the economy into less perilous terrain (although it would ultimately take the Second World
War to lift the country completely out of the Great Depression) but
also in restoring hope to a faltering nation. He was making people
believe again, restocking the one ingredient required to restore the
American Dream: hope. Roosevelt's triumph was in marketing as
much as economics.

How did he do it? How did he market something that could so
easily be tagged as socialist? Proving that words matter, Roosevelt
crafted a strange mix of soaring rhetoric and ideological flexibility
premised on balancing individual freedoms with a staunch concern
for the common good, and then he called this mixture *liberalism*.

When he first used the term, it surprised nearly everyone. Just
a few months before the election, Roosevelt needed a way to describe his hopeful agenda. He knew that the word *socialism* was too

damaged, too aligned with radicalism. Socialist parties had led revolutions in Europe and promoted radical challenges in the American Midwest and the urban Northeast. Should the government take over the railroads? The banks? Should it enforce more universal price controls? As one of Roosevelt's closest advisors said, "The danger that he might be tagged 'Red' with all that follows from such a labeling, made Mr. Roosevelt cautious about stating any objective except the 'preservation of capitalism.'"[1] Roosevelt was in need of a safe term.

So, rather suddenly, in the summer of 1932, Roosevelt started calling his plan "liberalism" and himself a "liberal." This verbiage quickly became a cornerstone of every one of his stump speeches. On July 2, 1932, accepting the Democratic Party's nomination for president, he said his party "is the bearer of liberalism and of progress" and that Democrats "must be a party of liberal thought, of planned action, of enlightened international outlook, and of the greatest good to the greatest number of our citizens."[2] A month later, he told an audience in Columbus, Ohio, "The kind of confidence we most need is confidence in the integrity, the soundness, the liberalism, the vision, and the old-fashioned horse sense of our national leadership."[3] What was needed was a politics of ethical activism whereby the government used its potential might on behalf of the common good but did so without overturning the capitalistic business ethos that had catapulted the United States to global prominence. It needed a balance, he said, and that balance he called "liberalism."

Hoover didn't like it. Hoover said that FDR's New Deal was, in fact, socialism. Knowing the root of the word *liberalism* was the Latin *liber*, meaning "freedom," and that the word had had a variety of meanings over the previous few centuries, Hoover said, "the spirit of liberalism is to create free men; it is not the regimentation of men. It is not the extension of bureaucracy" as Roosevelt's New Deal promised. Hoover suggest that Roosevelt's was "a false liberalism" that interfered with business. "Every step in that direction poisons the very roots of liberalism. It poisons political equality, free speech, free press, and equality of opportunity. It is the road not to liberty but to less liberty."[4] Hoover thought FDR was taking a long-standing philosophical tradition and bending it to his own political needs. Which he was.

But Roosevelt wasn't bothered by Hoover. He generally ignored him and used the word the way he wanted. Knowing the importance of avoiding the capitalism-versus-socialism binary, Roosevelt instead spoke of the "conservative and liberal" one.[5] This binary was new in American politics, with the effect of painting the Republican Party as the upholders of conservatism, a political loser at a time when there was little worth conserving. Proposing that his liberalism was a state of mind signifying acceptance of the modern world and not a specific political platform, Roosevelt worked to recruit "liberal-minded Republicans."[6] He ensured that business and professional people had a place in his vision, telling, for instance, the Business and Professional Men's League, "You represent a liberal and understanding point of view toward the relationship of business and Government."[7] Roosevelt claimed that his "liberalism" was a capacious term promoting a plan that would save capitalism from itself.

So far as we know, Roosevelt's use of the word *liberalism* wasn't tested by advisors or stolen from another politician. He knew of others who had used the term before, and that there was a philosophical and political tradition of liberalism throughout the Western world. He had read the *New Republic*, an American journal of opinion founded in 1914 to locate "a liberalism centered in humanitarian and moral passion and one based in an ethos of scientific analysis." And he was largely sympathetic with Great Britain's Liberal Party, which was Britain's parallel to the American Progressive movement from the early 1900s. And he knew the term had been used by the business classes throughout the nineteenth and twentieth centuries, making it suitably capitalistic without being absolutely laissez-faire. But the index of Roosevelt's public papers between 1928 to 1932 shows zero references to "liberal" or "liberalism."[8] Yet by the summer of 1932, Roosevelt had begun to imagine himself, over and over again, as the "bearer of liberalism and of progress." In early 1933, he wrote a campaign book called *Looking Forward.* The cover sheet announced, "We are about to enter upon a new period of liberalism and of sane reform in the United States. . . . As President of the United States I shall do my utmost."[9]

Why "liberal" and "liberalism"? His closest advisor, Rex Tugwell, once asked Roosevelt directly. According to Tugwell, Roosevelt just shrugged "and asked if it mattered."[10] Tugwell, left to his own imagination, thought that "liberal" was a masterfully vague term of convenience. It was forward-looking, it was active, and it easily countered "conservative." Its history evoked freedom and liberty but also generosity toward the common good. As such, Roosevelt used it throughout his entire presidency. The title of Roosevelt's public papers for 1938 was *The Continuing Struggle for Liberalism.*[11] He was the first self-professed white liberal.

The word *liberal*—if not Roosevelt's exact definition of it—had a long history before 1932, but it was mostly a European history, with several distinct meanings affixed to the word over time. On American shores, Helena Rosenblatt, in what is so far the best word history of *liberalism,* located a very small number of uses of the word *liberal* around the time of the American Revolution, when it characterized the elite's civic duty ("liberality") to preserve a government by the people. Thus it sat between ragtag democracy and elitist aristocracy.[12] Then the word basically disappeared from the United States for nearly a hundred years. Latter-day historians have supposedly identified some version of what *they* call a "liberal tradition" in the United States, but they are relying on the word's contemporary meaning. And while it might make sense to say that *liberalism* as we know it existed in the United States before the word came to mean what we think it means, no one in those prior ages would have known what you were talking about if you referred to the "liberal tradition" in America.[13]

Not so in France and England. That is where "liberalism" really grew up. And as with most words with a lengthy history, *liberal* came to assume multiple meanings that sometimes sat together awkwardly. At first the word was generally understood to signify someone with a kind and magnanimous spirit. In Shakespeare's time, *liberal* was widely used as a familiar synonym for personal generosity, both material and intellectual. To be liberal in the sixteenth and seventeenth centuries was to be broad-minded, and perhaps have a liberal education—that is, an education emphasizing the development of general intellectual capacities through the study of language, literature, history, philosophy, and the theoretical sciences, in contrast to vocational study that was designed to prepare students for a particular trade or profession. By the eighteenth century, religious tolerance was added to the characterization. People might possess different spiritual values and beliefs, but this was no justification for expulsion or worse. Slowly, a liberal was someone generally open to change, sometimes even welcoming it. The revolutions in France and the United States in the late eighteenth century added to the word's meaning a belief in several individual rights, most especially in the right to a representative government. The French Revolution, in fact, witnessed the world's first self-proclaimed "liberals," with *liberal* used as a noun and not an adjective. In Paris, Germaine de Staël (or, as she was more widely known, Madame de Staël) and Benjamin Constant were principal architects of a politics premised on what they called "liberal principles."[14] Grounded in characteristics like kindness, generosity, and compassion, de Staël and Constant articulated a political philosophy premised on the rule of law and civil equality, representative constitutional government, and a number of individual rights, including freedom of press and freedom of religion. It is important to point out that de Staël and Constant were not proponents of democracy because they, like many thinkers in the time of the French Revolution, believed that expansive democracy led to mob rule—like what they were actually witnessing during France's Reign of Terror. Because the rise of Napoleon in

France killed off any political alliances surrounding their liberalism, the first liberal party formed in Sweden in 1809, challenging King Gustav IV Adolph. Spanish liberals were the first to call their party "Liberal," forming the Liberales in 1810, after Napoleon installed his brother, Joseph, as king. Madame de Staël herself gushed about a "liberal impulse" sweeping across Western Europe during the early nineteenth century.[15]

All these meanings—generosity of spirit, widespread tolerance, upholding individual rights, ensuring a say in the direction of one's life, and in having representative government to help get one there—continued to underpin the meaning of the words *liberal* and *liberalism* throughout their existence. In some places, they still do.

In the late seventeenth century, however, a key addition to their meaning set in motion a dispute that would later cause significant friction. That addition was an emphasis on the right to own property. English philosopher John Locke gets pride of place in most accounts of this expansion of the meaning of *liberalism*, although he was not the only thinker to make the claim. Locke's contribution was suggesting that, in the seventeenth and eighteenth centuries, the key to individual freedom (*liber*) was a social contract premised on the notion that everyone has a right to life, liberty, and property. A government, Locke argued, must not only not violate these rights but in fact protect them, which, he said, was the primary reason people would support any government at all. If a government allowed people to own property and then protected their right to do so, people would be invested in the success of that government. Locke thought humankind's capacity for reason justified people's freedoms and made liberal government possible in the first place, but the key to preventing too much incivility in the name of acquiring power and wealth was giving people a stake in the game. However, Locke, who is claimed today to be the key philosopher of liberalism, never once referred to anyone as a "liberal" or coined anything close to a "liberalism."[16]

Liberalism's confluence of meanings, including the addition of property rights, stayed together fairly peacefully throughout the eighteenth and nineteenth centuries, when the primary power holders in most societies were royal and religious. Liberals in France, England, Spain, and Sweden easily embraced both the "generosity of spirit" meaning of the word and the more capitalistic defense of property rights. This worked because the liberals of that era saw economic mobility and capitalist growth as a means to enlarge individual freedoms and overturn entrenched structures of power. Wanting to maximize individual freedoms, *liber*, they saw capitalism as a tool to empower people, giving them the strength to push back against possible authoritarian intrusions. Britain's Liberal Party, which formed in 1859 and was for decades led by William Gladstone, believed in the freedom of markets and minimal governmental intervention, all in the name of creating a strong middle class that could challenge the aristocracy. But Britain's Liberal Party was not solely about economic growth. It also opposed expansive imperialism, pushed for religious toleration, passed laws that set up public benefits like state-run elementary schools, and supported some rights for working people. Britain's Liberals under Gladstone used markets to challenge entrenched powers and expand individual freedom. And in doing so, liberals in Britain and throughout Europe had much luck. Royal lines fell throughout the nineteenth century, and those that managed to survive often had their powers curtailed. The Roman Catholic Church went on the defensive, too. For many nineteenth-century liberals, unleashing capitalism was a means to an end, not an end unto itself.[17]

But this balancing act did not last into the twentieth century. And what split the meaning of *liberal* was another revolution, this one perhaps even more momentous than the political revolutions of the previous century. What we today call the Industrial Revolution (from, say, 1860 to 1929) was a great expansion of goods and services that fueled much of the economic growth in the United States and throughout the world.[18] If you look at graphs of measures like gross national product, the average number of calories consumed per person, and average life expectancy, you will see a line in the shape of a hockey stick. For a long time throughout human history, these factors had not changed all that much since the agrarian revolution twelve thousand years ago, and then suddenly, markedly, beginning around 1800, they shot upward. The Industrial Revolution birthed factories and corporations. It led to the manufacture and transport of a tremendous number of goods, supplying them at cheaper prices to greater distances. It electrified the world (literally), and made it seem smaller through communication breakthroughs like the telegraph and through transportation breakthroughs like trains and airplanes. As historian H. W. Brands writes, the leaders of the Industrial Revolution "turned a society rooted in the soil into one based in cities. They lifted the standard of living of ordinary people to a plane associated, not long before in America and for decades after elsewhere, with aristocracy. They drew legions of souls from foreign countries to American shores. They established the basis for the projection of American economic and military power to the farthest corners of the planet."[19]

They also, Brands notes, "threatened to eclipse American democracy."[20]

And this is when FDR's "liberalism" emerged. Whereas at one point capitalism had been a ticket to freedom from the yoke of church and state, now large-scale capitalism had become the yoke itself. In place of kings and popes, the new power holders were people Roosevelt tagged as "economic royalists." The wealthiest businesspeople had become so wealthy during the Industrial Revolution they manipulated stock markets and controlled politicians. They used their money and influence to get laws passed that were beneficial primarily to them. To quote Brands again, "never had such a small class wielded such incommensurate power. By the [nineteenth] century's end the imperatives of capitalism mattered more . . . than the principles of democracy."[21]

In response, by the last third of the nineteenth century, European liberals began to advocate for a stronger bureaucratic state to counterbalance the titans of big business. John Stuart Mill, another commonly cited "father of liberalism," fits here. Today, scholars have a hard time deciding whether Mill was a socialist or a liberal. The truth is that he was both, something perhaps impossible to imagine today. Mill was looking for a middle ground between the radicalisms of the left (most especially the emergent communism breathed into life by Karl Marx) and the free-market right. Mill advanced a version of liberalism in which the power of the state counterbalanced the ever-increasing power of the wealthiest classes.[22]

In Britain, the generation of Liberal politicians that followed Gladstone sought to demote the importance of property acquisition as a cornerstone of freedom. Led by politicians like William Beveridge, David Lloyd George, and a young Winston Churchill, and academics like J. A. Hobson and Leonard Hobhouse, this young generation of British Liberals enacted programs like old-age insurance for all Britons (not just wage earners), developed a greater number of public works programs, and put into place poor-law reform, stricter railroad controls, broader compulsory education, and unemployment and sickness insurance. The size and dynamics of the capitalists had changed. They were now as powerful as royal and religious aristocracies, if not more so. And British Liberals changed liberalism in response.[23]

This change didn't immediately translate to the United States, at least not under the label "liberal." The American parallel to these British Liberals usually falls under the label "Progressive." And that's largely because, in the US, liberalism had some largely forgettable early moments. In 1870, for instance, the Republican Party grew divided over the political corruption tolerated by President Ulysses S. Grant and over his plans to reconstruct the nation after the Civil War. Trying to project an image that Grant was an American Napoleon, a handful of politicians, including the wildly influential Charles

Schurz, founded the Liberal Republican Party. Schurz denounced "greedy politicians" and sought to "infuse a higher moral spirit into our political life."[24] The new party did not last long, in part because of its desire to grant amnesty to all former Confederate soldiers and end Reconstruction. The Liberal Republican Party was routed at the polls in 1872 and folded shortly thereafter.[25]

Four years later, a second group of Americans also utilized the label "liberal," tapping into a completely different thread signified by the word *liberal*. This second group of American liberals responded not to growth of capitalism nor the purported loss of a generosity of spirit, but more primarily to Roman Catholicism. As Catholic immigrants came to the United States in increasing numbers throughout the nineteenth century, they reacted to Protestant hostility by creating a parallel Catholic universe, including separate hospitals, schools, and charity organizations. Thinking it was providing services to a large number of citizens, the church demanded public funds for Catholic schools. Many Americans saw this as a direct challenge to American democracy. After all, schools were supposedly training centers for democracy. To protest the Catholics, up rose an organization called the National Liberty League, which adopted "Nine Demands of Liberalism." All nine attacked the Catholic Church. But they went further. Pushing the definition of religious liberty to its extreme, the National Liberty League made itself open to atheists and freethinkers—anybody but Catholics. It created liberal clubs across the country. A town in Missouri called itself "Liberal" in 1880, signifying it as a safe space for radical religious thought. There was even a Liberal University. But the National Liberty League quickly reached its limits, in part because Catholics countered smartly. Catholics simply called them "amoral libertines." The National Liberty League did not help when its members mocked the sanctities of Christian marriage and advocated (and practiced) pre- or extramarital sex as part of their "liberal" agenda. They quickly became seen as scandalous. The term subsequently went into steep decline in the 1880s. In 1885, the National Liberty League splintered, with one faction changing its name to the American Secular Union, others leaving the movement altogether.

Perhaps because of this scandalous tarnish, members of the American parallel to Britain's Liberal Party called themselves Progressives and not liberals. Making the same critique that the growth of big business was the primary deterrent to freedom, American Progressives sought to end political corruption by enacting election reforms that ensured a fair ballot of candidates and the public enactment of laws through initiatives and referendums. They adopted the progressive income tax, mandated the democratic election of senators, and passed laws enabling women to vote. They even tried to clean up cities by democratizing garbage collection and developing settlement homes. In short, these Progressive era reformers demanded the government play a larger role in the economy, usually for better (child labor laws, female suffrage, trust busting, cleaning up cities), but sometimes for worse (eugenics, racially defined "efficiency" efforts). "Progressivism was an explosion," writes historian Michael McGerr, "a burst of energy that fired in many directions across America." It channeled "a fierce discontent" at the ill effects of industrialization.[26]

One thing most Progressives did not do is call themselves "liberals." Some Progressive intellectuals did toy with the word, mostly around the circle of Herbert Croly's *New Republic*, which tried to show solidarity with Britain's Liberals. After all, their critiques were similar. For example, in 1909, Croly published an influential Progressive era book, *The Promise of American Life*, which damningly criticized laissez-faire economics, warning, "It is the economic individualism of our existing national system which inflects the most serious damage on American individuality." Croly concluded rousingly, "In so far as the economic motive prevails, individuality is not developed, it is stifled."[27]

Croly, however, rarely used the words *liberal* or *liberalism* to describe his vision. A few Progressives did, but sparingly. In 1916, for instance, President Woodrow Wilson called himself a "Progressive" like everyone else (the election of 1912 pitted four self-proclaimed

"Progressives" against one another). To differentiate himself, in 1917 Wilson called himself, briefly, a "liberal." When Wilson went to Europe to promote his peace plan for the end of World War I, he declared that "liberalism is the only thing that can save civilization from chaos," although it was unclear what he meant.[28] A host of writers immediately questioned Wilson's use of the word *liberalism*, thinking it tipped too much toward preserving the power of big business. Journalist Harold Stearns argued in his 1919 book, *Liberalism in America*, that Wilson was too in bed with the "plutocracy" of wealthy businessmen to promote what Stearns thought was a real liberalism (Stearns's full title was *Liberalism in America: Its Origins, Its Temporary Collapse, Its Future*.)[29] Left-winger Max Eastman similarly assumed that Wilson's vague definition was out of date and overly laissez-faire, calling Wilson's vision "the temporary twilight of liberalism."[30] Also in 1919, writer Will Durant said of the confused definition of liberalism in the United States, "The very word is in bad odor . . . it has come to betoken a mild and bespectacled indecision, as of a man who dispenses radical rhetoric but cannot forget that he has some shares in Bethlehem Steel."[31]

If the political understanding of the word *liberal* remained in dispute throughout the first quarter of the twentieth century, there were similar battles going on in religious circles, where the word also carried significant meaning, historically signifying those who advocated religious tolerance. Among Protestants, the great divide of the nineteenth century occurred between those who embraced scholarly challenges to the Bible, including questions about its historical accuracy and its scientific premises, and those who trusted the Bible as literal truth. Those who favored understanding the Bible as metaphor we generally today refer to as Liberal Protestants, but in the first decades of the twentieth century, they more often understood themselves as "modernists." They did claim to adhere to what they called "liberal" beliefs about things, as when geologist Joseph LeConte tried to reconcile his Protestant faith with his scientific knowledge by admitting that, at first, he had been "orthodox of the orthodox; later, as thought germinated and grew apace, I adopted a liberal interpretation of orthodoxy; then gradually I become unorthodox; then, in deep sympathy with the most liberal movement of Christian thought."[32] English theologian William Page Roberts may have been the first to come up with the label "Liberal Protestant" when, in 1886, he argued in a sermon that "Liberal Protestantism, Liberal Christianity, is not anti-dogmatic, is not anti-theological."[33] But the phrase never took off in the United States until the middle decades of the twentieth century. Indeed, philosopher William James hinted at the word's uncertain meaning for Protestants in 1902, when he referred, dismissively, to "the advance of liberalism, so-called," within American Protestantism.[34] It was clear that in religious circles, "liberal" was an orientation toward belief, not a solidified constituency.[35]

If some Protestants were using the words *liberal* and *liberalism* to signify a new orientation toward their faith, Catholics suffered no such equivocation. In short, Catholics equated the word *liberalism* with the Antichrist. In liberalism, Catholics saw an ideology premised on extreme individualism that was destined to prioritize humankind over God. In its view, the celebration of *liber*, taken to its logical end point, mandated religious pluralism, and that meant tolerating error. To Catholic ears, the rise of liberalism meant the end of faith, and that meant the end of civil society. The Vatican even placed some of John Stuart Mill's writings on its Index of Forbidden Books. In the modernizing world, the Catholic Church saw liberalism as its biggest enemy, although its understanding of liberalism was wildly different from that of most others who used the word.[36]

Before 1932, then, liberalism carried with it several sometimes contradictory definitions in the United States. There were a great many people who viewed the word favorably, and most people appreciated its nod toward "generosity of spirit" and its forward-looking disposition, especially in the throes of the Great Depression. In the political realm, the word possessed no fixed definition in the United States, although the British Liberal Party was perhaps the closest equivalent to what Roosevelt sought to do. Indeed, FDR and his advisors were keenly aware of the British Labour Party's attempts to rebalance private property rights, the public good, and state action. It was with this backdrop that Roosevelt rebranded the term.

Roosevelt was an unlikely author of American liberalism. Born to great wealth, he was nonetheless inspired by his distant relative, President Theodore "Teddy" Roosevelt, who voiced the ethos of Progressivism throughout his presidency from 1901 to 1909. FDR's famed first Hundred Days in 1933 initiated a tidal wave of legislation that affected multiple industries (banking, housing, farming) and many Americans (young men, artists, the unemployed, the elderly). And there was more after that first Hundred Days, too. The government bureaucracy in Washington, DC, ballooned with government investment in the economy totaling something close to three-quarters of a trillion dollars in today's money. FDR put Americans to work and created a social security network and engineered the modern welfare state. He created what we today call liberal democracy, a system designed to use government power to ensure individual freedom for the maximum number of people, a goal that was admittedly always a work in progress.

Two aspects of the New Deal story are vital for us. The first is that FDR did all this while consciously saving capitalism from itself. It was not just smash-and-grab socialism with government taking over the economy, as critics' cartoons sometimes suggest. No, the New Deal was a capitalistic enterprise with a significant dose of government regulation.[37] Roosevelt passed laws that reformed the banking industry, but he did not dissolve it. He buttressed agriculture, but he did not take over farms. Some initiatives did seek to control prices and manage the distribution of goods for some industries, but they were always understood to be temporary. Mostly he just regulated capitalism. As one of the first historians of the New Deal, William Leuchtenberg, described it, the New Deal crafted "a welfare state on a capitalist foundation."[38] As one of the most recent historians of the New Deal, Jason Scott Smith, put it, New Dealers were simply "reformers who were deeply interested in fixing the problems of capitalism."[39]

To fund the endeavor, Roosevelt did raise taxes on the wealthiest Americans—into the eightieth and ninetieth percentile for some. Roosevelt called those who paid this rate "economic royalists." But he did not freeze assets nor permanently direct wealth to specific industries. It is perhaps worth pointing out that communists were not happy with the New Deal, either. They knew Roosevelt was not radical enough to enact a complete state takeover of the economy or eliminate private property. And they were right. Roosevelt recognized that unregulated capitalism would lead to its own downfall, but too much regulation would stymie economic growth. Both were threats to individual liberty. This middle ground is what he called liberalism.

Roosevelt was president for more than a decade, well into World War II. In 1940, during his unprecedent third term, Roosevelt raised taxes on the wealthy to fund a dramatic expansion of the military and, during the war, the government did declare a national emergency and take over certain price measures. But these efforts were dismantled almost as soon as the war ended in 1945. Roosevelt's final gift to the American people, the GI Bill of Rights, offered "start over" funds to returning soldiers, government-funded higher education for those who had served, and low-interest home loans. Again, the key to Roosevelt's liberalism was to provide secure foundations that would keep capitalism working while protecting it from its greediest actors. He was not mandating a Moscow apartment but guaranteeing home loans and creating suburbs.

And it worked. At least for many Americans it did. Premised on foundations laid during the Great Depression and the Second World War, from 1945 to 1965 the United States had the largest per capita middle class it has ever had. Wealth was distributed more evenly than ever before. The gross domestic product grew at a substantial clip. Subsistence was no longer a rallying cry for many, if not all, Americans.[40]

No wonder FDR's liberalism triumphed. Historians sometimes have had a tough time making sense of all the changes proposed in Roosevelt's New Deal. Some see FDR as unprincipled, having no recognizable political theory. This is not true. In fact, the New Deal makes sense as an expression of a certain kind of liberalism, balancing concern for the oppressed while keeping the system upright. It was the president's wife, Eleanor Roosevelt, who summarized the new political philosophy best when she affirmed that liberalism "rests neither on a set of dogmas nor on a blueprint, but is rather a spirit which each generation of liberals must learn to apply to the needs of its own time." She added, "The spirit itself is unchanging—a deep belief in the dignity of man and an awareness of human frailty, a faith in human reason and the power of free inquiry, a high sense of individual responsibility for oneself and one's neighbor, a conviction that the best society is a brotherhood that enables the great numbers of its members to develop their potentialities to the utmost."[41] As FDR himself put it in 1935, "The faith of a liberal is profound belief not only in the capacities of individual men and women, but also in the effectiveness of people helping each other."[42]

In 1944, President Roosevelt mused that "we should have two real parties—one liberal, and the other conservative." This in fact is how it played out. Roosevelt was so successful at setting the terms of American political debate that, for a time, both parties embraced FDR's liberalism. Even the Republican candidate in 1948, Thomas E. Dewey, and the Republican president Dwight D. Eisenhower in the 1950s accepted the basic tenets of the New Deal. As we will see, other conservatives accepted no such thing.

———

Franklin D. Roosevelt was not alone in formulating this new understanding of liberalism. A second key figure in this rebranding effort was the country's foremost philosopher, John Dewey. If Roosevelt's role was to update the politics of Constant and Gladstone for the industrial era, Dewey's was to refresh the philosophies of Locke and Mill. If Roosevelt took as his cue the Great Depression, Dewey took as his the rise of totalitarianisms around the world in the 1930s. The country's most famous philosopher—Dewey appeared on the cover of *Time* magazine in 1928—Dewey spent the 1930s writing articles like, "The Meaning of Liberalism, "The Meaning of the Term: Liberalism," "Liberalism and Equality," "Liberalism and Civil Liberties," "The Future of Liberalism," and "A Liberal Speaks Out for Liberalism." His key book of the era was called *Liberalism and Social Action* (1935), which his disciple Sidney Hook imagined would be to the twentieth century what the Communist Manifesto had been to the nineteenth, suggesting it would be the work that set the terms of the debate for the rest of the twentieth century.[43]

Dewey made the case for FDR's version of liberalism on two grounds. First, he recognized that human reason, which sits at the root of modern liberalism's belief that human beings are capable of good, had never excited allegiances as much as had things like tradition, nationality, religion, or other forms of tribal belonging. This was a well-known problem to Progressive era thinkers, and one that Dewey himself had grappled with in previous books. Dewey sought to disentangle "religiosity," a human emotion he loved, from "religion," which he felt was humanity's attempt to contain that fervor in a box that promised uniform answers. The trick for Dewey was to get liberalism to tap into people's religious spirit without requiring a religious system, a god, or a guarantee of salvation. How could liberalism—sitting beside the certainties promised by authoritarians and communists—gain enthusiastic adherents when it could promise no eternal rewards? In *Liberalism and Social Action*, Dewey reminded people of a time when liberalism was a fighting faith, one that had overthrown monarchs and popes, committed to "the liberation of individuals so that realization of their capacities may be the law of their life."[44] The goal of liberalism, he wrote, was to pledge allegiance to "a social organization that will make possible effective liberty and opportunity for personal growth in mind and spirit in all individuals."[45] The other options on display in the 1930s were premised on squelching minoritized voices and denying individual freedom for too many people. He concluded, "Vital and courageous democratic liberalism is the one force that can surely avoid" the extremes of fascism and communism.[46]

The second argument Dewey made concerned how liberalism's nondogmatic philosophy (it was a spirit, not a plan) could sustain a democratic society. Who, in short, would define where one person's freedom ends and another's begins? Here, Dewey was particularly worried that capitalists controlled too much of the economy and would lobby politicians to bend to their will. In the United States, he wrote, "power rests finally in the hands of finance capital, no matter what claims are made for the government of, by, and for all the people," adding that "the distortion and stultification of human personality by the existing pecuniary and competitive regime give the lie to the claim that the present social system is one of freedom and individualism . . . for all."[47] In Dewey's mind, in the 1910s and 1920s, capital had become too powerful and liberalism had to serve as the antidote.

Dewey was farther to the left of Roosevelt. For Dewey, the New Deal was merely "trying to save the profit system from itself."[48] And he was not wrong. Dewey urged FDR to further constrain capitalism. "We must," Dewey wrote, "see that socialized economy is the means of free individual development as the end."[49]

FDR quietly ignored him.

Dewey eventually came around to FDR's vision. Throughout the 1930s, Dewey elaborated an activist definition of liberalism that called for strong government regulation of the economy, government challenges to capitalist elites, and an embrace of mass participation in social planning. He vacillated as to how much intervention was needed, and when. But Dewey concluded, like FDR, that liberalism "came into use to denote a new spirit that grew and spread with the rise of democracy. It implied a new interest in the common man and a new sense that the common man, the representative of the great masses of human beings, had possibilities that had been kept under, that had not been allowed to develop, because of institutional and political conditions."[50]

Throughout the 1930s, then, Roosevelt and Dewey had successfully co-opted and redefined the word *liberal*. For the remainder of the twentieth century, liberalism in the United States would be understood as walking a line between too much state control and too little. It would connote an activist government that, at least in name, was eager to right the wrongs imposed by entrenched powers (kings, popes, and now industrialists) who threatened individual rights. New Deal liberals recognized the importance of workers and their unions, thereby ending much of the Progressive era radicalism. But New Deal liberals also empowered business interests, ensuring that a sufficient number of Americans had vested interest in the success of the government. The fact that they embraced a spirit and not a policy gave wide range to debate and much ammunition to their enemies.

The high tide for white liberals extended from 1935 to 1965. They battled and won two wars—one against the Great Depression, another against Hitler and Tojo and Mussolini—and were engaged in a third, against communism in the Cold War. Armies of thinkers, activists, and doers were busying themselves putting into practice lessons from the 1930s and 1940s. In the post–World War II moment, white liberals and their political philosophy reigned supreme. Large-scale government projects appeared everywhere, including major infrastructure projects like the national highway system, major public health endeavors like Medicare, major expansions of higher education like tuition subsidies for GIs, and major investments in the foundational structure of capitalism like government insurance of home loans that spurred the postwar housing boom.

A flood of articles and books celebrated what one author called "the liberal tradition in America."[51] The great economist John

Kenneth Galbraith published a book of essays from the 1950s under the title *The Liberal Hour*.[52] Arthur Schlesinger Jr., the Harvard historian and John F. Kennedy consultant, defined the predominant liberal sensibility in his 1949 book, *The Vital Center*, as advocating a centrist position between communism and fascism, between pride and corruption, between oppression and stagnation. "The non-Communist left and the non-fascist right must collaborate to keep society truly free," Schlesinger wrote.[53] Barely able to contain his optimism, Schlesinger gushed, "I am certain that history has equipped modern liberalism . . . to construct a society where men will be both free and happy."[54] A year later, literary critic Lionel Trilling reported, "In the United States at this time liberalism is not only the dominant but even the sole intellectual tradition." Trilling confidently suggested that "it is the plain fact that nowadays there are no conservative or reactionary ideas in general circulation." Those who claimed not to be liberals, Trilling wrote, were simply expressing themselves "in irritable mental gestures which seek to resemble ideas."[55] Even for a sourpuss like Trilling, liberalism was the least worst option available.[56]

But a problem lurked. FDR and Dewey had fashioned modern liberalism at a time of economic decline and authoritarian threat. What would happen if those threats disappeared? After the war, it was no longer true that, as Roosevelt had said in 1936, "those who tilled the soil no longer reaped the rewards which were their right."[57] By the 1950s, the US had the largest middle class in its history. As historian Richard Hofstadter said in 1954, "a large part of the New Deal public, the jobless, distracted and bewildered men of 1933, have in the course of the years found substantial places in society for themselves, have become home-owners, suburbanites and solid citizens."[58]

In the 1950s, then, prominent liberals recognized the dissonance between the language of New Deal liberalism and the postwar reality. To keep the momentum going, they began to imagine something called "qualitative liberalism." It was Schlesinger's phrase, first used in a 1956 article entitled, "The Future of Liberalism: The Challenge of Abundance."[59] The "quantitative liberalism" of the New Deal, he wrote, focused on the "immediate problems of subsistence and survival." That battle was basically over and was, "in the main, a brilliant success." Schlesinger advocated transitioning to something he called "qualitative liberalism," although his definition remained vague: "to better the quality of people's lives and opportunities." Despite the skimpy definition, this liberalism expanded the necessary "conditions for freedom" toward a specific vision of high quality of life, which included inexpensive or free higher education, civil rights for all Americans regardless of local controls and despite community standards, city planning that prioritized business and consumer efficiencies over the preservation of neighborhoods, and the elevation of popular culture. "In education, law, politics, and economics the assumed necessities of the past were brought into question, and a wider vision of meaningful choice was offered to more people," wrote a political scientist in 1956.[60]

Postwar liberals were expanding the definition of "basic subsistence." And it's hard to argue with their ambition. Why shouldn't the wealthiest nation the world had ever known provide its citizens with the highest quality of life possible?

The key organization making the case for "qualitative liberalism" was Americans for Democratic Action. Founded in 1947 by left-leaning, noncommunist academics, politicians, and labor leaders, including Schlesinger, Galbraith, Eleanor Roosevelt, Walter Reuther, Reinhold Niebuhr, and Hubert Humphrey, the organization advocated progressive ideas on civil rights, government spending, and high taxation on the wealthiest Americans. Early on, it was "sometimes facetiously called 'the New Deal government in exile.'"[61] Sometimes Schlesinger's optimism was met by more tempered colleagues. For instance, Niebuhr, America's most famous Protestant theologian, advocated not "qualitative liberalism" but instead a "realistic liberalism" absent all notions of "the perfectibility of man and on the idea of historical progress," which, he said, "were basic to all the political miscalculations of the Enlightenment and were the source of its errors." Accusations of liberals' supposed desires for perfectionism were a common complaint coming from liberalisms' more religious challengers. Still, Niebuhr didn't challenge liberalism's premises "because only that philosophy, stripped of its utopian errors, leaves the way to the future open."[62] Even Niebuhr bought into FDR and Dewey's premises.

But one question postwar liberals didn't bother to ponder too much concerned *whose* definition of "quality of life" should prevail. With liberal ideals reigning supreme, "qualitative liberalism" was designed to embrace diversities of opinion—and then subsume them. Black Americans should be allowed to practice liberal democracy and have access to higher education and places of work, so that they, too, could move to the suburbs and work for a pension. The idea for Chinese immigrants was to stamp out their unique cultural inheritance (which ended, evidently, in communism) in favor of English-speaking Enlightenment-valued Americanism. Qualitative liberalism was open to all who embraced it, but it put them on a broad but bound highway that limited definitions of "the good life." This limitation would turn out to be one of liberalism's biggest liabilities.

These weak spots in the postwar definition of liberalism—centered on the dual questions of how much government intervention was acceptable and whose vision of the "good life" would prevail—sometimes had comical effect. In early 1949, for example, when William Attwood went on his search for a fixed definition of "liberal," he encountered all sorts of answers, including "'Don't do as I do, but do as I say.' That quotation must have been the words of a liberal," and "A liberal is one who is so tolerant that he has outgrown all old-fashioned convictions of inherent right and wrong, good and evil." Perhaps the best response of the liberal's middling position was "A liberal is a man who is constantly and simultaneously being kicked in the teeth by the Commies and in the pants by the National Association of Manufacturers."[63]

Still, throughout the 1940s and 1950s the overwhelming sentiment toward liberalism was absolutely positive. In 1960, Charles Frankel, the renowned *New York Times* journalist, wrote a piece called "A

Liberal Is a Liberal Is a—," arguing that self-proclaiming liberals were so successful in filling the label with positive sentiment that most Americans sought to be called "liberal." As Frankel put it, "the word apparently designates an attitude of mind and an outlook on the world which relatively few Americans are willing to say unequivocally that they do not share." He added, "Presidents Hoover and Truman, President Eisenhower and Senator Lyndon Johnson, Mr. Nixon and Mr. Stevenson, the late Senator Taft and Senator Humphrey. There is not one who has not had kind words to say about 'liberalism' and who would not bridle if he were called 'anti-liberal.'" Frankel went on, "For the fact is that anyone who today identifies himself as an unmitigated opponent of liberalism can hope at best for only local or regional power in American politics. He cannot aspire to influence on the national political scene."[64]

This was all about to change.

TWO

"I SMELL THE BLOOD OF A LIBERAL"

The Buckley Playbook

In 1958, William F. Buckley Jr., the thirty-three-year-old impresario who would become the key figure in making a coherent whole out of the various strands of 1950s conservativism, wanted to publish a book that could sit at the foundation of his cobbled-together right-wing movement. Somewhat allergic to deep thinking (he once called himself a "salesman" for conservatism), Buckley did not want to spend years crafting a weighty tome only a few intellectuals would read. Indeed, he didn't want to write a book about conservatism at all. Instead—and this was his master stroke—Buckley knew that what would unify his ragtag bunch of conservatives better than anything else would be to locate an enemy they could all agree on, and then pillory it mercilessly.[1]

Scrolling through his imaginary Rolodex of potential targets, Buckley knew communists would not do. He was of course staunchly anticommunist, but so was everyone else. This was the 1950s, after all. It was not beyond contemplation that the harshest enactor of McCarthyism was not Joseph McCarthy, but instead Democratic president Harry S Truman, who was so effective at ridding the federal government of communists during the late 1940s that Joseph McCarthy had little real work to do other than toot his own horn.

No, Buckley knew he would have to stay closer to home. He wanted a domestic target he could castigate as the true power holders in America, someone who could make conservatives look like plucky upstarts being put down by a powerful elite. So he threw together a few of his canned red-meat speeches from the previous two years, bound them together with an introduction, and sent them to friends and a publisher, seeing if anyone would bite.

His longtime publisher, Henry Regnery, did not like the idea of publishing a loose collection of canned speeches, so he passed. Buckley was miffed, because, as Buckley put it, "he has been in business twelve years, and the No. 1 and No. 2 bestsellers that he published were written by me!"[2]

Thinking a celebrity endorsement might help, Buckley sent the manuscript to one of America's most famous novelists and conservatives, John Dos Passos. Buckley was a sycophant of tremendous ability (he once wrote to Dos Passos: "I spent the day with Whittaker Chambers a week or so ago, and he told me the one thing he agreed with Sartre about is that you are the finest novelist of our generation").[3] Buckley then told Dos Passos he had identified "the people who rule our world" and that it was time to assemble against them.

Who were these people? Buckley made it clear with his proposed title: "I Smell the Blood of a Liberal."[4]

With Dos Passos's guidance, the book eventually made it into publication the following year. Adhering to Dos Passos's advice about the title, namely, that "'I smell the blood of a Liberal' doesn't seem quite right—but it's in the right direction," Buckley ended up calling the book, *Up from Liberalism*, blatantly stealing (without attribution) from Booker T. Washington's classic *Up from Slavery*.[5] The implied suggestion was that 1950s liberalism as imagined by the American right equated to 1850s antebellum chattel slavery. In Buckley's eyes, the "qualitative liberalism" as articulated by the likes of Arthur Schlesinger Jr. and John Kenneth Galbraith was destined to create a federal government so strong and so rigid that it would destroy individual freedom the same way slavery had for Black people a century prior. Unless we fought back, we would all lose our freedom as enslaved Black people had, Buckley argued. Buckley's book ended up being the urtext in the formation of the conservative revolt against liberals.

As weak as the book was (biographers continue to marvel that *Up from Liberalism* stands as Buckley's fullest description of the conservative movement's goals[6]), it brought together conservatives of many stripes—libertarians who hated government, traditionalists who wanted to preserve some aspect of the past, and the young angry white men and women who believed that their country was slipping away from the foundations upon which they were reared, which basically meant their right to assume (and proclaim) that the United States was premised on the Christian faith and that the benefits of being a white American would be perpetual. Importantly, the book gave conservatism a narrative: since the rise of FDR, Americans had been betrayed by a liberal elite that was in the act of creating an all-powerful state whose end goal was equalization, which meant, in short, the US was en route to becoming communist and all that it implied—no religious faith, equal rights for minoritized people, and the loss of the ability to control one's destiny, financial and otherwise. By crafting a story that made liberals the enemy of the people, Buckley sought to awaken a conservative movement he imagined was laying inert beneath the surface, in need of an organizing principle that was more attractive than antisemitism, racism, or religious intolerance. Dos Passos, who ended up writing the book's foreword, summarized it this way: "The 'liberal' mentality which Mr. Buckley puts over a barrel in this book is . . . the ideological camouflage of the will to power of this new ruling class."[7]

Buckley found an eager audience. His biographer later called it a "milestone not only in his own political development but in that of the conservative Right."[8] Writing twenty-five years later, in the anniversary edition, Buckley asserted that "a great, indeed a massive,

change was under way in the America in the late fifties, the beginning
of an endemic disenchantment with American liberalism or, if one
is after taxonomic nicety, call it Eastern Seaboard Liberalism." Its
characteristics were, Buckley said, "smugness . . . and by the arro-
gance of its misbehavior." Let others define conservatism, he recalled
twenty-five years on. Buckley's sole aim in *Up from Liberalism* was
to identify and poke fun of an enemy called "the Liberal" and "to
show that, after all, it was merely a scarecrow, frightening away much
that should have been welcomed, and utterly useless against the
real enemy," the godless communism that liberalism was inviting to
the gates.[9]

Ever since, the American Right has been following the Buckley
playbook: coming from all its various vantage points to train its
guns on a single target called "the Liberal," all while claiming to be
a repressed minority. And it has worked. By aiming together, these
conservative groups found one another. They found unity not in a
common cause but in a common enemy.

It was not obvious that "liberals," whoever they were, would be the
collective target of conservative ire. In the 1940s, the conservative
movement in America needed something, anything, to revitalize it.
The movement was in tatters. There were lots of people, across the
political spectrum, with conservative ideas. There was strong anti-
union sentiment here and there, culminating in the Taft-Hartley
Act of 1947, which curtailed union activity and organization. Many
people had vicious or genteel racist and anti–civil rights feelings,
whose manifestations led to the widespread resistance of the early
civil rights movement. Many people feared the growth of the federal government, high taxes, and regulations on business, seeing it
as a curtailment of their freedoms. And many saw the rise of legally
enforced religious pluralism—something widespread in the wake of
the Holocaust—and felt as though the country was slipping from

its supposed Christian roots. There were numerous hardline anti-communists, too.

But advocates for these causes were scattered across the political spectrum. Historically, the Democratic Party was home to most segregationists, at least at the federal level. The Republican Party, meanwhile, was the natural home of most small-government activists because of its general resistance to government regulations on business. Both parties were avowedly anticommunist. To those on the farther flanks of right-wing thought, the Republican Party might have earned their small-government sympathies, but it, too, had acquiesced to the New Deal Order. To them, most Republicans were liberals as well. Wendell Willkie, the 1940 Republican presidential candidate, simply proposed to modify the New Deal rather than overturn it. The Republican candidate in 1948, Thomas Dewey, was more of the same. The liberal order had so much general support it seemed futile for a major national party to resist it. Conservatives felt they had nowhere to go within the conventional two-party system.

There was, then, no conservative movement to speak of during the post–World War II era, nor a single cause to rally behind. When the famous radical Saul Alinsky reviewed the political terrain in 1946, he concluded, "Time need not be wasted on Conservatives, since time itself will take care of them."[10] What the right lacked, it turned out, was a common enemy and a siege mentality.

Some on the right had tried to locate a usable opposition. Terms were floated. Predictably, "socialism" was trotted out as a term of abuse, as Roosevelt had guessed it would be. In the immediate aftermath of World War II, Republicans wasted no time in smearing their opponents not so much as "reds" or "Bolsheviks" but instead almost always as "socialists." When Republicans took control of the US Congress in 1946, many of the victorious campaigns succeeded by red-baiting their opponents. Perhaps the most famous exemplar of this tactic was young Richard Nixon, whose 1946 campaign was premised on aligning his opponent to the labor movement and then suggesting that labor was in bed with communists.

But despite many Americans' worry about a "communist menace" in the United States, most Americans were simply too far removed from the possible threat to imagine it actually invading their shores. There may have been a political move toward more collective action since the New Deal, but the suggestion that there was a whole lot of "Marxist pollution" in Washington, DC, did not pass the smell test.[11] Harry Truman and Dwight Eisenhower may not have charmed conservatives, but only the wackos on the extreme right thought they were dupes of the Soviet menace. And movements are not made by wackos alone.

Those on the right needed another term that could lure mainstream conservatives.

"Collectivism" and "collectivists" had a good run. Ayn Rand's 1943 blockbuster *The Fountainhead* targeted it, with a vague "collectivism" countering American individualism. Rand fancied herself a philosopher, but it was as a novelist that she grew to great fame. *The Fountainhead*, which Rand began writing in 1936, right in the throes of the New Deal, positioned its hero, Howard Roark, as a classic American iconoclast. Played by a strapping Gary Cooper in the 1949 movie, Roark would rather blow up his own architectural designs than have his individual genius compromised for the common good. In Rand's prose, any notion of collective thought was little more than watered-down communism (from which she fled as a young child). It is not hard to see how the "collectivism" of Rand's childhood Russia made her an ardent defender-to-the-death of American individualism: anything that compromised one's individualism was simply greasing the slippery slope to Stalin. Collectivism, she said in *The Fountainhead*, was "the god of our century," adding, "To act together. To think together. To feel together. To unite, to agree, to obey. To obey, to serve, to sacrifice. Divide and conquer first. But then—unite and rule."[12] Her point was that savvy men would use the genial ideal of collectivism not for the good of the masses but instead to hoard power. These aspirational tyrants, she said, were typically cultural critics or the intellectual elite. They used media outlets or political power to craft opinions that would control the tastes of the common person and often bend them quietly to what the elite wanted. Usually these critics were people of limited talent. Out of anger they would shackle society's true geniuses. Tearing down their betters, these self-proclaimed elites would use their fancy words to craft a narrative that hid their true motive: power for themselves despite their limited abilities. Or at least that is how Ayn Rand imagined things.

Rand tapped into important strains of American frustration. For one, there was a general sense of antielitism that has long been part of the American lexicon. For another, the country has a long tradition of celebrating individual bravado and accomplishment, from Ralph Waldo Emerson to John Wayne. The New Deal and World War II had forced the country into acceding to elites and working toward the collective good. But those endeavors were in the past. The ethos of the postwar world was to return to valorizing the individual.

Making "collectivism" the enemy almost worked. Indeed, collectivism was one target in William F. Buckley Jr.'s first book, *God and Man at Yale*, from 1951. As Buckley wrote in its opening pages, "I myself believe that the duel between Christianity and atheism is the most important in the world. I further believe that the struggle between individualism and collectivism is the same struggle reproduced on another level."[13] Instinctively, he knew the importance of locating a proper enemy. "I will proceed on the assumption that Christianity and freedom are 'good,'" he wrote, "without ever worrying that by so doing, I am being presumptuous."[14] That caveat out of the way, onward to bludgeon the enemies!

But "collectivism" as a term of opprobrium did not stick. As with most attempts to coin a phrase, it is not entirely clear why it failed, and indeed, the historical record shows Buckley using the word well into the 1950s.[15] But there is some evidence to suggest that the word became too closely aligned with Rand herself, whose most popular novel, *Atlas Shrugged*, came out in 1957. As Buckley in the latter 1950s began to cobble together his movement, he sought to ostracize those on the outer limits of conservative thought, including the followers of Rand, who, Buckley felt, were too doctrinaire, too grossly materialistic, and flatly antireligion. (The first time Rand met Buckley, she said to him, "You are too intelligent to believe in God!" A devout Catholic, he avoided her ever after.[16]) In his effort to cut out Rand, he may have felt the need to cut out "collectivism" as well.

––––––––––

Before Buckley would go on to spend the better part of the 1950s (and 1960s and 1970s and 1980s and 1990s) clamoring about the horrors of the "liberals," two men played a key role in helping him reimagine the term: Whittaker Chambers and Joseph McCarthy. Neither was quite yet intentionally "triggering the libs," but they both repositioned the term in important ways. In short, Chambers used extremist argumentation to suggest that liberalism was simply a way station on the path to communism. McCarthy, on the other hand, suggested that liberals were not at all "of the people," as Roosevelt had portrayed them, but instead were elitists who mocked everyday Americans. Both moves would be crucial in opening the door for Buckley and his ilk to slide their movement into the political mainstream.

Chambers's story is fairly well known. Born in 1901 in Philadelphia, Chambers endured a childhood of poverty before making his way to Johns Hopkins University and then on to Harvard Law School. A communist intellectual the 1920s and 1930s (he joined the Communist Party in 1925), Chambers quit his editorship of the communist journal *New Masses* in 1932 to hold a variety of New Deal posts, while also serving as a spy for the Soviet Union. For most of the 1930s, he carried in his pockets photo negatives and secret phone numbers and invisible ink, and he worked with a web of prominently placed communists to get government information to the Soviet Union. In 1938, fearing for his life (an associate had been killed) and leery of the increasingly obvious danger of the Soviet strongman Joseph Stalin (1938 was a popular year for American communists to break with the party out of fear of Stalin), Chambers left the communist underground. He became a committed Christian and began working as a journalist, mostly for *Time* magazine. He worked his way up from book reviewer to book review editor to favorite of *Time*'s founder, Henry Luce, who helped him win a number of prestigious appointments. From 1946 to 1949, Chambers served as president of the Carnegie Endowment for International Peace. His move away from communism, however, was capped by a sensational trial in 1949 and 1950, where he publicly identified several members of the Communist Party in the United States, including Alger Hiss, a prominent New Deal bureaucrat and Roosevelt partisan who was much beloved by the Washington, DC, elite. A lengthy public trial ensued, culminating in Chambers supplying damning microfilm he had once hidden in a hollowed-out pumpkin on his farm. The microfilm, sometimes known as "the pumpkin papers," proved Hiss was a liar, and thus also a communist spy.

The lesson Chambers took from the story was not that all humans are flawed, nor that greed is a powerful motive. Instead, as spelled out in his 1952 bestseller *Witness*, Chambers concluded, first, that communists were everywhere in Washington, DC, and second, that all liberals were either closeted communists or unwitting accomplices.

In Chambers's telling, the advent of the Great Depression in 1929 marked a giant uptick in the number of communists in America. Most came from good, upper-crust families with easy access to power. They became important players in the federal government, shaping policy throughout the New Deal. With their common webs of social standing, they shared information and remained in the American elite. But despite their privileged background and Ivy League status, they were not capitalists. "All the New Dealers I had known were Communists or near-Communists," Chambers wrote fantastically in *Witness*. "None of them took the New Deal seriously as an end in itself. They regarded it as an instrument for gaining their own revolutionary ends."[17] Liberalism inevitably ends in communism, he argued.

Meanwhile, these supposed communists were duping liberals into helping them out. The "drift was prevailingly toward socialism," Chambers wrote, "though the mass of those who, in part directed, in part were carried along by it, sincerely supposed they were liberals."[18] But, he continued, these liberals "could not see that what they firmly believed was liberalism added up to socialism."[19] In Chambers's telling, the times were dire, and the end was near. "The simple fact is that when I took up my little sling and aimed it at Communism [by agreeing to testify], I also hit something else," Chambers wrote. "What I hit was the forces of that great socialist revolution, which, *in the name of liberalism*, spasmodically, incompletely, somewhat formlessly, but always in the same direction, has been inching its ice cap over the nation for two decades."[20]

Chambers added several other components to his argument, too, none perhaps more damning than the accusation that liberals were elitists. He saw a dire split "between the plain men and women of the nation, and those who affected to act, think and speak for them." The liberals who imagined themselves as "the enlightened and the powerful," who claimed to be "proponents of the open mind and the common man," instead had "snapped their minds shut in a . . . psychosis, of a kind which, in an individual patient, means the simple failure of the ability to distinguish between reality and unreality."[21] In a counterpoint to Lionel Trilling, Chambers was arguing that it the liberals who were insane.

Witness stood atop the *New York Times* bestseller list for thirteen consecutive weeks. Epitomized by the giant hulking man that was Whittaker Chambers, the argument was that *real* Americans were not slim, effete liberals, who were just closeted communists anyway. They were masculine, red-meat-eating Americans who utilized the language of individuality in order to make it on their own. The feminization of liberals began about here.

Chambers's contemporary Joseph McCarthy took it from there. Emerging as a national politician right after the Chambers/Hiss trial but before the release of *Witness*, McCarthy would unsparingly push the idea that liberals were elite oppressors of the common American. Interestingly, because he was a politician, he had to be careful about hurling the grenade of *liberal* because the term still had overwhelmingly positive connotations in the 1950s.[22] His 1952 book *McCarthyism, the Fight for America*, for instance, only mentioned "liberals" or "liberalism" once, in reference to Chinese communists. His book from the previous year, *America's Retreat from Victory*, used it a handful of times but often put it in quotation marks.

McCarthy catapulted to fame with a single speech in February 1950. He had planned to speak to the Ohio County Republican Women's Club of Wheeling, West Virginia, about housing issues or the elderly. But seeing the Chambers/Hiss trial changed his mind. He gave a blistering speech about Hiss and then, in a memorable moment, pulled out a piece of paper and said it contained the names of 205 communists "still working and shaping policy in the State Department." The following day, the figure dropped to 57 names. It would continue to fluctuate. Nonetheless, the nation was stunned by the possibility there were communists in the US government, and McCarthy became the key figure in rooting out the "communist menace." He used his position as chair of the newly created Permanent Subcommittee on Investigations to attack political enemies, many of whom were liberals within the Republican Party, even including President Eisenhower himself. McCarthy's mudslinging was clearly politically motivated and built on a mound of untruth. But after the revelation about Hiss, it was unclear who could be trusted. Were all liberals closeted communists?

What is fascinating about McCarthy was not solely his reign of terror but how he used his pulpit to attack the nation's elite. Of humble Wisconsin origins himself, his diatribes had a personal feel and were almost always about how the common American had been left behind by an overly educated, coddled elite. He was plainspoken and gritty, and he used that to tap into populist fears not only about communism but also about the anxieties of those who believed the elite did not respect them. And when it came to smearing "liberals," McCarthy was careful, almost always using a qualifying adjective. In 1950, for instance, McCarthy called out the "egg-sucking phony liberals."[23] The "egg-sucking" was probably an attempted reference to the more commonly used word "egghead," which was used to signify the experts who told the ordinary people how to live. But beyond the eggheads, McCarthy used the "phony" in "phony liberals" to distinguish from the *real* liberals, who were perhaps not so bad. As a writer for the *New York Times* put it in 1960, calling someone a "phony liberal" "carried the convenient suggestion, to be sure, that all liberals were phonies. But it also left the inference open that he had nothing against genuine liberals, if he could only find any."[24]

McCarthy was not alone in using qualifying adjectives, such was the goodwill of the term *liberal* in the 1950s. Southern senators called out *"Northern* liberals." In the South, real liberals were OK, but "Northern liberals" were those out to change the Southern way of life, most especially by ending the structures of racism. President Eisenhower himself attacked *"self-styled* liberals . . . with the irresistible impulse . . . to squander money—your money."[25] In Eisenhower's use, real liberals might be fine. Still, conservative Americans were now 90 percent of the way to seeing "liberals" as practically un-American.

McCarthyism also exposed something else—postwar American liberals were generally weak when on the defensive. Certainly several self-proclaiming liberals fought back against the smears of McCarthy. And many defended FDR's appropriation of liberalism to signify the use of governmental power to ensure individual freedom for the maximum number of people and that the New Deal was a practical example of how to do that. But perhaps because 1950s liberalism was in the midst of transitioning from Roosevelt's quantitative liberalism to Schlesinger's qualitative liberalism, or perhaps because of revelations like Alger Hiss's that demonstrated that real communists had in fact hidden under the banner of liberalism, liberals themselves scattered in a million directions when they were labeled enablers of communism. Some defended communism as a nicely intentioned economic policy gone wrong. Others defended it as a matter of free speech. Some said McCarthy was correct in trying to rid the nation of communists. Some were embarrassed by their past efforts to work in left-wing groups that courted communism. Many turned on one another. In short, their good standing as patriotic Americans was put on the defensive, with liberals having to prove their loyalty in ways conservatives never did. And they were not particularly good at it. Their rationales were often too nuanced and filled with caveats. The use of qualifiers left 1950s liberals vulnerable to tagline politics. And McCarthy excelled at that kind of simple politics.

By the mid-1950s, then, Chambers and McCarthy had crafted a one-two punch in redefining "liberal" from its New Deal/World War II definition. Chambers supposedly showed how liberals were little more than the dupes of communists, and McCarthy argued that liberals were phonies who used fancy words to say nice things about the common people while secretly disdaining them. Both men feminized their opponents. Both imagined them as un-American. Perhaps there is an irony here that, just as liberalism is a temperament as much as a policy program, right-wing antiliberalism is also just a mishmash of opportunistic criticisms. To conservatives, though, *real* Americans were not effete liberals who apparently could not even defend themselves without requiring qualifying explanations.

Ironically, it would be a man who grew up in a mansion of 114 rooms who would solidify the notion that liberals were enemies of the common people. William F. Buckley Jr. would also have the most fun at the expense of liberals for the remainder of the twentieth century. Buckley's genius was not in trying to usurp the "liberal" label and return to some original meaning (other conservatives had tried that and failed) but instead in ceding the term while simultaneously redefining liberals in a certain way, in effect pigeonholing the American left as "liberals" bent on the destruction of America. He used some sound critiques of liberalism (bureaucracies were annoying, paying taxes was frustrating when the rewards were so hard to see) and combined Chambers's intellectual work (liberals want to lead you to communism) with Mc-Carthy's efforts to stir up the anxieties of the "common man" (liberals are a smug elite trying to turn you into sheep). Buckley then grafted an extreme version of New Deal politics onto them while arguing—like Ayn Rand—that liberals' true intent was to take away Americans' freedom. And Buckley did all this with a grace and elegance and vocabulary that made even many liberals question themselves.

The son of a very wealthy, very Catholic Connecticut oilman, Buckley came of age reading the work of his father's friend, the conspiratorialist Jay Alfred Nock, on something called "the remnant." In Nock's telling, the remnant was a small group within society who understood beauty and compassion and individual heroism. Everyone else had succumbed to the ethos of the dominant culture. They were sheep. At his father's urging, Buckley read Nock's lectures about how individualism had to trump community. Buckley's father hated Roosevelt, seeing him as a class traitor, a wealthy man ruining what was great about America. Buckley Sr. took particular joy when his daughter Patricia, William Jr.'s sister, took the blue ribbon in a horse-riding competition but did not salute the guest of honor, President Franklin D. Roosevelt.

While coming of age, young Bill Buckley knew he wanted to become a right-wing partisan, but he was not sure how. His father wanted him to become part of the intellectual elite, to get a doctorate and profess knowledge. Buckley was not interested. He saw academia's limited reach. Great books take time to have their ideas seep into culture and are usually only read by a handful of people. As Buckley put it when pressured to pursue a higher academic degree, "I *know* what I think. The question is whether this [degree] will be helpful to me as a salesman."[26] He knew he wanted to oppose Roosevelt's internationalism and his welfare state, but Buckley did not think academic life was the best route. Buckley became a popular writer instead and used his writing to champion the cause of right-wing conservatism.

In his first book, *God and Man and Yale* (1951), Buckley took for granted what conservatism stood for, simplifying it to the two Cs: Capitalism and Christianity. He tried to show how professors at Yale, his alma mater, taught the New Deal and steered young people away from free-market capitalism. Contrary to what their (mostly wealthy) parents believed, Yale was teaching liberal economics and religious tolerance. After quoting Nock in the final chapter, Buckley concluded by pleading alumni not to give money to Yale: "If the majority of Yale graduates believe in spiritual values and in individualism, they cannot contribute to Yale so long as she continues in whole or in part to foster contrary values." But alumni "who believe atheism and socialism to be values superior to religion and capitalism" could rest easy and give abundantly.[27]

It was clear that dualistic thinking was a part of Buckley's modus operandi. Buckley went on to coauthor a book defending McCarthyism (while carefully dismissing McCarthy himself) before beginning one of his most enduring ventures, the creation of *National Review*, a magazine that served as the flagship outlet for conservative thought until the advent of Fox News in 1996. And, because of the way it conditioned the discourse used by the conservative elite, it was *National Review* that helped redefine "the liberal" in the American conservative imagination.

From his very first fundraising letters in the mid-1950s, Buckley's intentions were clear: in his telling, liberals owned what he called "the thought-industry"—what we today might call "the mainstream media," as well as the professoriate and the influential political and cultural magazines. He often referred to the "sorry situation of today where the liberal appears to have a monopoly on sophisticated information, while the conservative so often appears as a rather inarticulate fellow with a heavy chip on his shoulder."[28] The mainstream media had become "breeding grounds of little state lovers who see the beginning of civilization as starting in 1933," the year of the New

Deal.[29] Buckley was direct when he said he was trying to prevent "another generation of Liberal indoctrination."[30]

He wanted to start a journal of contrary opinion, one that would legitimate conservative thought, one that would reach an intellectual elite but not be too highfalutin to be impenetrable to a broader audience. Buckley wanted to attack New Deal liberalism for, in his mind, making nice with the Soviet Union and creating an atmosphere wherein high taxes and government regulations were the norm. In his telling, "Liberals" sought to replace the "free market-place" with "social engineers" who were eager to give away entrepreneurs' hard-earned money.[31] And their confidence made him sick: "Although there is marked smugness among the Liberals today, a smugness born of their conviction that they have met and vanquished the opposition once and for all, they are still more or less poised to go to work against the remnant."[32]

The original mission statement of *National Review*, which has become a classic document in modern conservative thought and is still quoted frequently, minced no words. *National Review*, Buckley wrote, "stands athwart history, yelling Stop, at a time when no one is inclined to do so, or to have much patience with those who so urge it." And what was it trying to Stop? Liberals. As Buckley put it, "energetic social innovators, plugging their grand designs, succeeded over the year in capturing the liberal intellectual imagination. And since ideas rule the world, the ideologues, having won over the intellectual class, simply walked in and started to run things."[33]

And this "Liberal Establishment" (another of Buckley's coinages) was threatening the very premise of American democracy. "Instead of covetously consolidating its premises" of Christianity and capitalism, "the United States seems tormented by . . . the relationship of the state to the individual, of the individual to his neighbor, so clearly enunciated in the enabling documents of our Republic." Liberals had departed from the country's founding principles, he contended. This left conservatives like himself in quandary. "Radical conservatives in this country have an interesting time of it," Buckley wrote, "for when they are not being suppressed or mutilated by the Liberals, they are being ignored or humiliated by a great many of those of the well-fed Right." He proposed with *National Review* to create "a responsible dissent from the Liberal orthodoxy."[34]

"We begin publishing, then," he concluded his mission statement, "with . . . a despair of the intransigence of the Liberals, who run this country."[35] Buckley's assault, the founding assault of the modern American conservative movement, was against a group he always called "the Liberals." His despair was tempered with a kind of grudging respect, though: he always capitalized the *L* in "Liberal." But the capital also served another, perhaps more important purpose: it set "the Liberals" apart, as a unified group with a plot against America.

———————

Buckley beat the drum against "the Liberals" throughout the 1950s, making *National Review* the central location of respectable conservatism in America. He gracefully culled the antisemites, the lovers of Ayn Rand, and the conspiratorial anticommunist John Birchers from the right (at least for a while), while keeping the conservative movement going through a steady attack on "the Liberal Establishment."[36] *National Review* featured a weekly column tearing apart the liberal media. In a 1957 television interview with Mike Wallace, Wallace asked Buckley if he would ever become a revolutionary. Buckley answered: "I am already a revolutionary against the present liberal order." He wanted to overturn "the revised view of society pretty well brought on by FDR."[37]

It would take a few years before *National Review* became financially stable, and its finances were almost always buttressed by income generated from Buckley's speeches. It was out of these speeches that Buckley crafted *Up from Liberalism* in 1959. The first thing that becomes apparent in *Up from Liberalism* is that a book supposedly defining the tenets of conservatism devotes 217 of its 229 pages not

to conservatives but to taking down liberals. Buckley coyly defined
them in ways that few self-proclaiming liberals would recognize:

> They are men and women who tend to believe that the human being
> is perfectible and social progress predictable, and that the instrument
> for effecting the two is reason; that truths are transitory and empir-
> ically determined; that equality is desirable and attainable through
> the action of state power; that social and individual differences, if
> they are not rational, are objectionable, and should be scientifically
> eliminated; that all people and societies should strive to organize
> themselves upon a rationalist and scientific paradigm.[38]

Although there are certain aspects of this definition that 1950s
liberals would claim, the kernels of truth devolve into overstate-
ment (perfectibility? transitory truths?). Buckley went on to name
some liberals, too: Eleanor Roosevelt, Arthur Schlesinger Jr., Joseph
L. Rauh, James Wechsler, Richard Rovere, Edward R. Murrow,
Chester Bowles, Hubert Humphrey, Adlai Stevenson. All these
people were certainly on the political left in the 1950s, but it is
unlikely any of them would have agreed with Buckley's definition
of liberalism.

That was not the point, however. Chapter after chapter in *Up from
Liberalism* tells stories that would have irritated conservative Americans into action—about professors supposedly teaching socialism
to tuition-paying students, about newscasters not taking both sides
of a story, about an elite putting forward a policy or program that
ignored the people on the ground. "The Liberals" were smug and
self-righteous. They were against us. They were running the country
headlong into a dreary "age of modulation." And when one protested
their assumptions, one "runs the gravest risk of triggering the liberal
mania; and then before you know it, the ideologist of openminded-
ness and toleration is hurtling toward you, lance cocked."[39] Conservatives, beware the wrath of "the Liberal." A certain siege politics was
part of the conservative revitalization from the beginning.

Beyond simply sounding the alarm against "Liberals," Buckley did perform some intellectual work in the book. For instance, he posited a useful critique that liberals lionized democracy too much. Popular democracy, Buckley argued, did not necessarily bring about good governance. Buckley also accused liberals of using federal power to overturn local control, even when local control might appear to outsiders to be retrograde while making sense at the micro level. And he even, in the book's final twelve pages, tried to craft a vision of conservatism. But he found himself cornered. He wanted to celebrate free-market capitalism, but he could not lionize it too much for fear that capitalism's radical results would upset true conservatives who wanted to conserve an older way of communal life. In the end he was forced to admit that "conservatives are bound together for the most part by negative response to liberalism."[40]

So there it was: from the beginning, modern American conservatism was bound together not by any forward-looking vision but instead by a collective opposition to something called "liberalism," a word whose definition was, in the conservative imagination, not written by FDR but instead by William F. Buckley Jr. Knowing the strength of oppositional politics, that was the drum Buckley beat for the remainder of his life. It would change the world.

———————————

With Buckley's prodding, then, by the early 1960s "liberals" had become the archenemy of the newly animated conservative movement. Countering the image put forward by FDR, John Dewey, and Arthur Schlesinger Jr., liberalism in the conservative imagination came to represent radical socialized government, which would always eventually lead to communism. It perpetuated a tyranny of the elite, which, in their telling, silenced the common man. It controlled the outlets of information, which meant that truth had to be located elsewhere and that so-called experts could not be trusted. It stood for loose, not fixed, principles, which meant liberals advocated change at the cost of tradition. And it stood for federal control over local control. These would be the talking points of the right for the next seventy-five years.

At the same time conservatives were giving liberalism this counterdefinition, they were also redefining liberals as a feminized, overly intellectual pompous elite. Liberals were supposedly indecisive and self-serving, but often in ways that would eventually protect their power. A liberal in the conservative imagination wore professorial glasses, did no hard labor, and allowed their ideals to distract them from reality. They were women from the do-gooder society who knew (by implication) nothing of global politics or Keynesian economics. They would be pitied if they weren't perpetuating a plan to destroy America.

And the spread of these right-wing counterdefinitions occurred quickly. A year after *Up from Liberalism*, the conservative standard-bearer Barry Goldwater centered antiliberalism in his manifesto, *The Conscience of a Conservative*. On the very first page, Goldwater argued that "America is fundamentally a Conservative nation. The preponderant judgement of the American people, especially of the young people, is that the radical, or Liberal, approach has not worked and is not working."[41] By equating "Liberal" with "radical" he was following the slippery-slope tradition provided by Chambers and Buckley. Goldwater similarly warned that, despite the widespread conservatism of the American people, "the radical ideas that were promoted by the New and Fair Deals under the guise of Liberalism still dominate the councils of our national government." During Goldwater's presidential run in 1964, Goldwater's press secretary even handed out gold pins to reporters that read "Eastern Liberal Press." The stunt may have been designed to ensure fairer coverage by reminding the reporters that they, too, had a position on the issues and needed to put their own opinions in check. More likely, though, the stunt was designed to make Goldwater's supporters laugh at the buffoonery of the liberal elite and respect the gall of someone who was willing to poke them in the ribs. It was classic us-versus-them politics.

The politics of antiliberalism began to appear in other conservative venues in the early 1960s as well. Conservative activist Phyllis Schlafly's breakout book of 1964, *A Choice Not an Echo*, attacked the Republican Party for doing little more than echoing the Democratic agenda, accusing them of "liberal me-tooism."[42] Conservative evangelical leader Billy James Hargis began to expand evangelicals' understanding of "liberal" in the early 1960s, transitioning it from having just a theological meaning to having a more expansive definition: it was John F. Kennedy and his "liberal associates" who were spending so much on welfare programs that they were making the United States ripe for a communist takeover, he said in one speech.[43] In 1965, Hargis wrote an entire book called *Distortion by Design: The Story of America's Liberal Press*.[44] As we'll see in later chapters, both Schlafly and the religious right would develop these critiques more completely in the 1970s and 1980s, but the reimagining of conservativism's bogeyman began early.

There were several ironies in the right-wing attack. For one, conservatives' claim to speak for the common American often emanated from a group of wealthy Ivy League–educated elites. Buckley had gone to Yale. Goldwater's family owned a department store. Schlafly had married into a wealthy St. Louis family. These backgrounds were hardly "common." For another, even though conservatives claimed to be defenders of an unchanging "truth," they had few qualms about massaging the truth to fit their own ends.

But perhaps the greatest irony of all was that conservatives were making the argument that liberalism nurtured authoritarian communism during a period of unbelievable economic growth. From 1945 to 1970, the gross national product grew at an average annual rate of 3.9 percent. The average American commanded 50 percent more real income at the end of the period than at the beginning. More interestingly, this postwar rise in income meant that the mass of Americans could, for the first time, enjoy discretionary income and have great control over the direction of their lives. That conservatives could slowly begin to win turf in this period based on an argument premised on the threat of liberalism testifies to the importance of crafting narratives and shifting the meaning of words. It also suggests that other factors were at play. The areas where these arguments spread fastest, especially as the 1950s proceeded into the 1960s, were the Sunbelt and the suburbs, consciously white Christian areas that were intentionally so (and, adding to the list of ironies, were areas that had grown quickly as a direct consequence of all manner of government intervention, including the GI Bill, the placement of defense industries, and the development of the federal highway system). Despite these ironies, the threat of "big government" spoke to many Americans' fears of intervention both in the economy and in social matters. Using a new and open-ended definition of threatening "liberalism" allowed for a big tent of opposition, no matter how good the economy nor how much your side might be winning. There was always something to be angry about and only one place to put the blame.

One final irony: at the same time conservatives were redefining liberals as radicals advocating socialism, self-proclaimed liberals such as Arthur Schlesinger Jr., Adlai Stevenson, and Joseph Rauh were, more often than not, perhaps the harshest anticommunists of all, leaving the progressive left in America wildly adrift. The progressive left, then and now, saw postwar liberals as irreparably conservative, in bed with corporate capitalism and eager to fight far-off imperial adventures against communism. And it was this left-behind left that would have the next go at American liberals. And they, too, would redefine the word *liberal* to their liking.

THREE

"PLEASE DON'T EVER CALL ME A LIBERAL"

The Left against Liberalism

I cheered when Humphrey was chosen,
My faith in the system restored.
I'm glad the commies were thrown out
Of the AFL-CIO board.
I love Puerto Ricans and Negros
As long as they don't move next door.
So love me, love me, love me, I'm a liberal.

PHIL OCHS, "Love Me, I'm a Liberal" (1966)

In early 1963, *Playboy* magazine published the transcript of a raucous debate between William F. Buckley Jr., and the novelist and left-wing intellectual Norman Mailer. The title when it appeared in print must have seemed obvious to *Playboy*'s silk-robed, pipe-smoking publisher, Hugh Hefner. To Hefner, Buckley versus Mailer was nothing short of "The Conservative versus the Liberal," two young guns, both in their thirties, debating the future of America from the right and the left.[1]

But Hefner, so often prescient at recognizing the tenor of certain components of the American population, had missed major rumblings within the American left. When Mailer saw the title, he was furious. For Hefner had failed to understand that, by the early

1960s, Americans on the left had developed considerable disdain for those they labeled "liberals." Indeed, beginning in the 1950s and lasting throughout the 1960s, the American left not only defined itself in opposition to the right—which it deemed ignorant and retrograde because of McCarthyism, Goldwater, and white Southern racial oppression—but also and perhaps more important in opposition to those they saw as middle-of-the-road "liberals." Just like their counterparts on the right, the left began the post–World War II era by articulating clear critiques of postwar liberalism only to recognize the rhetorical utility of a broader critique against liberals by the mid- to late 1960s. Rather than being the gateway to socialism (as the right understood liberals), leftists like Mailer felt that postwar liberalism had embraced corporate capitalism at the expense of small-business owners and individual capitalistic pioneers. Rather than spending the taxpayer's dollar too freely, leftists argued that fears imposed by the Cold War had hemmed in social and political boundaries, signifying an end to the expansions of the New Deal state. Instead of bringing about unjustified leveling, leftists argued that postwar liberals' political calculations had limited their ability to push for egalitarian things like civil rights and greater income equality. Postwar liberals in the left-wing imagination were problem solvers, not dreamers, bureaucrats, not people of action. So afraid of being labeled a communist, postwar liberals had, according to their peers on the left, created a culture that rebuffed any kind of artistic or political voice that threatened the status quo. Instead of quelling totalitarianism, liberalism was verging on becoming what it most feared—an all-encompassing, authoritarian way of being that squelched all opposition.[2] Historically, the US was at its most progressive when liberals and leftists found common cause. Now, wrote Norman Mailer in 1959, "the shits are killing us," forever memorializing the dreary sentiment of radical revolt against what it saw as the liberal malaise.[3]

In response to Hugh Hefner's title, Mailer fired off one of the all-time great letters to the editor. "I wish you hadn't billed the debate between William Buckley and myself as a meeting between a conservative and a liberal," he wrote. "I don't care if people call me a radical, a rebel, a red, a revolutionary, an outsider, an outlaw, a Bolshevik, an anarchist, a nihilist or even a left conservative, but please don't ever call me a liberal."[4]

———————

By the 1960s, then, leftists, too, disdained liberals, but with a completely different understanding of what liberals and liberalism stood for. If the right saw liberals as dupes of communists and useful cannon fodder in bringing together their insurgent movement, the left saw them as bland moderates working in the service of corporate capitalism, people eager to retain safety and security and the status quo, reformers at best but reformers who acted only to stave off bona fide change. To those on the left, liberal freedom came to mean mostly just the freedom to purchase. It had little to do with spiritual soaring, authentic joy, or egalitarian politics.

Mailer was nowhere near as central as Buckley in bringing together a movement on the left. No one was. But his critique of liberals reflected the tone for much of the left's postwar rebellion against liberalism. He, like many, began with plausible critiques against New Deal liberalism as being overly bureaucratized and premised on rational thought and slow change when people were anything but rational and change in the twentieth century happened quickly. But that critique evolved over the 1950s and early 1960s into a more open-ended understanding of American liberalism as the foundation of the corporate rat race, vanquishing its opposition (socialism) so badly that it all but ceased to exist as a political option in America. Labor unions, once the vanguard of the left, were toothless, now simply a weak subset of what leftist sociologist C. Wright Mills called "the power elite." (Those on the left conveniently ignored the fact that unions were toothless largely because of the 1947 Taft-Hartley Act, against which self-proclaiming liberals fought mightily.) As put forward by artists as varied as Jackson Pollock and Andy Warhol, even the artistic scene had been bought off by Madison Avenue or exorcised by Joseph McCarthy and the House Unamerican Activities Committee. Liberals had even outlawed the American Communist Party. As Mailer said in his 1962 debate with Buckley, postwar American liberalism had created "a deterioration of desire, an apathy about the future, a detestation of the present, an amnesia of the past. Its forms are many, its flavor is unforgettable: it is the disease which destroys flavor."[5]

By the 1960s, most people on the left imagined liberals as little more than tinkerers, pretty happy with how things were going, unwilling to sacrifice security to address major inequalities. They blamed the double whammy of the good postwar economy and the red-baiting of McCarthyism for the fact that liberalism had seemed to sever ties with its radical left-wing fringe, thus cutting off its radical ballast. Liberals were now no longer pushing for things like national health insurance or the end of racial segregation (at least not fervently). Instead, they had embraced a consumerist individualism that was more akin to historic conservatism.

To those on the left, the liberal order had grown so bad in postwar America that what leftists would seek in the 1950s and 1960s was, as Mailer put it, "nothing less than making a revolution in the consciousness of our time."[6] The beatniks, or Beats, would yearn for something they called "the New Vision." The radical student organization Students for a Democratic Society (SDS) would seek "participatory democracy." Whatever it was called, it was a turn against what those on the left saw as the hallmarks of postwar American liberalism: slow change, rationalized progress, security. Much like their mirror image on the right, the postwar left was a scattershot group filled with a variety of goals that changed depending on whom you asked. But throughout the 1950s and 1960s, the left increasingly defined itself in opposition to the liberal order. And the utility of that critique would, by the end of the 1960s, lead the left to fashion an image of the liberal with which no self-respecting liberal would agree. But that didn't matter. What was important was justifying their own critique of America.

The postwar left's topography of American political thought was laid out earliest by Saul Alinsky, the Chicago-based community activist and latter-day political theorist. In the immediate postwar days, Alinsky began to see a widening gap between himself on the left and those in the center of American political life, whom he saw as drifting rightward. The turf was no longer simply small-government conservatives on the right versus FDR liberals on the left. Instead, he now saw three parts. He saw conservatives on the right versus liberals in the middle versus radicals on the left, and he sided with the radicals.

Alinsky developed his topography in his 1946 book *Reveille for Radicals.* "A Conservative wishes to conserve the status quo, Liberals ask for change and Radicals fight for change," he wrote in the book's opening pages.[7] According to Alinsky, the conservative vision was close to dead in 1946, so it did not merit much attention. The real fight was between "the Radical" and "the Liberal." Alinsky did not name names, so it is hard to know exactly whom he was imagining when he pilloried "the Liberal." But he spared no punches in calling them elitists. And inauthentic. And talking a good game but being unwilling to shed blood. In words that would become thematic for those on the political left, Alinsky wrote, "Liberals like people with their head. Radicals like people with both their head and their *heart.* Liberals talk passionately of the rights of minority groups; protest against the poll tax, against lynching, against segregation, against anti-Semitism, and against all other inhuman practices of humanity. However, when these same Liberals emerge from their meetings, rallies, and passage of resolutions and find themselves seated next to a Negro in a public conveyance they instinctively shrink back slightly." Liberals, he concluded, had "radical minds and conservative hearts."[8]

To Alinsky, the distinction was partly stylistic. In his telling, "Liberals" were worried about respectability. They were concerned about security and preserving the status quo, and they were also concerned about appearing too far left that they might be accused of being communists. McCarthyism had taken a toll. Centrists were fearful of losing what had been gained since the Great Depression (modest wealth, carefully guarded security), so they refused to put any of it on the line to extend the bounty to others, even though they knew it was the right thing to do.

To Alinsky, what was tragic was that this moderation-out-of-fear had severed a key alliance between the left and moderates. Now "Liberals" (notably again honored with a capital L) rationalized away anything that might cost them much. Alinsky hated that they "lay claim to the precious quality of impartiality, of cold objectivity, and to a sense of mystical impartial justice which enables them to view both sides of an issue." And because there are at least two sides to every issue, "Liberals are hesitant to act. Their opinions are studded with 'but on the other hand.' Caught on the horns of this dilemma they are paralyzed into immobility. They become utterly incapable of action. They discuss and discuss and end in disgust," he ended in disgust.[9]

Alinsky concluded his taxonomy with a collection of fantastically dismissive one-liners: "the difference between a Liberal and a Radical is that the Liberal is one who walks out of the room when the argument turns into a fight."[10] He quoted the "old description" that "a Liberal is one who puts his foot down firmly on thin air."[11] And he pointed out that "Liberals" are ultimately afraid of what it takes to make change: power. "Every issue involving power and its use has always carried in its way the Liberal backwash of agreeing with the objective but disagreeing with the tactics," he wrote.[12]

What is surprising about Alinsky's 1946 book is that the people then claiming the mantle of liberalism—the recently deceased Franklin D. Roosevelt, for instance, or Henry Wallace—had just battled the Great Depression and won the Second World War by connecting individualist freedoms to social responsibilities. These were not exactly people hiding from Adolf Hitler or shirking experimental solutions to large-scale problems. Still, to Alinsky, in the immediate postwar era these men and women of action had recoiled at the dangers of totalitarianism and had begun to think the cost of continued courage was too great. In the aftermath of Hitler, "Liberals" had grown content to have saved the system, even if it meant leaving some Americans behind—Black people, women, the poor. "Radicals," as Alinsky understood them, were more eager to toss out the system or reconstruct it significantly in an effort to build a more egalitarian one.

He may have been on to something. As Alinsky was writing *Reveille for Radicals*, the Democrats, led by Roosevelt, were demoting Henry Wallace as too radical in favor of the far more moderate Harry S Truman. By the time Alinsky's book came out, Roosevelt was dead, Vice President Truman had become president, and Wallace had been fired as secretary of commerce, going on to leave the liberals and the Democratic Party behind in order to create a Progressive Party that advocated left-wing dreams: conciliatory policies to the Soviet Union, immediate desegregation of public schools, a national health insurance program. Alinsky's topography seemed spot-on.

Alinsky's book also gave the postwar left a name it would cling to: "radicals." Being a "radical" safely removed left-wingers from being tarnished as socialists (at least some of the time) and distinguished them from "liberals" who, in their mind, had given up the struggle for radical justice. There would be "radicals" on the left all the way to today's antifa. No self-respecting leftist wanted to be called a liberal.

The vital event that drove a wedge between liberals and leftists was the Cold War. At a basic level, the promises of Soviet communism and those of the American social democratic left could be easily paralleled. Both advocated for greater income equality, easier access to higher education and medical care, racial desegregation, less reliance on the corporate order to ensure basic security. This made any hankering for social justice subject to the slippery-slope arguments readily pointed out by those on the right, and postwar liberals were eager to avoid that. Many moved away from left-wing dreams.

At a deeper level, though, postwar liberals were less afraid of being accused of communism than of what their experience had taught them during the previous two decades: political ideologies that pushed too far inevitably led to totalitarianism. The political realities of Nazism and fascism and Stalinism seemingly made the case plain. Hannah Arendt's influential 1951 book *Origins of Totalitarianism* described how fanaticism on the right and left had equally led to a totalitarian state. After witnessing the rise of Hitler and Joseph Stalin, the postwar world needed, Arendt concluded in good liberal fashion, "a new guarantee which can be found only in a new political principle, in a new law on earth, whose validity this time must comprehend the whole of humanity while its power must remain strictly limited."[13] What the world needed, she suggested, was middle-of-the-road liberalism that protected against the fanatics.

Many onetime leftists followed Arendt's argument, abandoning what they now perceived to be "radical" social democratic economic goals in favor of individual rights and a defense of the preservation of private property. The shadow of totalitarianism loomed large for liberals: the "common man" so lionized in the 1930s by FDR as being subject to whims beyond his control and in need of a federal safety net was now suddenly pilloried as the "mass man" of the 1950s, someone susceptible to manipulation and demagoguery and who might unknowingly seek the firm ground of utopian visions or authoritarian certainty. Rather than seeing the "common man" as the salt of the earth, liberals' experiences during the 1930s and 1940s had shown them how manipulable human beings could be, how attracted they were to the allure of certainty. To liberals, the common people needed protecting from the extremes; they needed a secure liberal center that would prevent the poles from gaining too much support. Harvard historian Louis Hartz outlined this centrist position in *The Liberal Tradition in America*, offering up an explanation for why the US had, so far, yet to succumb to the polarities of totalitarianism. The answer, he argued, was the country's supposed historical commitment to liberalism. Arthur Schlesinger Jr. located what he called "the politics of freedom" in his 1949 book *The Vital Center*, a politics safely between communism on the left and fascism on the right, totalitarianisms both.[14] The left-liberal alliance that had made the New Deal possible in the 1930s frayed as liberals prioritized the demands of freedom over equality for fear that too much socialism would lead to communist fanaticism. Warding off authoritarianism was a primary concern of American liberals in the 1950s and early 1960s.[15]

Another way of saying this is that, as with the critique from the right, there was a kernel of truth in the left-wing critique against postwar liberalism. Liberals' fear of the specter of totalitarianism led them to turn against proposals that would have aligned with the liberalism as outlined by FDR. There was little in the New Deal that would have pushed back against something like national health insurance. Now liberals fell victims to the argument that it was simply "socialized medicine." There was little in FDR's definition of liberalism as the use of governmental power to ensure individual freedom for the maximum number of people that would have prevented ending racial segregation in the South. Now liberals acted with caution out of fear that pushing for the end of segregation would be seen as "communist leveling" and leaders like Martin Luther King Jr. and Bayard Rustin were dismissed as communist agitators. As with the right, though, the left would decide against haggling over a "true" meaning of the word *liberal*, instead capitulating it willingly to those they saw as their opposition and then redefining it as a way of setting themselves apart.

McCarthyism was key in this retreat. The rabid anticommunism of the right, on the one hand, and the liberal anticommunism of the center, on the other, allowed McCarthyism to have powerful influence in the 1950s. It is hard to overstate how important McCarthyism was in this era, not in eradicating communists, which the Truman administration had already done by the late 1940s, but instead in provoking fears among onetime leftists, which essentially narrowed the political spectrum, carving off the left and moving the political center to the right. Everyone left of center carried the potential of being tarnished as a socialist unless they took drastic action to declare themselves pure. Alinsky admitted in the 1970s, "Few of us [radicals] survived the Joe McCarthy holocaust of the early 1950s."[16] So effective was this purge that, by the early 1960s, Alinsky found no one to "pass on the torch of experience and insights to a new generation."[17] As historian Doug Rossinow has put it, "In the first half of the 1950s most liberals treated anyone with even a light reddish hue as a plague carrier."[18] Can you blame them when, as Eleanor Roosevelt put it, "I am beginning to think that if you have been a liberal, if you believe that those who are strong must sometimes consider the weak, and that with strength and power goes responsibility, automatically some people consider you a Communist"?[19] From 1950 to 1960, subscriptions to nearly all the left-wing journals of opinion plummeted. Subscriptions to the *Nation* fell from 39,439 to 23,148. *New Republic* subscriptions tanked from 52,022 to 23,633. And the *New Leader* went from having 43,000 subscribers in 1945 to just 15,900 in 1960.[20]

John Higham, a budding historian in the 1940s and 1950s who was also something of a political radical, perhaps best expressed the tortured position of a liberal in the 1950s. In a letter to his University of Wisconsin mentor Merle Curti, Higham admitted that he saw himself "in the broad liberal tradition," but, in the 1950s he became "an aristocratic liberal, who has come to think of the tyranny of mass opinion as the worst of the dangers confronting us."[21] The liberal retreat gave the left a wide berth to redefine the center as they saw fit.

––––––––––––

The American left, for a time at least, was stranded. Because politics was where they were most exposed (communists!), the loudest radicals of the era emerged as social and cultural outsiders. The Beat poets epitomized this reaction. As protestors against social norms, the Beats sought a more authentic society, what writer Jack Kerouac called "a New Vision" of American life. The "old vision" was stilted, prone to status approval, and out to deny basic human impulses. And who, pray tell, was denying that new vision? As Beat writer William Burroughs put it, "the word liberal has come to stand for the most damnable tyranny, a snively, mealy-mouthed tyranny of bureaucrats, social workers, psychiatrists, and Union officials."[22]

Among artists, Andy Warhol poked fun at the heightened value of consumer culture in the postwar era, his multicolor depictions of Campbell's soup cans probing questions not only about the consumption of high art (and the distinctions between high art and low) but also about the reigning values of postwar liberalism. Freedom in Cold War America was, he suggested, the freedom to consume the same items as everyone else. Roy Lichtenstein's cartoonish art, meanwhile, mocked the aggressive nature of the Cold War, suggesting that a simplified version of war had real-world manifestations that people refused to acknowledge. Cold War liberalism was literally killing people, even if most Americans would rather pay attention to cartoons. And if the artistic critiques grew too radical, liberals had an answer: the New York ad agencies on Madison Avenue would co-opt the message and use it to sell Coca-Cola.[23]

By the mid-1950s, some leftists had slowly begun to reclaim the social democratic tradition. But they had to perform a careful balancing act. How could they advocate greater social democracy and social equality without being dismissed as communists? The periodical *Dissent*, established in 1954 by a group of New York intellectuals that included Irving Howe, Lewis A. Coser, Rose Laub Coser, and Meyer Schapiro, sought to fill this gap. In some ways, *Dissent* was *National Review*'s reflection in the mirror of a fun house. Instead of running from socialism, *Dissent* wanted to restore its name. *Dissent* wanted to create space for a noncommunist left, where an expansive social safety net existed and strong regulations protected consumers and small business owners from large-scale corporate capitalism. Equality would weigh more heavily than freedom. "The purpose of this new magazine is suggested by its name," read *Dissent*'s opening salvo, "to dissent from the bleak atmosphere of conformism that pervades the political and intellectual life of the United States; to dissent from the support of the *status quo* now so noticeable on the part of many former radicals and socialists."[24]

Unlike *National Review*, which required an enemy to coalesce right-wing forces, *Dissent* did not initially name an enemy. Instead, it sought to "engage in a frank and friendly dialogue with liberal opinion."[25] This was a mild attempt to reconstruct the former New Deal alliance.

But that changed quickly. By the end of 1954, Howe, *Dissent*'s guiding light, published a hit piece called "The Shame of U.S. Liberalism." It was a collection of thoughts Howe compiled after the US Congress passed a bill outlawing the American Communist Party. "Democracy had suffered a blow," wrote Howe, and "liberalism had struck it."[26] He mourned "the creed to which so many of his friends had turned in their gradual loss of belief" in socialism. In voting to shun radicals, "liberalism had resigned its moral claim. It had committed moral suicide. . . . After August 1954 American liberalism could never again speak, except with the most vulgar of hypocrisies, in the name of either liberty or liberalism."[27]

Throughout the 1950s, it became increasingly clear who was *Dissent*'s real enemy, and it wasn't conservatives. For his part, Norman Mailer used the pages of *Dissent* to attack liberal individualism numerous times, most effectively perhaps in a scathing review of David Riesman's *Individualism Reconsidered*, a collection of essays whose overarching argument was that Americans needed to recommit to "individuality" and to people's "private selves," not toward "greater social participation and belongingness." Not doing so, Riesman implied, would lead to the triumph of mass men, the shock troops of authoritarianism.[28] Mailer called Riesman "the professional liberal's liberal," adding, "while I happen to have met no particular person who has been influenced by him, I have seen his name in many references, blurbs, and occasional columns, all exceptionally laudatory, by such intellectual deacons of the liberal body as Arthur Schlesinger, Jr. and Max Lerner." As if calling the guy a phony wasn't bad enough, Mailer also found the book boring: "I believe I can say with no conscious smugness that I learned almost nothing else in these five hundred pages." Most important, though, Mailer hated the deal American liberals had made when they gave up social democracy, substituting "what-is for the more elusive what-should-be." Liberals, in Mailer's mind, had gotten it wrong in assuming it was the threat of communism that caused postwar Americans to be anxious. Instead, Mailer suggested, "it makes equal sense to argue that the increasing anxiety of American life comes from the covert guilt that abundance and equality remain utterly separated."[29] Mailer would echo this complaint numerous times in the pages of *Dissent* and elsewhere, as would many others on the left.

Dissent was not alone in protesting the liberal order from the left. Another group of left-wing activists including A. J. Muste, Bayard Rustin, David Dellinger, and Roy Finch were crafting their own magazine, eventually called *Liberation*. Its prospectus rued the country's "decline of independent radicalism and the gradual falling into silence of prophetic and rebellious voices." *Liberation* demanded instead "a creative synthesis of the individual ethical insights of the great religious leaders and the collective social concern of the great revolutionists."[30]

Liberation first appeared in April 1956, and, although it never had more than a few thousand subscribers, the activist tradition from which it stemmed meant it was physically distributed at every major protest event of the late 1950s and into the 1960s. Its masthead read like a who's who of the midcentury radical left. Dorothy Day and Lillian Smith both wrote for *Liberation*, as did Michael Harrington, Paul Goodman, William Appleman Williams, Tom Hayden, Staughton Lynd, and C. Wright Mills. Martin Luther King Jr.'s "Letter from Birmingham Jail" was quickly published the pages of

Liberation, too, demonstrating an alliance of radicals among secular and religious activists.

There were other emerging left-wing outlets as well, including local venues like the *Village Voice*, cofounded by Mailer, which emerged in 1955 and carried forward an ironic sensibility whose goal was to be a thorn in the side of bureaucratic liberals. By the late 1950s, there was a solid critique of liberalism emerging from the left. It protested liberals' supposed embrace of corporate capitalism at the expense of small-business owners, its reticence to push social democratic policies and civil rights legislation, and its increasingly militant support in fighting the Cold War in numerous hot spots abroad. Socialist party leader Michael Harrington gave these voices a name in a 1959 pamphlet entitled "The New Left: The Relevance of Democratic Socialism in America." The name "New Left" had emerged in England and France, but Harrington sought to imagine a version in the US that was capable of navigating the terrain between Soviet-style communism and American liberalism.

———————

The liberals who were dismissed as overly individualistic by the left and as quasi socialists by the right did not cede the definition of liberalism easily. They fought back. They tried to protect the sanctity of their supposed tradition (even by labeling it "a tradition"). Their philosophical underpinnings remained the notion that liberalism was still the exhibition of a generosity of spirit and the expansion of individual freedom. They still largely bought into FDR's redefining of the term to signify the role of governmental power in ensuring individual freedom for the maximum number of people. They also argued that liberalism had to be on guard against radicalisms right and left, which might bring about fascism or communism, both of which would lead, in their minds, to totalitarianism. Their politics remained generally those outlined in Schlesinger's *Vital Center*, which was fearful of mass politics, instead favoring gradual change premised on preserving a version of consumerist corporate capitalism that maintained egalitarian stopgaps, like high taxes on the wealthy and a social security net. John Kenneth Galbraith sanctified the place of regulated corporate capitalism in his book *American Capitalism* (1952). And with the rise of a more bellicose Soviet Union after the invasion of Hungary in 1956 and the launch of its Sputnik satellite in 1957, liberals doubled down on their bet that socialism and its celebration of the masses was the greatest threat to humankind. "For the moment," wrote Columbia literary critic Richard Chase in 1960, "a revolutionary politics or economics makes no sense to contemporary America. What does make sense is the liberal virtues: moderation, compromise, countervailing forces, the vital center, the mixed economy."[31] Galbraith marked as much when he titled his 1960 collection of essays *The Liberal Hour*.[32]

And no one marked the liberal hour more than John F. Kennedy. In 1960, two days after famously speaking to hostile Protestant ministers in Houston about his capacity to lead the nation while being a Roman Catholic (albeit a "bad" Catholic, as his wife Jackie said), candidate Kennedy flew to New York to accept the nomination for president from the small Liberal Party of New York. He used the opportunity to attack those on the left and the right who were attacking him for being a "liberal," doing so by pointing out their false definitions of the term. "If by 'Liberal,'" Kennedy lampooned his enemies from the right, "they mean . . . someone who is soft in his policies abroad, who is against local government, and who is unconcerned with the taxpayer's dollar," then he was "not that kind of 'Liberal.'" Instead, ever the politician, he harked back to FDR and courted the left. "If by 'Liberal,' they mean someone who looks ahead and not behind, someone who welcomes new ideas without rigid reactions, someone who cares about the welfare of the people—their health, their housing, their schools, their jobs, their civil rights, and their civil liberties—someone who believes that we can break through the stalemate and suspicions that grip us in our politics abroad, if that is what they mean by a 'Liberal,' then I'm proud to say that I'm a 'Liberal.'"[33]

Calling liberalism "not so much a party creed or a set of fixed platform promises as it is an attitude of mind and heart," Kennedy proclaimed he had the liberal's "faith in man's ability through the experiences of his reason and judgment to increase for himself and his fellow men the amount of justice and freedom and brotherhood which all human life deserves." Trying to reunify the left and the liberals in common cause, he called the "basic issue" of the 1960 election whether or not the country "will fall in a conservative rut and die there, or whether we will move ahead in the liberal spirit of daring."[34] Judging by his tone, it could have been 1932 and Dwight Eisenhower could have been Herbert Hoover.

Conservatives were having none of it. They tried to tar him as an "ultra liberal" who would usher in communism. But the *Nation* dissented, suggesting that, while Kennedy had "healthy liberal leanings," he was moving the political center of American politics to the right. The area "left of Kennedy" was "rapidly becoming a vast area indeed," its contributor wrote.[35]

Kennedy thus presented radicals with a choice: trust that he was going to braid together the left and the middle, or remain marginalized. Kennedy's appeal to the left was mostly campaign propaganda. He never strongly advocated for civil rights until forced to do so. He amplified, not soothed, tensions with the Soviet Union. And he did not expand many domestic social services or engage in any important poverty alleviation programs. He became what the left dismissed as a "corporate liberal."[36]

For his part, Kennedy was in a bind, politically. Three decades prior, Roosevelt had been able to push through the most important elements of the New Deal by brokering deals with the Democratic Party's Southern wing. Perhaps most important, FDR allowed local control over the rollout of many federal projects, which allowed Southern racial segregation to persist. Thus, as expansive as FDR's liberalism may have been rhetorically, it was bound by political compromises that enshrined racial segregation.[37] As the Democratic Party cautiously began to embrace desegregation in the 1940s and

1950s, Southern Democrats loomed as an increasingly large challenge to any racially progressive liberalism. Kennedy, not yet ready
to cut this Gordian knot to risk losing the votes of Southern Democrats, spoke of an expansive liberalism that included desegregation
but did not embrace it until he was forced to do so by the actions
of civil rights activists, and even then only in limited, politically
conscious ways.

This awkward position did not go unnoticed, especially by the
young. For them, Kennedy's Cold War liberalism seemed, as one
political scientist put it, "middle-aged, middle class, and muddled."
It was filled with "bumbling platitudes, of Madison Avenue" and "the
age at large" had "played havoc with American idealism."[38] The cor-
poratization of postwar American liberalism, the priority of security
over equality, forced young idealists to look elsewhere for inspiration.
As with those on the right, the ideological contours of a nonliberal
left took many competing and often irreconcilable forms. That meant
the primary thing sewing them together was a collective animosity
toward the status quo, which meant, in their eyes, against liberalism.

—————

In 1960, C. Wright Mills, a left-wing sociologist from Columbia
University who saw himself as the ultimate rebel, drafted a short
but influential article entitled "Letter to the New Left." It has been
misread ever since. Mills spent the 1950s analyzing and bemoaning
the absence in America of any political opposition to what he called
"the power elite," the power brokers from the political, business,
and military classes who, despite their different job descriptions,
all emerged from the same background and moved freely from one
category to the next. It was "no exaggeration," he wrote, that "smug
conservatives, tired liberals, and disillusioned radicals" had carried
on a "wearied discourse" in which the "sickness of complacency has
prevailed [and] bi-partisan banality flourished." The triumph of the
liberals in the 1940s and 1950s had led to a "style of cultural work

that is in effect an intellectual celebration of apathy," he wrote, un-enthusiastically.[39] Postwar liberals were so business friendly that all that was left of conservatism was the lunatic fringe. And they were so good at smearing left-wing radicals as communists that radicalism had largely disappeared. To Mills, liberals had even recruited the traditional agent of change from the left, the working classes. Now labor leaders sat at the table of the power elite. They were mostly powerless, junior partners for sure, but at least they were at the table.

So where would radical change come from? After a trip to England reignited his hopes that a younger generation might be able to protest the monotony of modern life, Mills wrote a hopeful letter, mostly directed to young people in England, but also, he hoped without optimism, to those in the US, too. "I have been studying, for several years now, the cultural apparatus, *the intellectuals*—as a possible, immediate, radical agency of change," Mills wrote, astonished at this turn of events. "For a long time, I was not much happier with this idea than were many of you; but it turns out now, in the spring of 1960, that it may be a very relevant idea indeed."[40] He wouldn't be wrong.

His timing was spot-on, too, because, also in 1960, an organization emerged that would serve as a key organizer of youthful rebellion against the liberal order. Students for a Democratic Society (SDS) was begun by Robert "Al" Haber, a twenty-four-year-old graduate student at the University of Michigan who revived it from older organizations that were mostly connected to the labor movement. But the New Left wasn't terribly interested in the redistribution of wealth, at least not as a primary concern. It was more interested in allowing the flourishing of individual authenticity. Theirs was an intellectual and spiritual movement as much as if not more than a materialistic one. The young intellectuals saw politics as a way to achieve a moral society, not solely solve problems, which it perceived to be the liberal's goal. The youth saw direct action as the key to change, not elections.[41]

Haber, a self-described "radical" in the Saul Alinsky tradition, took the helm of SDS seeking to articulate "radical alternatives to the inadequate society of today."[42] He hired a young reporter from the *Michigan Daily* named Tom Hayden to help. In 1962, Hayden drafted the *Port Huron Statement*, a long-winded attempt to put a politics and a style behind the mood of the emerging New Left. Its central argument was that liberalism's lofty goals of economic equality, social justice, and the expansion of democracy were worthy but had stalled in light of McCarthyism and the fear of totalitarianism. The country needed to move beyond liberal pronouncements and toward something called "participatory democracy." Since the Great Depression, wrote Hayden, liberals had centralized power and used experts to enact a philosophical utilitarianism, trying to use reason and bureaucratic measures to pursue the greatest good for the greatest number. And it had worked—to an extent. But its fears of mass men and totalitarianism prevented it from finishing the job. Instead, it had "instilled quiescence in liberal hearts," partly a reflection of "the extent to which misery has been overcome," but also "the eclipse of social ideals" because of the perpetual and unfounded fear of communism.[43] As SDS complained, "not even the liberal and socialist preachments of the past seem adequate to the forms of the present."[44] As Hayden saw the situation, large-scale material problems had been solved, but the fears buried within postwar liberalism led to stultifying control and the decline of individual expression. To push through the malaise, SDS argued that the whole system needed to be decentralized, which would allow participants to put into place their variety of opinions. Cycling through the various mechanisms of power in American life—politics, economy, the military (Hayden acknowledged his reliance on Mills)—Hayden found centralized control everywhere, all part of a single mechanism that robbed people of their individuality. His goal, then, was "changing the conditions of humanity in the late twentieth century, an effort rooted in the ancient, still unfulfilled conception of man attaining determining influence over his circumstances of life."[45]

This goal would be achieved, Hayden argued, through a politics of action, not by bureaucratic procedure. Partly this argument was a punt. Hayden really had no political philosophy to advocate other than "participatory democracy," so he promised to follow men and women of action and let an ideology emerge later. The point was to unite in opposition to the supposedly stultifying liberal order that had imposed slow and halting nonrevolutionary change amid bureaucratic anonymity. Unfortunately for SDS, no political ideology ever emerged, to somewhat disastrous results. Throughout the decade, leftists tore themselves apart in their pursuit of myriad individualized lines of philosophy. The only thing they had in common was that they all saw postwar liberalism as an emblem of an unfulfilled promise.

SDS was only the beginning of the student revolts of the 1960s. By 1964, animated by the *Port Huron Statement* and the emerging civil rights movement, Mario Savio, a graduate student at the University of California, Berkeley, stood on top of a police car that had come on campus to arrest the leader of one of the campus's political organizations. Savio's impromptu speech and its improbable location kicked off what became known as the free speech movement, a rebellion that quickly extended beyond Berkeley and beyond free speech. Despite its varying goals—end the Vietnam War, reimagine higher education, mandate equality—the free speech movement had several calls but, beneath the surface, only one unifying principle: to fight against mainstream liberalism. According to Jack Weinberg, one of the Berkeley leaders, the student recruits started "as liberals, talking about society, criticizing it, going to lectures, donating money. But every year more and more students find they cannot stop there. They affirm themselves; they decide that even if they do not know how to save the world . . . they must let their voice be heard. They become activists, and a new generation, a generation of radicals, emerges."[46]

The Vietnam War heightened the tone of (and the stakes for) the students. In April 1965, shortly after Lyndon Johnson launched the air war against North Vietnam, SDS led a March on Washington in protest. Twenty-five thousand people turned out to listen to SDS president Paul Potter ask, "What kind of system is it that justifies the United States or any country seizing the destinies of the

Vietnamese people and using them callously for their own purposes? What kind of system is it that disenfranchises people in the South, leaves millions of people throughout the country impoverished and excluded . . . that creates faceless and terrible bureaucracies and make[s] those the place where people spend their lives and do their work? . . . We must name that system, we must name it, describe it, analyze it, understand it, and change it."[47]

SDS named the system a year later. Carl Oglesby, the SDS president after Potter, said the men who engineered Vietnam "are not moral monsters." No. "They are all honorable men. They are all liberals." Consumed by the logic of capitalism to take and to consume, Oglesby said liberals had allied with right-wing dictators and undermined popular regimes. And if that sounded anti-American to some people, Oglesby said, "Don't blame *me* for *that!* Blame those who mouthed my liberal values and broke my American heart."[48] As Allen Matusow, one of the leading historians of the 1960s, put it, Oglesby's speech was tantamount to "a declaration of war against liberals," who were "now irrevocably the enemy."[49]

The use of antiliberalism as the left's primary unifying principle would go on. In 1968, the leader of Columbia University's SDS chapter, Mark Rudd, mocked the university's vice president, David Truman, for wanting to hash out their differences at a conference rather than through protest, saying, "He gives us this alternative because he is a very *li-ber-al* man." Rudd said he rejected what he called the "basic liberal conception" of mediation, instead preferring to invade and occupy.[50] The following academic year, from fall 1968 to spring 1969, there were nearly three hundred major student protests at more than 230 college campuses around the country.

Partly this was a generational battle. Postwar liberals like Arthur Schlesinger Jr., David Riesman, and even JFK came of age under the shadow of totalitarianism. Many were anticommunist out of guilty feelings that they, in their youth, had been seduced by communism's unachievable promise. As supposedly wizened realists, postwar liberals now recognized communism's evil and sought to intervene wherever they saw it spread. They saw regulated capitalism as the least worst way of economic organization and so, in the postwar era, when the economy was good, they favored piecemeal reforms rather than large-scale overhauls that might bring the nation closer to communism. They understood the compromises liberals had been forced to make regarding segregation in order to achieve the New Deal. Gradualism was key for them because unforeseen consequences and eager confidence men were always there to take advantage of a hidden loophole. Plus, they had to adhere to political realities. Such was how the postwar generation of liberals understood human nature.

More than this, however, they feared the rise of a left that was unhinged from commitments to discussion, moderation, and reform. In his 1968 Columbia University commencement speech, historian Richard Hofstadter defended the ideals of "freedom, rationality, inquiry, [and] discussion," and hoped for a "willingness of society to support and sustain institutions part of whose business is to examine, critically and without stint, the assumptions that prevail in that society"—basically, liberalism.[51]

The younger generation rejected each pillar of this definition of liberalism. Smaller, piecemeal reforms had failed to root out the worst of American poverty. Aggressive anticommunism led to far-flung adventures that perpetuated totalitarian regimes rather than supported democratically elected ones. Gradualism wasn't working, either, especially when it came to civil rights, women's rights, a fairer distribution of wealth, and the general opening of American culture. Even looking back, in the 1970s and 1980s a host of New Left historians saw businessmen behind every theory of liberalism. This view started early, with Crawford B. Macpherson's *The Political Theory of Possessive Individualism: Hobbes and Locke* (1962) analyzing liberal theory as a reflection of the capitalist market. But perhaps the best example was R. Jeffrey Lustig's *Corporate Liberalism: The Origins of Modern American Political Theory, 1890–1920* (1982), which demonstrated by its very title how liberals were in bed with capitalism.

In 1971, Saul Alinsky wrote *Rules for Radicals*, which said of the New Left, "Most of them are products of the middle class. They have rejected their materialistic backgrounds, the goal of well-paid job, suburban home, automobile, country club members[hip], first-class travel, status, security, and everything that meant success to their parents. They have had it. They watched it lead their parents to tranquilizers, alcohol, long-term-endurance marriages, or divorces, high blood pressure, ulcers, frustration, and the disillusionment of 'the good life.'" Politics had failed them. "The search for freedom does not seem to have any road or destination," he wrote.[52]

From Alinsky to the Beats to *Dissent* to SDS, thinkers on the left developed an argument in the 1950s and 1960s that liberalism had failed to redeem its promise for the full development of the potentialities of every individual. There were still too many poor people. Too many Americans were alienated not only from the goods they produced but also from others within their society. There was too much unhappiness, too much unfulfillment. In this, they followed Karl Marx's classic critique of liberalism—that it was little more than an attempt to rationalize power for the bourgeois. Liberalism, the New Left argued, had not only failed to curb the worst abuses of capitalism but had enabled it and, even worse, given it moral cover. Real-life liberals disagreed with this understanding of the term, of course. But those on the left continued with their definition anyway.

———

In January 1967, in an attempt to unify countercultural hippies and political radicals, a group of leftists organized the "Human Be-In" in Golden Gate Park in San Francisco. It was an attempt at "a union of love and activism," as one of the founders said. Headlined by Jefferson Airplane and the Grateful Dead, the music was great, but when things turned to politics, the tenor changed. By the late 1960s, all politics seemed to smack of attempts to justify liberalism. The New Left, after beginning with its admirable and pointed critique of postwar liberalism, had by 1967 spun into a disparate variety of movements, some of which seemed legitimate, many of which seemed farcical (in 1968, members of the Youth International Party nominated Pigasus the Pig for president). When the political activist Jerry Rubin tried to give a speech at the Human Be-In, his political tone hit the wrong note for the Grateful Dead's guitar player, Jerry Garcia, who asked, "Why enter this closed society and make an effort to liberalize it? Why not just leave it and go someplace else."[53] *Liberalism* was a blanket term for any kind of traditional politics, one that signified the perpetuation of a blasé life filled with unfulfilled promises and a paucity of joy.

There were a great number of ironies in the New Left's rejection of liberalism, perhaps foremost among them being that their critique of liberalism's supposedly overorganized, overbureaucratized society invited those on the left to push back against government reforms, an instinct that would lead them to accept many of the calls for deregulation made by those on the right (and, later, by those advocating economic neoliberalism).

The two decades following World War II led to a clear divorce between the left and the liberals. And, as divided as the left was, its members typically found common cause only in making an enemy out of their version of liberals. Why "make an effort to liberalize" America when the results had already been so tragic?

FOUR

MY WHITE LIBERAL PROBLEM—AND OURS

Putting the White *in* White Liberals

In early 1964, James Baldwin, the powerful voice of the civil rights movement who had just appeared on the cover of *Time* magazine as the person finally able to tell white liberals what Black people wanted, received an invitation to speak at a roundtable hosted by the then-liberal magazine *Commentary*.[1] Although it wasn't explicit in the invitation, Baldwin was the roundtable's designated Black person.

Invitations like this were a dime a dozen for Baldwin in 1963 and 1964, but this one sounded interesting. Founded in 1945 to be a distinctly Jewish voice of liberal anticommunism, *Commentary* at the time operated on high intellectual terrain. Its authors were professional sociologists, philosophers, economists, and political scientists, all of whom professed some version of midcentury liberalism. But in late 1963, *Commentary*'s editors detected a growing anger coming from the Black community and a rising backlash against civil rights coming from many white people in America. They thought it was a good time to take stock. It was unclear what feedback they imagined they'd receive from Baldwin, but it's clear they weren't expecting what Baldwin had in mind.

The main question these white liberals wanted answered was: why were they continually hated when they tried so hard? Why was the alliance between white liberals and Black liberals faltering at such a pivotal moment? It seemed that no matter how much white liberals did when it came to questions of race, especially in the aftermath of the considerable support white liberals had given to the Montgomery bus boycott, the nationwide sit-ins, and the Freedom Rides, they were simply hated more and more. Support the March on Washington? Virtue signaling. End legal segregation in the South? Too little, too late. White liberals meant well and used their power to make change. Why, in early 1964, were they so despised by so many Black Americans?

Norman Podhoretz, *Commentary*'s editor, thought he knew the answer. He suspected, not completely incorrectly, a growing divide between some (mostly white) liberals who thought that, on matters of race, true liberalism simply promised an end to racial discrimination and an equitable sharing of opportunities, while other liberals (mostly Black) wanted some form of reparation, some affirmative action, a payment for past misdeeds. But Podhoretz wasn't sure that was quite right. So he set up the roundtable, which he titled "Liberalism and the Negro."[2]

Baldwin accepted *Commentary*'s invitation, knowing he would be sitting alongside intellectual heavyweights Nathan Glazer, Gunnar Myrdal, and Sidney Hook—white liberals all. Other major luminaries dotted the audience. Baldwin was at a key point in his intellectual development, one that, significantly, mirrored that of much of Black America. Baldwin had begun 1963 as the white liberal's hero. His chart-topping book, *The Fire Next Time*, to which the *New Yorker* had devoted its *entire* November 17, 1962, issue, gave liberals one last chance to make real progress on civil rights. Baldwin wrote in the book's stirring finale, "If we—and now I mean the relatively conscious whites and the relatively conscious blacks, who must, like lovers, insist on, or create, the consciousness of the others—do not falter in our duty now, we may be able, handful that we are, to end the racial nightmare, and achieve our country, and change the history of the world."[3] And if that didn't happen? *"No more water, the fire next time!"*[4]

Throughout 1963, however, Baldwin, like many Black Americans, changed his mind about white liberals. The fire had come. Hope had soured. Mounting white backlash to Black progress taught Baldwin that even something as transformative as the about-to-be-enacted Civil Rights Act of 1964, which outlawed legal segregation in the South and employment discrimination nationwide, would not end racism.[5] White liberals were finally and only out of duress listening to Black America, and still only halfway. They still refused to own up to their part in the national nightmare. It was as if there were two civil rights movements: one aimed at ending legal segregation in the Jim Crow South, powered by Black and white liberals together, and another aimed at ending racism in America, powered almost exclusively by Black people. White liberals apparently did not want to confront myths about their own supposed greatness. They did not want to rebuild institutions designed to keep themselves in power and Black Americans subservient. They did not want to acknowledge that the language of tolerance was just a happy facade put on a system premised on oppression.

For Black Americans, it was exhausting having to educate white people all the time, especially when success seemed so amoebic. The years 1963 and 1964 were key years in this intellectual transition for many Black Americans, years when "white" was permanently affixed to the increasingly derogatory stereotype of "the white liberal," the one who had let them down, the group that had focused on process instead of results, who worried about deliberation more than Freedom Now! "White liberal" as stereotype was born as an unqualified term of abuse in 1963 and 1964.

———————

The *Commentary* roundtable at New York's Town Hall was a perfect vehicle for Baldwin to explain all this. Plus, he'd specifically get to say it to editor Norman Podhoretz, who, the year before, had used the closing words of Baldwin's *The Fire Next Time* to launch one of the most controversial essays of mid-twentieth-century American life: "My Negro Problem—and Ours." Podhoretz's piece admitted that white liberals were profoundly racist but blamed it on their historic conditioning and past experiences with Black people. But by 1963, they were trying hard to overcome it; Black people just needed to be patient, Podhoretz urged. He argued that the glacial pace of progress was the necessary price for changing white attitudes; indeed, miscegenation might be the only answer to white racism, and that could take generations. He also argued that Black people were retarding progress by protesting too loudly. Baldwin, who had actually encouraged Podhoretz to write the piece assuming Podhoretz would have too much sense to do so, hated the essay.[6]

After introductions, all the white liberal panelists somewhat remarkably laid bare some of the flaws in, well, white liberalism. It was quite an interesting moment, as some of the fiercest defenders of midcentury liberalism worked through the shortcomings of their own political philosophy in what can only be seen as an attempted inoculation. Nathan Glazer, a Harvard sociologist, put it succinctly: "Liberalism assumes the existence of certain mechanisms for the solution of problems: it assumes reasonableness; it assumes also a kind of good will; it assumes an acceptance of the principle of the fundamental equality of all men." Where these assumptions didn't exist, as in the segregated South, liberalism was bound to struggle. To illustrate the point, Glazer read a newspaper from Jackson, Mississippi, where "housewives" complained that textbooks were "brainwashing" kids into believing "prejudice is wrong." Glazer concluded, "What does liberalism do or say in the face of what seems to be mass commitment to evil?"[7]

This was an astute critique. Liberalism works best when people agree on how to get at the truth, when everyone respects the findings of experts, when people are capable of engaging in reasonable debate and willing to do so. But when there's a "mass commitment to evil" and, even worse, the construction of falsehoods designed to defend or obscure that evil, liberalism will suffer. Reason often suffers in the face of powerful emotions like fear and anger.

Gunnar Myrdal, the world-famous scholar of American race relations and the principal author of the groundbreaking *The American Dilemma*, pointed to another flaw in liberalism: its prioritization of individual rights over the well-being of the collective. Displaying some sympathy to the cause of civil rights activists, Myrdal said that "we should not be so stupid as to think" outlawing discrimination will solve the problem: "It won't." But progress had been made, Myrdal insisted, because of slow-moving cultural changes in how white people perceived Black people. Myrdal went on to advocate a poverty program to raise up *all* poor people in America—Black, white, and everything beyond and between. Black people did not need special treatment once granted legal equality, he argued: reparations should be distributed to all who suffer, but the Black case should not be singled out.[8]

Sidney Hook, head of the Department of Philosophy at New York University and plausible heir to John Dewey as the country's most recognizable philosopher, began by attempting to rob Baldwin of his own experience: "On the basis of your experience, Mr. Baldwin, you say that the attitudes of the American people to the Negro haven't changed. But on the basis of my experience, I say that the attitudes of large sections of the American people *have* changed." Hook said there was a "revolution of rising expectations" that came from white Americans being educated that racism was wrong. Echoing Podhoretz, he said that Black people just needed patience.[9] Myrdal and Hook both suggested that, with time, enough Black individuals would make enough headway to convince white Americans to change their minds.

To Baldwin, this was the typical nonsense of the white liberal. The dual premises of prioritizing individual rights and promoting reasonable debate were exactly the things Baldwin knew wouldn't work. White liberals were always resorting to gestures of goodwill, always talking about progress made, education ongoing, laws to be enacted. Trust the process, they said. But they conveniently ignored the question of why the institutions were constructed to move as slowly as they did, and they ignored the pain and suffering that went on during the seemingly endless deliberations. How could Black people be expected to trust the institutions of change when those institutions had let them down so many times before? "I'm delighted to know there've been many fewer lynchings in the year 1963 than there were in the year 1933, but I also have to bear in mind—I have to bear it in mind because my life depends on it—that there are a great many ways to lynch a man," Baldwin said, mentioning specifically the degradation of poverty and perpetual second-class citizenship, even for someone as famous as him.

Baldwin then settled into his key argument: large numbers of Black people were realizing that violence and direct action were the only way to provoke change, liberalism be damned. White liberals had missed their chance by dallying, and the fire had come. "The impulse in American society," Baldwin said, "has essentially been to ignore me when it could, and then when it couldn't, intimidate me; and when that failed, to make concessions." The problem was not a Black problem, Baldwin said. It was a white problem. White people were simply incapable of seeing Black people as fully formed human beings. Conservatives saw Black people as an abomination. Liberals saw them as a problem. No one saw them as human. "The way white Americans look on each other," he said, "is not the way they look on the black population here."[10]

To Baldwin, liberals' "real attitudes" were "revealed when the chips are down." A white liberal was "someone who thinks you're pushing too hard when you rock the boat, who thinks you are bitter when you are vehement, who has a set of attitudes so deep that they're almost unconscious and which blind him to the fact that in talking to a black man, he is talking to another man like himself."[11] White liberals were not "wicked," they simply had reflexes to tinker and modify but also to perpetuate racial hierarchies within institutions of power. How can you change something that has become a reflex? "What strikes me here," Baldwin said, "is that you are an American talking about American society, and I am an American talking about American society—both of us very concerned with it—and yet your version of American society is really very difficult for me to recognize. My experience in it has simply not been yours."[12]

"White liberals," Baldwin concluded, are "a kind of affliction." White liberals had given him a platform to write his books. This was true. But then they asked him to write about the Black experience only. They asked him to be a Black voice, not an American voice. They saw him as only one thing. They denied his full humanity. My "major premise," he summed up, "is simply this: that in terms of my own experience and the experience of people around me, the liberal record is a shameful record. And the reason it is so shameful is that white liberals—with some exceptions—have been unable to divest themselves of the whole concept of white supremacy and that this concept is reinforced by all the institutions in which power is located." For things to change, "all American citizens will be forced to undergo a change, and all American institutions will be forced to undergo a change too." He finished: "I repudiate most of the standards by which Americans live, and I don't see any hope—not for *my* freedom, but for *our* freedom, as long as we live by these standards."[13]

"I don't agree," thundered Sidney Hook immediately. All the other white liberals pushed back against Baldwin's conclusions, too.[14]

But coming to Baldwin's defense that night was the only other Black person invited to speak, the famous psychologist Kenneth Clark, who sat in the audience. Clark, whose research was famously quoted in the US Supreme Court's *Brown v. Board of Education* case of 1954, stunned the crowd and the panelists by saying that Baldwin was "helping some of the rest of us cope with this difficult problem of facing the American liberal with the fact that in relation to the Negro he had never been as liberal as he likes to profess."[15]

Indeed, Clark said, the only way he could make sense of them was by removing the "liberal" part of "white liberal." White liberals were simply people wearing masks of good intentions to hide their undergirding racism. "We can go right down the list of areas of American life that are not controlled by out-and-out bigots but that are controlled by individuals who define themselves as liberals," Clark said, "and find that the predicament of the Negro in each of these areas is incomprehensible." "White liberals," Clark continued, his words as sharp as a knife, were "a curious and insidious adversary— much more insidious than the out-and-out bigot."[16]

Clark was, he admitted, "forced to agree with James Baldwin" that the white liberal "*is* an affliction."[17]

————————

Beginning in the 1950s, many Black Americans had grown conscious of white liberals trying to help their cause. White liberals were not, in the 1950s, generally reviled, as they would be from 1964 onward. They were simply a new audience, mostly Northerners who bought into the rhetorical imperatives of World War II, the "Americans All" language of the Cold War, and the heartfelt convictions of the early civil rights activists. Feeling that Jim Crow was a dark stain on American ideals, white liberals favored the end of legal segregation in the South. They might not be antiracist activists, but they sought an end to public discrimination. They wanted, at least rhetorically, a more color-blind society, where Black Americans had the same opportunities as white Americans. Commitments varied. Some marched in the streets and sat next to Black activists at sit-ins. Some simply bought into the rhetoric and lived their lives, showing support when they could.

Black comedians were some of the first to recognize white liberals as an emerging group within postwar America. In the 1950s, Dick Gregory, Bill Cosby, and a handful of other Black comedians recognized that they could perform racial satire and develop an audience of sympathetic white Northern liberals willing to simultaneously affirm their convictions and congratulate themselves for being not as bad as the outright bigots. Dick Gregory developed jokes like this one: "Last time I was down South, I walked into this restaurant and this white waitress came up to me and said, 'We don't serve colored people here.' I said, 'That's all right, I don't eat colored people. Bring me some fried chicken.'"[18] White liberals would laugh, proud both of recognizing the idiocy of Southern bigotry and for supporting edgy Black comedians.

Black activists saw the development of this new type as well. They, however, were keenly aware of the historically vexed relationship between Black activists and white moderates. Quakers in the 1830s—some of the most ardent abolitionists—nonetheless had separate prayer benches for nonwhite Friends. One Black believer, Sarah Douglass, said of the Quakers, "Many, very many are anxious to take up the cross, but how few are strong enough to bear it."[19] A few decades later, another Douglass, Frederick Douglass, had great hopes for white friends, Quakers and non-Quakers alike, friends he called "liberal-minded." Often, they were nice to him in person and made promises for racial reform, but then they almost always allowed other concerns to precede his. Abraham Lincoln was perhaps foremost among these sorts of allies. No John Brown was he.[20]

A century later, a youthful and then-radical Ralph J. Bunche sparred with his boss, Gunnar Myrdal. Bunche saw weakness in the interracial leadership structure of organizations like the National Association for the Advancement of Colored People (NAACP). Black people always had to keep a "weather eye" on white sympathizers because they were either "cautious liberals or mawkish missionary-minded sentimentalists." In this supplicant relationship, nothing got done: "lacking the courage and conviction to face the harsher realities, [the liberal] seeks to find release and solace in counterfeit substitutes, in political and social *ersatz*. He recognizes and revolts against injustices, but seeks to correct them with palliatives rather than solutions; for the solutions are harsh and forbidding, and are not conducive to spiritual uplift."[21]

Langston Hughes voiced a similar complaint. In the 1940s, Hughes developed a fictional character named Jesse B. Simple, who

asked basic questions that exposed the idiocy of American race relations. Simple became the key figure in Hughes's *Chicago Defender*
columns throughout the 1940s and 1950s. In one 1949 column, Simple asked a friend, "Just what is a liberal?" His interlocutor answers,
"Well, as nearly as I can tell, a liberal is a nice man who acts decently
toward people, talks democratically, and often is democratic in his
personal life, but does not stand up very well in action when some real
social issue like Jim Crow comes up." Simple then ponders whether
liberals should have a mascot, like Republicans have the elephant and
Democrats the donkey. Simple suggests "the ostrich" because "old
ostrich sticks his head in the sand whenever he don't want to look
at anything. But he leaves his hind parts bare for anybody to kick
him square in his caboose." Simple concludes magnificently, saying
that a liberal "can pull his head out of the sand and say, I see a new
day ahead for America! I see the democratic dawn of equal rights
for all. . . . Indeed, my dark friend, democracy cannot overlook you."
But when Black people ask for housing in a white neighborhood, the
ostrich will "stick his head right back down in the sand."[22]

A similar rebuke came from Gwendolyn Brooks, the first African
American to win a Pulitzer Prize. In her 1960 poem "The Lovers
of the Poor," Brooks mocked wealthy white liberals who wanted to
support civil rights but were turned off by the sight of actual Black
poverty. These fictional "Ladies from the Ladies Betterment League"
were thoroughly imbued in liberal values. Their mothers had said,
"You'd better not be cruel! / You had better not throw stones upon
the wrens!" But when they arrived in Black neighborhoods, "all deep
and debonair," they couldn't help but inadvertently show "the pink
paint on the innocence of fear." They were turned off by the smell,
"the urine, cabbage, and dead beans." They had "never seen such a
made-do-ness as / Newspaper rugs before!" As they leave, the white
liberal ladies "look, / In horror, behind a substantial citizeness," allowing "their lovely skirts to graze no wall, / Are off at what they
manage of a canter." They suggest that next year, instead of visiting
in person, "Perhaps the money can be posted."[23]

Black thinkers were obviously frustrated by white liberals but didn't use the phrase "white liberal" as a term of abuse. There seemed to be bigger fish to fry, such as the out-and-out bigots lynching Black people across the South. And anyway, during the 1950s, change seemed possible. The US Supreme Court's ruling in *Brown v. Board of Education* was decided unanimously by nine white male judges and premised on liberal values. Meanwhile, Rosa Parks and the Montgomery bus boycott were marketed by the likes of Martin Luther King Jr. to, among other things, appeal to the conscience of Northern white liberals. More than a hundred white reporters came to Montgomery to report to their mostly white audiences across the country.

There was real hope that, this time, white liberals might be able to help Black activists end segregation and create a more equal society. This was the hope Baldwin aired in the final pages of *The Fire Next Time*. This was the hope of King's "I Have a Dream" speech. Hubert H. Humphrey, mayor of Minneapolis in the 1940s and a US senator throughout the 1950s, urged civil and human rights at the 1948 Democratic convention and was now a party stalwart. To his fellow white liberals who complained that civil rights were moving too fast, Humphrey had retorted, "We are 172 years too late!"[24] White liberals were flocking to the cause, marching in the streets, writing letters to the editor. Would white liberals finally and at long last put self-interest aside and give up what was necessary to create a more color-blind society?

––––––––––

The answer, at least as far as Black people saw things, would be no, with 1963 and 1964 as crucial years. Despite sometimes acknowledging successes like the passage of the 1964 Civil Rights Act and the flood of young white volunteers helping the cause, there were nonetheless numerous reasons for the shift in Black perception of white liberals, most of them circling around the idea that whereas many white liberals believed the civil rights movement was about ending legal segregation in the South, most Black people believed the civil rights movement should be about ending racism in America. White liberals were aiming too low, perhaps too afraid to make changes that would notably impact their own lives. The Black freedom movement's Northern march, the attempts to desegregate Northern schools, and the calls for integrated housing above the Mason-Dixon Line were only a few of the most potent issues bringing a different understanding of civil rights to the forefront of white liberal conscience. And it was there the civil rights movement had run aground.

And so, starting in late 1963 and early 1964, the Black community grew increasingly militant, either through Black nationalism or through more confrontational tactics. In 1964, the predominantly Black Mississippi Freedom Democratic Party (MFDP) went to the Democratic National Convention and demanded to be seated in place of the predominantly white "official" Mississippi state delegates. When Lyndon Johnson refused to seat the MFDP, Black leaders like Robert Moses and Fanny Lou Hamer dramatically signed off from white alliances for a while. As Black people began to understand, civil rights advocacy was fine when it was "down there" and nonviolent and didn't cause disruption to beloved institutions. But when it moved closer to home? In a January 1963 article in the *Atlantic* entitled "The White Liberal's Retreat," white sociologist Murray Friedman suggested that "the liberal white is increasingly uneasy about the nature and consequences of the Negro revolt." Friedman damningly concluded, "In the final analysis, the liberal, white, middle-class society wants to have change, but without trouble."[25]

The year 1963 bore out this assessment. The more radical demands for equality were rebuffed. Political action had to be navigated though hostile waters in Congress. And so, by late 1963, the stereotype of the "white liberal" emerged within the Black community as a figure of widespread derision and even hate. As usual, James Baldwin was in the forefront. In his 1964 play *Blues for Mister Charlie*, the white bigot Lyle goes to his friend, the white liberal Parnell, for help. "Parnell, you're my buddy," bigot Lyle says. "You know more about me than anybody else in the world . . . You—you ain't going to turn against me are you?" "No," answers white liberal Parnell, "No, I'll never turn against you. I'm just trying to make you think."[26]

That Baldwin's opinion of white liberals evolved so quickly, from the tortured and tenuous hopefulness of *The Fire Next Time* in very early 1963 to the dismissed stereotype just eighteen months later is revealing of the epochal changes in America in 1963, and in the Black conception of the white liberal.

In a similar fashion, we can chart quite easily the change in tone about "the white liberal" in the words used by Martin Luther King Jr. He has been lionized as someone able to speak from the deepest well of the American liberal tradition, of its promised freedoms and our ability to use reason and moral persuasion to build a society capable of equality. But even someone as famously patient as King began in 1963 and 1964 to fall back on the emerging stereotype of the white liberal. His frustration had become too much.

From his earliest days on the national scene, King, like other Black liberals, tried to cajole white liberals for support. In 1957, in one of his first national speeches, King called on white liberals to be more forthright in their support of the Black freedom struggle. "What we are witnessing today in so many northern communities," he said, "is a sort of quasi-liberalism which is based on the principle of looking sympathetically at all sides." That would never be enough, he argued. "It is a liberalism so bent on seeing all sides," he said, "that it fails to become committed to either side."[27] King blamed white liberals for the lack of momentum after the Montgomery bus boycott, saying the movement had a "pressing need for a liberalism in the North that is truly liberal, that firmly believes in integration in its own community as well as in the deep South."[28]

In these early years, King balanced hope with frustration. In a 1960 speech, he targeted "white northern liberals," saying, "There is need for the type of liberal who not only sides up with righteous indignation when a Negro is lynched in Mississippi, but will be equally incensed when a Negro is denied the right to live in his neighborhood, or join his professional association, or secure a top position in his business."[29]

This balance between cajoling and being honest about the likelihood of a deep alliance emerged perhaps best of all in his 1963 "Letter from Birmingham Jail," one of the most powerful pieces of protest literature ever written. King's "Letter" was famously inspired when a prison guard smuggled him a newspaper featuring a letter by seven Christian ministers and a rabbi objecting to King's direct social protests, saying confrontation was delaying civil rights rather than speeding it up. King targeted his response at two overlapping groups. One was white religious leaders. Their weak support for civil rights showed their lack of "the sacrificial spirit of the early church," a lack that would prompt the white church to become "dismissed as an irrelevant social club with no meaning for the twentieth century." The other group King was "gravely disappointed with" was white liberals. By 1963, he had "almost reached the regrettable conclusion that the Negro's great stumbling block in the stride toward freedom is not the White Citizens Councilor or the Ku Klux Klanner but the white moderate who is more devoted to order than to justice; . . . who constantly says, 'I agree with you in the goal you seek, but I can't agree with your methods of direct action'; who paternalistically feels that he can set the timetable for another man's freedom; who lives by the myth of time; and who constantly advises the Negro to wait until a 'more convenient season.'"[30]

"Maybe I expected too much," King concluded.[31] By 1963, King had grown tired of trying to cajole unwilling spirits, to rouse the conscience of those who might have something to lose. The weakness of the white liberal was debilitating. Black people might just have to go it alone.

From then on, King's dismissiveness toward the "white liberal" grew. He more often fell back on the pessimism within his prophetic religious tradition, a tradition that suggested that the oppressed are the only ones who will ever be willing to bear the burden of the struggle against their oppressors because they are the only ones with a firm interest in doing so.[32] He increasingly called them "moderates" instead of "liberals," suggesting their abandonment of the historic meaning of liberalism. In *Why We Can't Wait*, from 1964, King was harsh in his assessment of white liberal requests, saying that Black leaders were constantly "being asked [by] moderates if we could be trusted to hold back the surging tides of discontent [from Black people] so that those on the shore would not be made too uncomfortable by the buffeting and onrushing waves."[33] It is hard not to think that this was King's response to Podhoretz's "My Negro Problem—and Ours." King increasingly began to see white liberals as obstacles rather than friends. Even *after* passage of the Civil Rights Act of 1964 and the Voting Rights Act of 1965, King referred to the "de facto" school segregation in the North as "a new form of slavery covered up [by] certain niceties." He openly hated the "rationalization" of police brutality among white liberals, seeing them as "polite" accomplices.[34] In 1967, King wrote, "Our white liberal friends cried out in horror and dismay: 'You are creating hatred and hostility in the white communities in which you are marching. You are only developing a white backlash.'" King mocked the hypocrisy: "As long as the struggle was down in Alabama and Mississippi, they could look afar and think about it and say how terrible people are. When they discovered brotherhood had to be a reality in Chicago and that brotherhood extended to next door, then those latent hostilities came out."[35]

King learned the hard way that genuine change only comes with increasing tension, and white liberals were opposed to that friction. "Society needs nonviolent gadflies to bring its tensions into the open and force its citizens to confront the ugliness of their prejudices and the tragedy of their racism," King wrote.[36] White liberals were simply unwilling to confront that ugliness.

One could easily suggest that King's language was tactical, that he himself didn't lose faith in the white liberal but that his dismissiveness was designed to curry favor with the increasingly radical people he was trying to lead. Either way, it testifies to the growing image of the "white liberal" as someone who is only ever a partial friend, easier to mock and distort in order to maintain power. The myth of the white liberal was set.

If someone as firmly planted in the liberal tradition as King could turn against white liberals, radical voices were eager in 1963 to say, "I told you so." "The white liberal differs from the white conservative only in one way," said Malcolm X in a famous speech from 1963. "The liberal is more deceitful than the conservative. The liberal is more hypocritical than the conservative." After all, "the white liberal is the one who has perfected the art of posing as the Negro's friend and benefactor; and by winning the friendship, allegiance, and support of the Negro, the white liberal is able to use the Negro as a pawn or tool in this political 'football game' that is constantly raging between the white liberals and white conservatives."[37]

Stokely Carmichael said much the same thing. "We are the maids in the kitchens of liberal white people," he told mostly white liberal students at Berkeley in 1966. "We are the janitors, the porters, the elevator men; we sweep up your college floors. . . . Are the liberals willing to share their salaries with the economically insecure black people they so much love?"[38] Malcolm X and Stokely Carmichael both rejected white liberal support in their organizations.[39] "We don't want you working in our ghettos one summer and going to Europe the next summer," Carmichael told an audience of white liberal Harvard students, adding, "if you really are sincere about helping Negroes in America, then try to reform some of the white supremacists in your own neighborhood."[40] In Carmichael's view, having white liberals work in Black neighborhoods perpetuated the myth that Black people cannot do the work themselves.

For radical voices like these, the problem with white liberals was more than just lack of reliability. It was their dubious goals. When it came to questions of race, the white liberal dream was integration. Most Black radicals rejected that as kumbaya assimilation. Most of them sought some version of Black Power, Black nationalism, or Pan-Africanism, all premised on a semblance of cultural, social, or political separation from the white world. In his signature speech on "Black Power," Carmichael concluded that white liberals "perpetuate a paternalistic, colonial relationship."[41] Like all anticolonial actions, Black Americans needed to demand freedom and independence, and then take it if it wasn't freely given.

To Black radicals, then, white liberals offered a poisoned olive branch. Calls for reform were designed to pacify. As Eldridge Cleaver understood the situation, some "Black Americans are too easily deceived by a few smiles and friendly gestures, by the passing of a few liberal-sounding laws which are left on the books to rot unenforced."[42] Radical voices like Cleaver and Carmichael generally targeted their critiques at large systems like capitalism or colonialism: white liberals were bad, but they were simply subservient to larger historical forces. Still, harping on white liberals helped display their own radical credentials. It is not hard to see the rhetoric as both generally true through their lens but also as self-serving rhetoric, designed to inflame. Once again, justifiable critiques of white liberals had evolved into a rhetoric of oppositional politics, with white liberals portrayed as the imagined oppressor.

———————

Amid the creation of this stereotype, actual white liberals protested. They were, as Hubert Humphrey had said, too slow in showing up, but they were there now, passing laws and making change. Still, no matter how hard they tried, they couldn't shake their image as halfway friends, impediments to real change.

In a famous dustup in 1963, for instance, Attorney General (and perceived white liberal) Robert Kennedy invited James Baldwin,

Kenneth Clark, Lorraine Hansberry, and a handful of other Black leaders to his New York City apartment to try to get a better sense of what Black people wanted. The tense, no-holds-barred, two-and-a-half hour meeting was punctuated by Kennedy's desire to rattle off a variety of political achievements and to locate realistic policy goals—the liberal methods of process, rational thought, and slow change. Baldwin, Hansberry, and the other guests believed that policy changes, which at that point were always curtailed by the political realities of kowtowing to white Southern congressmen, were not the point. The point was for the president of the United States of America to make Black civil rights a moral issue of right versus wrong, and to do so instantly. One proposal that made no sense to Kennedy was to have the president personally accompany the University of Alabama's Black students through campus. Kennedy saw political grandstanding. "They don't know what laws are," Kennedy said later, "they don't know what the facts are—they don't know what we've been doing or what we're trying to do. . . . It was all emotion, hysteria—they stood up and orated—they cursed—some of them wept and left the room."[43] Kennedy didn't have time for anguish. He wanted achievable goals that could be touted in a reelection campaign.

It was about this time that Norman Podhoretz published his inflammatory essay "My Negro Problem—and Ours," an essay that explored the white liberal's journey on matters of race. In some ways, it is worth forgiving the essay's blatant racial prejudices (the notion, for example, that all Black people have "superior physical grace and beauty") because working through ingrained racism is actually the point of the essay. Podhoretz tried to understand how it was that white liberals like himself could understand in their bones the moral correctness of the Black freedom movement yet still live in fear of Black people, how his own "twisted feelings" about Black people "conflict with the moral convictions I have." He assumed this imbalance was typical for white liberals (making the perhaps white liberal assumption that his personal experience represented the American experience at large). Podhoretz's essay concludes, "it used to be asked of white liberals, 'Would you like your sister to marry one?'" Now that he was older, he aimed the question at his daughter. His answer? "'No, I wouldn't *like* it at all. I would rail and rave and rant and tear my hair. And then I hope I would have the courage to curse myself for raving and ranting, and to give her my blessing." His last sentence? "How dare I withhold [my blessing] at the behest of the child I once was and against the man I now have a duty to be?" But it was still unclear what Podhoretz would do even when he clearly knew what was right. This was the anguish of the white liberal.[44]

In a very real sense, white liberals were eager to admit past errors and fight for change. They held councils, marches, fundraisers. They wrote letters to legislators, presidents, and op-ed boards. Many had sat at lunch counters with Black compatriots integrating Woolworths and other segregated facilities. Many had petitioned their lawmakers to make change. They had crafted the language that turned into the Civil Rights Act of 1964. When the Black freedom movement shifted from ending segregation to winning voting rights, white liberals endorsed laws and marched in Selma. When housing became the issue, they reformed housing laws and walked picket lines. They could not single-handedly change America, but they had used their considerable power to push for change, and some things had changed.

Many white liberals contended that they were not given the credit they were due. They argued, not incorrectly, that they were being stereotyped and disparaged as unidimensional. They were not back-lashers, after all. Their enthusiasm for the Black freedom movement may have flagged when the movement adopted nationalist or sep-aratist tones, but that was a philosophical transition away from the creation of a color-blind society.

As at the *Commentary* symposium, white liberals themselves were torn about the natural progression of their philosophy. Some advo-cated solely for the legal equality of Black Americans: once legal equality was achieved, then the civil rights movement would turn to educating Americans about equality and the civil rights movement would be over. Other liberals thought more radical measures would be needed, endorsing Whitney Young's notion of "a domestic Marshall Plan" for Black America. This plan would then bring Black Americans to a place where they could compete fairly with white Americans. Reinhold Niebuhr, for one, believed that it was this kind of "coercion" that would be needed to effect lasting change. But white liberals were split. Most wanted the ends of reparations without the cost. As President Lyndon B. Johnson famously put it, "You do not take a person who, for years, has been hobbled by chains and liberate him, bring him up to the starting line of a race and then say, 'you are free to compete with all the others,' and still justly believe that you have been completely fair." Johnson, at least rhetorically, wanted "not just legal equity but human ability, not just equality as a right and a theory but equality as a fact and equality as a result." But then, in this tortured speech that so profoundly started by suggesting the need for reparations, he ended by saying that Black people needed to work to uphold their own family structures.[45]

Those white liberals who believed legal equality was enough would move increasingly to the right over the 1960s and 1970s. They would soon be captured by the Republican Party as one component of its so-called silent majority. When in 1964 President Johnson cut the Gordian knot tying the South to the Democratic Party, the Republican Party became the home not only of the South but also an increasing number of onetime liberals who considered reparations of some sort a step beyond their understanding of liberalism. Meanwhile, those who favored a more reparative commitment to racial equality continued within the Democratic Party. They would fight to maintain and expand programs like affirmative action and fair-employment practices.

———————

Regardless of what they actually did, though, attempts to defend the work of the "white liberal" almost always fell short. As for those on the right and the left, the phrase had become a cudgel, a way for

Black people to safely vent frustration. And after 1964, it became a near slur. Lerone Bennett Jr., the historian, journalist, and intellectual provocateur, made the case clearest in a 1963 article in *Ebony* assessing "The Mood of the Negro." The article detailed the growing radicalism of Black Americans but saved its final paragraphs to target "middle-class white liberals" (which he put in quotation marks). Bennett raged against Podhoretz's essay "My Negro Problem" before quoting a civil rights leader who wished white liberals "a fond farewell, with thanks for services rendered, until you are ready to re-enlist as foot soldiers and subordinates in a Negro-led, Negro-officered army under the banner of Freedom Now."[46]

The essay proved so powerful that a publisher asked Bennett to develop it into a book. *The Negro Mood* came out in 1964. What is strikingly different about the book is that Bennett's critique of white liberals had grown exponentially. Bennett allotted roughly a third of the book to a chapter entitled, "Tea and Sympathy: Liberals and Other White Hopes." The essay, by far the hardest-hitting in the book, seethed and, pointedly, didn't use quotation marks anymore. Its assessment of white liberals was brutal: "In all crises, at all times, white liberals have two basic aims, to prevent polarization and to prevent racial conflict." And: "The white liberal is Augustine praying before his conversion, 'Give me chastity and continency, but not yet.'" And "This is the white liberal: a man of Shadows, a friend of freedom who pauses, calculates, hesitates."[47]

Bennett's analysis centered on the argument that white liberals always have chosen and always would choose unity of nation and security of self over moral correctness that comes with costs, and that Black people have throughout American history typically paid the price for that reticence. In the Compromise of 1877 that ended Reconstruction, "it was necessary to throw Negroes overboard to reconcile the North and the South," Bennett wrote, not unfairly. The relationship between white liberals and Black people, he concluded, "is a history of bad faith," one of "betrayal."[48] Bennett reported that in 1964 "the reputation of white liberals in the Negro community is at an all-time low."[49]

Some Black activists continued to work with white liberals. But their speeches and essays often morphed into rebukes. In June 1964, for example, a group of Black and white artists and thinkers met in New York City to clear the air. The forum was filled with intellectual and artistic heavyweights, including Charles Silberman, James Wechsler, Leroi Jones, Ossie Davis, and Ruby Dee, but it was Lorraine Hansberry who stole the show. Hansberry, of *A Raisin in the Sun* fame, confessed that she had been raised on liberal values but, by 1964, was wise enough to know "there is a problem about white liberals." They hid so far behind their methods of seeking knowledge and learning all perspectives on an issue that they forgot to *feel*. They were, she said, unable to empathize with the deep longings of people trapped in the prison of history. "Since 1619," Hansberry said, "Negroes have tried every method of communication, of transformation of their situation from petition to the vote, everything." Nothing had worked. She pointed to white liberals' hypocrisy. "The problem is," she said, "we have to find some way . . . to show and to encourage the white liberal to stop being a liberal and become an American radical." Hansberry did not question white liberals' sincerity, just their commitment.[50]

Historian David Chappell argued in 2004 that one major rift between white liberals and many civil rights activists, liberal or radical, was that many of the Black activists had a prophetic sensibility about human nature, a notion that human beings tended toward corruption and greed. Their experience and their religious faith had conditioned them to think this way. White liberals, on the other hand, tended to be more optimistic, thinking humans could be educated and improve. Their alliance in the early years of the civil rights movement was, Chappell suggests, "more an alliance of convenience than one of deep ideological affinity."[51] Viewed in this light, the alliance's unraveling after 1963 may not seem as baffling as it sometime has. That it unraveled, though, goes without question.

Following the publication of James Baldwin's *Commentary* symposium, the letters to the editor the next month proved revealing about
the state of the white liberal in 1964. "We grieve for you," wrote
the associate editor of the radical *Liberator Magazine*, "because we
think you might be sincere but also misguided as to what the . . .
real problems of our culture are." A reader named Donald F. Joyce
congratulated James Baldwin for trying "I fear in vain" to convey how
Black Americans feel, while the white liberals on the panel remained
"academic and clinical." Joyce added, "As a self-incriminating portrait
of 'white liberals,' I feel that the panel was a brilliant success. It revealed that the white liberal is emotionally unprepared to be liberal
when confronted with straight talk about the Negro." Another reader
said the discussion reinforced his own "prejudices on the subject of
liberal, a term which seems to have become a semantic trap, useless
for any kind of significant discourse."[52]

As the critique moved from pointed and specific to rhetorical and
utilitarian throughout the 1960s, the "white liberal" eventually became
a scapegoat symbolizing all unfulfilled dreams. In a 1969 discussion
between James Baldwin and Dick Gregory in front of a London
audience, Baldwin was asked about the role of "the white liberal"
within the civil rights movement. Baldwin was by now completely
dismissive. "To my ear as a Black man," Baldwin said, "a White Liberal is immediately suspect because it is indistinguishable from, and
one has got to face this, you might say the white missionary." The
white liberal was just reproducing the colonial order of the past four
hundred years, nothing more, nothing less—we'll save your soul while
stealing your natural resources and your labor, while also making you
fight on our behalf.[53]

But Baldwin's best swipe might have come in his discussion of
the white liberal's dream film, *Guess Who's Coming to Dinner* (1967),
produced and directed by Stanley Kramer, who was famous for his
liberal "message films." In this film, the characters played by renowned actors Spencer Tracy and Katherine Hepburn, Matt and
Christina Drayton, serve as stereotypical white liberals dedicated to

racial equality. Their ideals get tested when their daughter, Joanna (played by Katharine Houghton), brings home a Black man, John Prentice (played by Sidney Poitier), and announces her intention to marry him. John's résumé is impeccable—a doctor, a humanitarian, a World Health Organization volunteer. As is the way he treats their daughter—with kindness, deference, respect. Kramer intentionally made him so perfect that the only objectionable thing about him could be his race. Released just six months after the US Supreme Court's *Loving v. Virginia* decision, which legalized interracial marriage throughout the country, the film tested the question of how far civil rights should go. Christina generally takes their daughter's announcement well, but Matt is slower to come around. There are some interesting twists, as when both the Draytons' Black maid and John's father object to the marriage. But it is Matt's delay that is deemed important. Matt the white liberal doesn't want to be hurried into deciding. He needs time. As Tillie the maid puts it, "Civil rights is one thing. This here is somethin' else." Finally, good sense prevails. Matt chides Joanna and John for "attaching so much importance to what her mother and I might think . . . because in the final analysis it doesn't matter a damn what we think. The only thing that matters is what they feel, and how much they feel, for each other." In 1960s America, that was a bit naive. When the racists come, and they will, Matt advises, "the two of you will just have to ride that out . . . you'll just have to cling tight to each other and say, 'screw all those people!'"[54]

It was left to James Baldwin, once again, to explain to white liberals what was wrong with this celebration of racial advancement. In a 1968 article, Baldwin reported that "Black people particularly disliked *Guess Who's Coming to Dinner*" because "they felt that Sidney was, in effect, being used against them." Black people "have been robbed of everything in this country," Baldwin said, and now white liberals were robbing them of their best actor (literally: Poitier won an Oscar for his performance) to make a fairy tale about American race relations. Baldwin had to remind his Black friends that "this movie wasn't made for *you*."⁵⁵ White liberals, for Baldwin at least, had learned nothing.

By the second half of the 1960s, then, many Black activists had developed a cast-in-stone, politically useful image of "white liberals." According to everyone from Martin Luther King Jr. to Malcolm X to Lorraine Hansberry to James Baldwin, white liberals were soft at the core, committed to the cause in word but not in deed, generally mealymouthed partial allies who could be helpful only in some circumstances. As Lerone Bennett put it, "He is all negation, the white liberal: now is not the time, this is not the place, the weapon you have is too large or too small. . . . He wants results without risks, freedom without danger, love without hate. He affirms tomorrow, denies yesterday, and evades today. He is all form, all means, all words—and no substance."⁵⁶

Black thinkers didn't dwell too much on liberal accomplishments. And when they did, it was always with caveats, talking of things still to be done, or skipped over because of the kinds of compromises white liberals always felt compelled to make. By the late 1960s and early 1970s, the Black image of the white liberal was the young woman who wanted to march in the parade but then went back to her comfortable home when it was over, the man who professed to be for the cause but then left when the police showed up. They were halfway friends. By the late 1960s, to a large number of Black people, white liberals were a front for four hundred years of oppression.

As the 1960s moved into the 1970s, this lack of trust in a plausible middle ground populated by well-meaning white people pushed Black thinkers into at least two directions. Both were, in a sense, born out of a politics of resentment. First, that rejection went predictably toward radical Black nationalism, to dashikis and Afros, toward James Baldwin's departure from the United States and Angela Davis's harboring of guns to protest a racist judicial system and the formation of ethnic studies departments in universities that fashioned what later became known as identity politics. But that resentment also went toward a Black conservatism that took as gospel the trope that institutional assistance was little more than white liberal paternalism that ought to be rejected.

In either case, by the middle-to-late 1960s Black leaders had, fairly or unfairly, landed on an image of white liberals that proved generally useful to prod the more extreme elements within their movement. In this aspect, they paralleled almost exactly what had happened on the right and the left. For all these groups, the specter of the white liberal had worked to unify people with disparate policy goals and then helped push them away from the center. It would only be a matter of time before political analysts and culture watchers sought to more cynically pick up on the phenomenon.

FIVE

RADICAL CHIC AND POSITIVE POLARIZATION

White Liberals as Out-of-Touch Elites

"Mmmmmmmmmmmmmmm," started Tom Wolfe, gobbling down some delicious little Roquefort cheese morsels rolled in crushed nuts. The writer was at Leonard Bernstein's Upper East Side apartment in 1970, attending a fundraiser for the Black Panthers, the contrast almost too much to bear between the finery on display in the luxurious thirteen-room Park Avenue duplex and the guns-and-pancakes grit of the Black Panthers. Before settling into one of the most humorous takedowns of white liberals in American history, one that enshrined liberals as elitist, pretentious, and out of touch, Wolfe felt compelled to appreciate the appetizers a bit more: "It's the way the dry sackiness of the nuts tiptoes up against the dour savor of the cheese that is so nice, so subtle." Then came the knife: "Wonder what the Black Panthers eat here on the hors d'oeuvre trail? Do the Panthers like little Roquefort cheese morsels wrapped in crushed nuts this way, and asparagus tips in mayonnaise dabs, and *meatballs petites au Coq Hardi*, all of which are at this very moment being offered to them on gadrooned silver platters by the maids in black uniforms with hand-ironed white aprons?" Wolfe was curious how "that huge Black Panther there in the hallway, the one shaking hands with Felicia

Bernstein herself, the one with the black leather coat and the dark glasses and the absolutely unbelievable Afro, Fuzzy Wuzzy-scale in fact—is he, a Black Panther, going to pick up a Roquefort cheese morsel rolled in crushed nuts from off the tray, from a maid in uniform, and just pop it down the gullet without so much as missing a beat of Felicia's perfect Mary Astor voice?"[1]

When Tom Wolfe learned the that editors of *New York* magazine didn't put a word limit on articles—"until it gets boring!"—Wolfe penned a 25,000-word comedic hit piece that catapulted him to fame.[2] His target? White liberals. He had a ready audience, too. By 1970, almost everyone could find something to hate about white liberals, from the "godless communism" detected by those on the right, to the plastic meekness detected by those on the left, to their dangerous halfway friendship as experience by Black Americans. But Wolfe developed a different critique. Wolfe's argument was that, after being put on the defensive on multiple fronts throughout the 1960s, by 1970 white liberals were clamoring for respect any way they could, even by demonstrating affection for bona fide radicals. It wasn't now that they were too cautious, pragmatic, or defensive of the postwar culture the New Deal helped create, but rather, in Wolfe's portrayal, the white liberal was now effete, naive, and all too eager to support provocateurs. Wolfe's liberals were generally not the same people as those liberals who had been criticized in earlier iterations except in one important way: the way in which it was useful for those on the right to bundle them together. In Wolfe's memorable phrasing, liberals were not dangerous buffoons about to accidentally bring about communism; instead, they were fools unwittingly and ridiculously celebrating a moment of "radical chic," when it was hip for comfortable, well-heeled white liberals to give high fives to burn-the-house-down agitators. Everyone knew it was all show. But nonetheless, there they were, on a quest to hush their critics and reassert authority. Then along came Wolfe to pull the rug out from under them, poking bare-knuckled fun at the clash of cultures that occurs when white liberals pose as friends of the poor and the marginalized. By 1970, white liberals were no longer to be feared. Instead, they were to be mocked. How genuine was their commitment to the cause when they still had *meatballs petites au Coq Hardi* and uniformed servants?

On those servants: "Lenny and Felicia are geniuses," Wolfe reported, speaking of America's greatest composer and his wife, because they chose *white* South Americans: "Obviously if you are giving a party for the Black Panthers . . . you can't have a Negro butler and maid."[3]

On entertainment: Best stick with jazz. A mariachi band performing at a fundraiser for Cesar Chavez was a faux pas, as Andrew Stein had learned at his fundraiser for the grape growers on his father's estate in Southampton. "After all," Wolfe wrote, "mariachi bands, with those Visit Mexico costumes on and those sad trumpets that keep struggling up to the top of the note but always fall off and then try to struggle back up again, are the prime white-tourist Mexicans." And Stein's was a party for La Causa, "the fighting *chicanos.*"[4]

On attire: "Obviously one does not want to wear something frivolously and pompously expensive," Wolfe wrote, suggesting how wealthy many white liberals were in the popular imagination. "On the other hand one does not want to arrive 'poor-mouthing it' in some outrageous turtleneck and West Eighth Street bull-jean combination, as if one is 'funky' and of 'the people.'" Felicia Bernstein hit the ideal note with "the simplest little black frock imaginable, with absolutely no ornamentation save for a plain gold necklace. It is perfect."[5]

And on radical chic itself, on white liberals clamoring for a voice in American society when everyone seemed to have turned against them: "Only radical in style; in its heart it is part of Society and its traditions. Politics, like Rock, Pop and Camp, has its uses; but to put one's whole status on the line for *nostalgie de la boue* [literally, nostalgia for mud] in any of its forms would be unprincipled."[6]

Wolfe argued that this was a chic and not just a onetime Leonard Bernstein thing when he wrote, "as Lenny and Felicia are this evening, or as Sidney and Gail Lumet did last week, or as John Simon

of Random House and Richard Baron, the publisher, did before that;
or for the Chicago Eight, such as the party Jean vanden Heuvel gave;
or for the grape workers or Bernadette Devlin, such as the parties
Andrew Stein gave; or for the Young Lords, such as the part Ellie
Guggenheimer is giving next week in *her* Park Avenue duplex; or
for the Indians or the SDS [Students for a Democratic Society] or
the G.I. Coffee Shops or even for the Friends of the Earth." Yes, the
rich white liberal elite were being found out and were struggling for
relevance. Radical chic was their method.

"Panther night at the Bernsteins," as Wolfe cruelly called it,
was, then, in his telling, merely performance art. As Wolfe and
his audience well understood, the move would only backfire, too,
and for several reasons. First, it was just too easy to mock. Wolfe
barely broke a sweat penning his laugh-out-loud description. Even
famously unfunny President Richard Nixon could find humor in the
party. Wolfe received an adoring letter on White House stationery,
signed by Raymond K. Price Jr., special assistant to Nixon, saying,
"I've seldom enjoyed a magazine article as much as your 'radical
chic' piece. I've been watching the phenomenon develop with a
mixture of horror, fascination and amusement, and your treatment
of it is one of the deftest bits of literary dissection I've ever seen.
Truly a classic."[7]

But radical chic would backfire for another reason, too: because
embracing radicalism forced liberals into positions they could not
defend. The Bernsteins' supposed support for the Black Panthers,
for instance, led them straight into the treacherous waters of Black-
Jewish relations, which were being tested mightily in 1970 as Black
radicals vocally detested white liberal (often Jewish) leadership in
civil rights organizations and saw Israel as a colonizing force stealing
land from darker-skinned people. In this context, supporting the
Panthers could be seen as disrespecting Israel.[8]

But there was a third, key reason radical chic was destined to fail:
by 1970, the stereotype that white liberals were out-of-touch elites,
mockable by nearly everyone, was almost impossible to shake, and

Wolfe's piece hit them at their weakest. It is, of course, easier to mock than to understand, but understanding was beside the point. Close readers of Wolfe's essay would have spent at least ten pages working through a fairly rigorous discussion of the Panthers' political philosophy, with white liberals clearly rejecting the Panthers' long-term goals. When Don Cox, the Panthers' field marshal, said he didn't think equality could be achieved "within the present system," Leonard Bernstein laughed at him: "So you're going to start a revolution from a Park Avenue apartment!" Most of the white liberals left the party unconvinced. They remained true to liberalism's principles of change within a stable system that acknowledged the value of middle-ground positions.[9]

None of that mattered when Wolfe published his piece. It was the mocking that everyone remembered. After all, the piece "wasn't really about the Panthers at all," as Wolfe admitted on William F. Buckley Jr.'s television show, *Firing Line*. Instead, it was about "a social phenomenon," it was about mocking white liberals who still thought they were the American elite. The piece was designed to expose their inauthenticity, their distance from "real" America, for the ignorant way they tried to assert control when they had long lost that right. For many Americans, the late 1960s and early 1970s were a time of tearing things apart, a time of frustration about the Vietnam War, civil rights, women's rights, dreams unfulfilled, lost promises, and the assassination of nearly everyone who proposed a way forward. If there can be such a thing as a national mood, dark was its color and cynical its tone. And if all that disparate anger and frustration could converge on a single focal point, if it could find a single recipient, the result would be explosive. And, for reasons both simultaneously understandable and unjustified, the primary focus of much of that ire landed on white liberals, who had supposedly let everyone down.

After Wolfe's article, no one wanted to be at Lenny's party.[10] Bernstein himself spent countless hours fighting back, arguing that it had not been a party but a *meeting*, and that white liberals were not dupes and did not believe in the politics of the Black Panthers. His archives contain 203 letters about the event, almost all handwritten, almost all frustrated missives protesting outsiders' interpretations.[11] But these attempts to clarify were laughed at; Bernstein was missing the point. Few people cared about the Black Panthers at the party; they were simply enjoying a hilarious takedown of a group that could stand to be taken down a notch. The more Bernstein protested, the funnier it was.

Wolfe's piece, in short, demonstrated the culmination of a new tactic for attacking white liberals, especially for those on the right. Up until the mid-1960s, liberals had been criticized for their politics, for their halfway measures, for their appeals to moderation in the face of existential threats. But from the late 1960s onward, any attempt to rescue a unified liberal tradition confronted a different challenge: they were now mocked for their style, their smugness, their supposedly elitist, above-the-fray way of existing in the world. They were now dismissible as an aging, snooty dowager living an extinct way of life. This was clearly untrue. Not every white liberal owned a huge Manhattan apartment. Not every white liberal liked Petit Roquefort cheese morsels rolled in crushed nuts. Not every liberal was so easily offended. But Wolfe's critique and others like it led to the creation of a relatively unified stereotype of white liberals as not just political buffoons but also as snobs who didn't bother to get their hands dirty while still enjoying a sentimental version of the good life. All stereotypes emerge from some truth, but only sometimes do they consume their subject. "That damn Radical Chic thing is the albatross around our family's weary neck," said Jamie Bernstein, son of Leonard and Felicia, nearly forty years later. "Our mother never recovered from the heartbreak and shame of this incident. No one was all the way happy again."[12] The critique of white liberals that developed in the late 1960s and early 1970s led to a full-scale backlash against them, making clear that the white liberal was perfectly expendable, their day gone, the torch of authority ready to be claimed by someone else.

But who would claim it? Who would be able to focus all the anger of the late 1960s onto a single, eligible recipient? Or would everyone fail, leading to a society with no dominant cultural authority?

———————

Although Wolfe's essay wasn't strictly political, political analysts were among the first to recognize the uses of trolling liberals for their stereotyped way of being rather than their articles of faith. In doing so, in recrafting the image of the white liberal as out-of-touch elitists who foolishly embraced a variety of wrong-headed radicalisms, they could blame white liberals for all the supposed extremes of the 1960s—even despite the fact that those movements were begun, ironically enough, as protests to postwar liberalism. And, as was typical when it came to owning the libs, those on the right struck first. In doing so, the right began to exchange its stuffy, William F. Buckley-esque nerdy appearance for a souped-up populism geared toward issues of identity, siege mentality, and deep-seated anxiety. Today's Republican populism was born here.

Following the rule that it is easier to find a common enemy than common ground, Republican activists consciously and vocally tried to figure out how to use the growing resentment against white liberals even when liberal policies were still widely favored. This strategy emerged in 1968, through a twenty-seven-year-old political analyst named Kevin Phillips. Seeking a job, Phillips handed Nixon staffer Patrick Buchanan a book manuscript instead of a résumé. Upon reading it, Buchanan quickly realized Phillips knew more about reading political maps than anyone in the party. He hired him. The party consulted the manuscript throughout the campaign, perhaps helping glide Richard Nixon to the presidency. The next year the manuscript became the surprise 1969 bestseller *The Emerging Republican Majority*. Filled with graphs and notes and analysis of dozens of election returns from previous decades, Phillips's central message was that changing racial, demographic, and political patterns in the

US favored Republicans, and that Republicans would need to press those advantages to win. Specifically, Philips argued that Republicans could, with slight modifications to their message, win over the entirety of South and the Midwest and therefore safely ignore the more liberal coasts by focusing on the politics of resentment against white liberals. "The whole secret of politics," Phillips told Garry Wills, is "knowing who hates who."[13]

As Phillips saw things, Republicans could realign the electoral map for generations by gaining the votes of an emerging white middle class, the former working-class Americans who had just moved to the suburbs and who were actively revolting "against the caste policies and taxation of the mandarins of Establishment liberalism."[14] These were people who had achieved economic success in the postwar years and who simultaneously sought to close the door behind them (especially with regard to Black and Brown people) and resented those who they perceived looking down on them as nouveau riche—white liberals.

According to Phillips, Republicans could win these voters by training their rhetoric of resentment on each of these groups, one explicitly, the other more carefully. When it came to focusing ire on Black people, Phillips warned that Republicans would have to be careful because many Americans had embraced the idea that overt racism was contrary to American ideals. Republicans, therefore, should stick to coded language like "states' rights" and "law and order" when speaking about race. Everyone recognized this as "dog whistle politics"—talking about race without talking about race.[15] But it could be effective nonetheless. Republicans could win votes by paying attention to many white people's exhaustion with and resentment toward Black civil rights (or, for that matter, their outright racism), but Republicans had to avoid looking like outright bigots. George Wallace, the Alabama governor and 1968 presidential aspirant, was less cautious. He won many votes but had limited national appeal. There was a way, Phillips argued, to steal George Wallace's votes without becoming George Wallace.

But when looking at "who hates who" Phillips identified a second group Republicans could be far more overt about hating—white liberals. Phillips argued that Republicans could win the presidency not only by ignoring the Northeast, but by using the region as a *"provocateur* of resentment elsewhere."[16] Mock them, make them the enemy, make them appear contrary to American values. It would spark "a populist revolt of the American masses." In Phillips's mind, stoking hatred against northeastern white liberals was the trigger that would "unfold the multiple sectional conflicts and group animosities" that would spark the political excitement of those in the South and Midwest.[17] "Who needs Manhattan when we can get the electoral votes of eleven Southern states?" he asked. "Put those together with the Farm Belt and the Rocky Mountains, and we don't need the big cities. We don't even want them."[18]

Phillips labeled these potential resentful Republicans "the great, ordinary, Lawrence Welkish mass of Americans from Maine to Hawaii."[19] But unlike earlier eras of political transformation, the key to drawing these voters over to the Republican Party was tapping into their notion that the cultural changes of the 1960s—not just civil rights, but advances in women's rights, the expectations of children, the expanding provenance of the federal government, the basic codes of society—were the fault of white liberals. In Phillips's telling, if Republicans could make it appear as if white liberals were pushing all the social changes, they could drive a wedge between the white working class and the middle and upper levels of the middle class.

The key was *not* to focus on policy but on liberals themselves, on the "people who make their money out of plans, ideas, communication, social upheaval, happenings, excitement." These were the "research directors, associate professors, social workers, educational consultants, urbanologists, development planners, journalists, brotherhood executives, foundation staffers, communications specialists, culture vendors, pornography merchants, poverty theorists, and so forth." They were not, tellingly, people who got their hands dirty for a living. "This is not a movement *in favor of* laissez faire or any ideology; it is *opposed to* welfare and the Establishment," he said.[20] After all, in Phillips's mind, "the Establishment" was composed not only of "social workers" trying to clear a pathway up the economic ladder for those less fortunate but also of "pornography merchants" eager to adulterate "classic American values" to fit their culturally libertine tastes. Phillips's point was to yoke them together so Republicans wouldn't have to talk about policy.[21]

In several revealing passages, Phillips actually endorsed many of the New Deal and Great Society landmark programs, including specifically Medicare, Social Security, and expanded aid to education.[22] They were popular. Republicans should steer clear of talking about rolling back popular policies, even if they were perceived as "liberal." Instead, the key to Republican success was building resentment against the white liberals who were supposedly ushering in social and cultural changes. "The emerging Republican majority," Philips wrote, "spoke clearly in 1968 for a shift away from the sociological jurisprudence, moral permissiveness, experimental residential, welfare and educational programming and massive federal spending by which the Liberal (mostly Democratic) Establishment sought to propagate liberal institutions and ideology—and all the while reap growing economic benefits."[23] By not advocating any political policy but by uniting a bloc of voters around a common hatred, Republicans could win for generations.

Was Phillips right? This has been long debated in Republican circles. In 1970, Republicans were too explicit in their use of race as a tool of resentment, and voters punished them in the midterm elections, although midterm losses are typical for the party with presidential power, so it is unclear whether the politics of race really was important. Regardless, President Nixon thought it was. Nixon read Phillips's book over the winter congressional holiday in 1969. He wrote his staffers, "Use Phillips as an analyst—study his strategy—don't think in terms of old-time ethnics, go for Poles, Italians, Irish, must learn to understand Silent Majority. . . . don't go for Jews & Blacks."[24]

In the presidential campaign of 1972, Nixon focused his attacks most solidly on the havoc supposedly wreaked by white liberals. As one Nixon staffer put it, "We should increasingly portray [Democratic nominee George] McGovern as the pet radical of Eastern Liberalism, the darling of the *New York Times*, the hero of the Berkley Jet Set: Mr. Radical Chic."[25] For his part, Nixon sought to appeal to "those millions who have been driven out of their home in the Democratic Party," adding, "come home not to another party, but . . . to the great principles we Americans believe in together."[26] He was reelected in the third-largest landslide in American history (only FDR in 1936 and Ronald Reagan in 1984 have surpassed him in percentage of electoral votes won). Ever since 1972, Phillips's analysis has largely held up.

By the 1980s, coded racial animosities combined with antiliberal, small-government language had pushed Republicans to dominance in the South and Midwest, and it has remained so for at least fifty years. Republicans have attacked large social welfare programs in general terms but usually have been notably quiet about Medicare and Social Security. In 1980, Republican strategists added religious conservatism and antifeminism to their litany of pressure issues ("who hates who"), although they have done so not necessarily by openly embracing evangelical or patriarchal policies but by labeling anything outside them as "liberal" and using culture war rhetoric to stoke resentments. Phillips's road map has been a boon for Republicans; it located and molded the perfect target in the vague but adaptable specter of the white liberal.

Sometimes a script finds its perfect actor.

Kevin Phillips's book came out in July 1969, shot to the top of the *New York Times* bestseller list, and was immediately embraced throughout Republican circles and feared by those on the left. Nixon claimed initially he hadn't read it when in fact he had. For him, Phillips was too straightforward. Nixon wanted to portray himself as above politics. But one Republican who seemed to understand the book's message and his role in it was Nixon's vice president, Spiro Agnew. Within a year of its release, Agnew would be doing his utmost to act out Phillips's script, with Nixon perhaps directing but certainly watching and approving.[27]

Both Nixon and Agnew were sons of grocers whose fathers were strict disciplinarians, and both believed that their economic and social class had slowed their progress compared with wealthier peers. Both worked their way through college, both were the only students in their yearbooks who were wearing neckties.[28] In their minds, everything they achieved had been accomplished by dint of their own hard work, their wealthier and better-connected peers be damned. They both imagined themselves as the epitome of first-generation success, paying no attention to any historical or structural advantages they may have had.

Agnew worked his way through Maryland politics starting from his local Parent-Teacher Association, not with ideological commitment but through constant triangulation—as governor, he was a liberal Republican, more in favor of racial integration than any other candidate. But all of Agnew's policies were bound by one central message: order prevented lawlessness, and a politician's job was to provide security. In a way, Agnew's vision was the polar opposite of qualitative liberalism, which took security for granted and instead sought to enhance life and make it more sophisticated and worth living. For Agnew, chaos was always too close at hand, and controlling it was government's primary purpose. If Agnew appeared open to racial integration, it was out of an attempt to quell disorder, not promote egalitarianism.

But that sensibility changed quickly. In the first nine months of 1967, there were 164 civic uprisings concerning race, 33 of them so violent they required the state police to intervene, and 8 that required the National Guard. Already a skeptic of liberalism, after the uprisings Agnew began to believe that liberal efforts to give people what they wanted would inevitably be abused. In 1968, after riots in Baltimore erupted when Martin Luther King Jr. was assassinated, Agnew "came to believe that whenever he gave dissenters an inch, they took a mile, and anarchy was loosed upon the land. So he would no longer give an inch," in the words of historian Rick Perlstein.[29] Liberalism's efforts to improve the quality of Americans' lives was bound to be abused by ne'er-do-wells. Liberals were buffoons to think otherwise.

When Agnew was tapped to be Nixon's running mate in 1968, he understood his role. He was Nixon's bulldog, saying things the presidential candidate couldn't. Despite Nixon's long history of red-baiting, for instance, in 1968 it was Agnew who called Democrats "squishy soft" on communism. But anticommunism, once meat and potatoes for the Republican Party (and its vision of liberals), no longer sufficed. Communism stoked fear in some people, but it no longer seemed to pose an existential threat that would move voters. Then, just months after the release of Phillips's *The Emerging Republican Majority*, Agnew set his sights on a different target. After a few buildup speeches taking jabs at white liberals, he unleashed his first lengthy tirade the day before Halloween in 1969. It would remain a staple in his arsenal for as long as he remained vice president.

The tirade began by spelling out two diametrically opposing sides. In Agnew's telling, his side, Nixon's side, consisted of respectable people, the working classes, those who in some way take orders for a living, those who thought the social upheavals of the 1960s emerged from people trying to gain something for nothing. Agnew gave these frustrated Americans a voice, saying things like, "It is time for the preponderant majority, responsible citizens of this country, to assert *their* rights."[30] The Vietnam War was not particularly popular among the American people in general. It didn't poll well. But it polled better than those who *opposed* the war. If the war was bad, the antiwar left was far worse, claimed the pollsters. Agnew recognized this perfectly. The world was changing. Black people, women, young people all were demanding rights, and in those struggles Agnew's side only saw the deterioration of American values. "Yippies, hippies, yahoos, Black Panthers, lions and tigers alike—I would swap the whole damn zoo for a single platoon of the kind of young Americans I saw in Vietnam," he said in one speech.[31] He claimed to speak for the "responsible" Americans who put their heads down, did their job, and then thanked their lucky stars they were born American.

But it was his characterization of the other side that really animated Agnew. There, always painted in devious colors, were the vocal protestors, those who broke the law through civil disobedience. "Hating what they call 'middle-class' justice, they will openly disrupt a courtroom; hating capitalism, they will blow up a bank; hating law, they will attack law enforcers," said Agnew, adding that "these are dangerous and heinous crimes. But the very fact that they are openly committed makes them easy to identify and to contain."[32]

Alas, the real villains weren't the activists willing to put their lives on the line for what they believed. At least those people were honest. No, Agnew's harshest words were for "those who characterize themselves as liberal intellectuals," that "glib, activist element who would tell us that our values are lies." The liberals were "arrogant . . . asking us to repudiate principles that have made this country great."[33] Liberals were the "effete corps of impudent snobs." They were the "nattering nabobs of negativism" who refused to celebrate America's traditional values.[34] His beef wasn't with the welfare state, it was with those who mocked his values and made him feel stupid for having them in the first place.

As Agnew set up the pieces, it was "liberal" values versus American values, an existential battle to the death. The language would have been familiar to longtime conservatives, but the prior enemy had been communism. Now the enemies were liberals, people who had supposedly abandoned the working class, told them what to do, and redirected their earnings either to their own coffers or to the undeserving. Following Phillips's suggestion, Agnew hardly said anything about policy. He spoke about "values" and how "theirs" were different from "ours." They were "political hustlers . . . who would tell us our values are lies." They "disdain to mingle with the masses who work for a living." They "are vultures who sit in trees and watch lions battle, knowing that win, lose, or draw, they will be fed." They were "ideological eunuchs," "parasites of passion."[35] Agnew loved alliteration.

Then came perhaps his most startling line: "If in challenging [them] we polarize the American people, I say it is time for a positive polarization." It was time to declare open war against white liberals: "It is time to rip away the rhetoric and divide on authentic lines."[36]

"Positive polarization" is a strong phrase coming from a sitting vice president. But in the middle of battles over the supposedly revolutionary demands of Black Americans and the heating up of dissent surrounding the Vietnam War, it hit the right note for many Americans.

Nixon saw the emotions the speech stirred and loved it. Within weeks, Nixon asked Agnew to tour the country to expound on the theme.

And, in a brilliant act of political gamesmanship, Agnew extended the definition of his hated "white liberals" to include another group: the media. In speech after speech, Agnew lambasted nearly every journalist in the nation for possessing a "liberal media bias." Journalists, Agnew said, were not objective reporters of fact. They were partisans denying the opposition airtime and dismissing legitimate critiques of the liberal order. The argument, true or not (and his proof, when provided, was highly selective), was that the news reflected its creators, and, because of that, he argued, in the words of historian Nicole Hemmer, journalists simply sought "to perpetuate liberal ideas and persuade the public to accept liberal policies."[37] Agnew repeatedly went after what he called the "closed fraternity of privileged men, elected by no one" who shaped public opinion. He called the "big-city liberal media . . . dishonest," adding, "to a man these commentators live and work in the geographically and intellectual confines of Washington, D.C. or New York City." They were not true Americans who lived, for example, in the South or the Midwest; they were coastal elites trying to convince you that their ideas were right and you were stupid, he alleged. The complaint also contained quiet doses of antisemitism, with urbane New York City elites trying to use their power to control Middle America. Whereas one of William F. Buckley's efforts in the 1950s and 1960s had been to rid the American right of blatant antisemitism, its allure remained strong for many American conservatives, even if it, too, now had to be executed in the manner of dog whistle politics.[38]

The tactic of tarring the press was all the more brilliant considering what some Republicans were in fact quietly trying to do. Despite the rhetoric of being for the common man, the Republican Party was still the party of big business, low taxes, government deregulation, and a reduced social safety net. Yet men like Nixon and Agnew now saw the opportunity to redraw the political map by aligning culturally with the white working classes. It was, economically at least, bait and switch. And some people recognized it. In fact, Kevin Phillips eventually left the Republican Party in the mid-1970s for its overt lying to the working classes, for using working-class resentments to get elected but then perpetuating aristocracies of wealth. For Agnew to question the objectivity of the media—the people who might possibly report on this sleight of hand—meant that Republicans could always question the motives of anyone making the case against them. When the press questioned Nixon's plans in Vietnam? Liberal media bias. When the Watergate scandal emerged? As North Carolina senator Jesse Helms put it, the account of the break-in at Democratic National Committee headquarters at the Watergate complex in Washington, DC, during the 1972 presidential campaign and its subsequent cover-up by the Nixon administration was just a story from "the incredible New York *Times*-Washington *Post* syndicate, which controls to a large degree what the American people will read and learn."[39] Thus began a long disinformation campaign that put spin at the center of all debate and discounted the rational basis of liberal thought.

Although Agnew is better known for his alliterative rants, he did have something interesting to say about liberal political philosophy. He contended that radicals and liberals, whom he worked hard to equate, had pushed liberal philosophy too far, favoring uninhibited individual rights over communal consensus. Agnew, on the other hand, argued there was no such thing as an individual's "natural right" and "it is only when society acknowledges it as a right and backs it by the power of the state and the respect of a majority of its responsible citizens that the right exists." While one might wonder what Thomas Jefferson and his Declaration of Independence might have to say about Agnew's denial of "self-evident truths" and "un-alienable Rights," another key question here is: who gets defined as a "responsible citizen"? Agnew skipped over these quibbles, staying on attack, saying, for instance, that "liberals" were "so blinded by total dedication to individual freedom that they cannot see the steady erosion of the collective freedom that is the capstone of a law-abiding society."[40] They had, supposedly, favored individual rights over social order. The irony is that Republicans of Herbert Hoover's generation had feared liberals because of their supposed overly gen-erous concern for the common good. But evidently that was only a concern when it came to economic matters. Now that Republicans were moving away from economic matters toward cultural and social ones, preserving the norms of community emerged as paramount. Liberals couldn't win.

But of course they couldn't. From Phillips to Agnew to Wolfe, liberals were now openly mocked by a large part of the population, and not only or even primarily for their economic associations but now for their cultural image. In the late 1960s and 1970s, writers and politicians on the right had expanded their understanding of the terms to associate *liberals* and *liberalism* with cultural effeteness and political radicalism. And Agnew was masterful at weaponizing this new definition. Even the lion of the liberals, Arthur Schlesinger Jr., penned a piece in the *New York Times* called "The Amazing Success Story of 'Spiro *Who?*'"[41] Agnew appeared on the cover of *Life* on May 8, 1970, next to the words, "Spiro Agnew Knows Best," the joke being that Agnew was now the tough-love father giving America "the good, old-fashioned, parental Talking-To." *Life* said of Agnew's speeches, "if, in the process, he is maybe further polarizing the country, wid-ening the rift with the young'uns, at least the oldsters are finding in him a great source of solace."[42]

And, *Life* continued, perhaps suggesting whom Agnew understood to be the "reasonable citizens" worthy of full citizenship: "When his avid listeners rose in ovation, they were all lily-white, middle-class, status-torn, money-worried, equality aggrieved parents."[43]

———

Sometimes a script finds its perfect actress.

Phyllis Schlafly was born in Missouri in 1924, her mother working as a teacher throughout the Great Depression to support the family after her father lost his job as a machinist and salesman. After her mother put her through Catholic schools, Schlafly graduated from Washington University in St. Louis in 1944 and grew interested in politics, especially Catholic anticommunism. She worked at the conservative think tank the American Enterprise Institute, as well as on a handful of Republican political campaigns, often crafting language that would red-bait Democratic opponents. In 1949, she married the wealthy attorney John "Fred" Schlafly Jr., and she began grassroots organizing from their southern Illinois home, mobilizing women to conservative causes, especially anticommunism. She ran for Congress several times, losing handily each time. But it was at the 1960 Republican National Convention where, as a delegate, she found her place in the party, leading a revolt of people she called "moral conservatives." Schlafly had located a wedge within the Republican Party between conservatives and moderates, one she was eager to exploit.

Although Schlafly is best known today for her work against the Equal Rights Amendment in the early 1970s, it was her self-published 1964 book, *A Choice Not an Echo*, that catapulted her to prominence within conservative circles. If William F. Buckley Jr., was the intellectual architect of modern antiliberal conservatism and Phillips the political mastermind, Schlafly was the grassroots suburban organizer. *A Choice Not an Echo* eventually sold more than three million copies and was widely credited with helping secure Barry Goldwater's presidential nomination in 1964. Schlafly had once been a member of the John Birch Society and, although she resigned amid fears the affiliation would tarnish her reputation (she at times denied membership altogether), members of the Birch Society purchased and distributed copies of the book widely, including up to 300,000 in California right before the 1964 Republican primary.[44]

The major theme of *A Choice Not an Echo* was that liberals had taken over not only the Democratic Party but the Republican Party as well. Republicans, as she saw things, had succumbed to "liberal me-tooism."[45] These liberals had stolen the party from those she understood to be true conservatives, who were devout anticommunists and favored an almost libertarian philosophy about government, concerning not only the size of the federal government but also its reach into matters better left to the states (like race relations). Coming before Republicans en masse had located the bogeyman within liberalism, the book was not shy about sounding conspiratorial, opening with the shocking declaration that, "from 1936 through 1960 the Republican presidential nominee was selected by a small group of secret kingmakers who are the most powerful opinion makers in the world."[46] These "kingmakers," in her explanation, favored liberal politicians because they had a financial stake in the welfare state: "Since the New York kingmakers dominate the consortium which fixes the interest rate the Government has to pay on its obligations, they have no incentive to see deficit financing stop."[47] What she demanded, as her title reflected, was *A Choice Not an Echo*. Barry Goldwater, in her mind, was "the man the left-leaning liberals most fear," and that made him the only true choice.[48]

Schlafly was quickly recognized as an organizer to be reckoned with. Her biographer, Donald Critchlow, tells a story of Schlafly getting on an airplane with the famous actor-comedian Bob Hope. When the pilot announced there was crowd who wanted autographs from a passenger, Hope instinctively stood up. But then the pilot apologetically told him it wasn't him they wanted but Schlafly.[49]

An even bigger moment for Schlafly, the one that propelled her fame beyond conservative circles, came a few years later, when she almost single-handedly organized the defeat of the Equal Rights Amendment (ERA) to the US Constitution. In 1972, the Senate had passed the bill, setting its course to be ratified by three-fourths of the states. A year later, thirty states had done so, leaving it just eight short of becoming a part of the Constitution. Then Schlafly showed up. She wasn't really interested in feminism as an issue, but she recognized that the energy of grassroots conservatism had moved from anticommunism, the Cold War, and government bloat to social issues. Schlafly dove into the movement, forming the STOP ERA (Stop Taking Our Privileges ERA) organization as her bullhorn. A brilliant tactician, Schlafly didn't invent a rationale for her antifeminism, she simply countered every point made by the most famous feminist at the time, Betty Friedan, whose book *The Feminist Mystique* (1963) had helped set the tone of the women's liberation movement.

With STOP ERA, Schlafly followed the Buckley playbook and Agnew's "positive polarization" to a tee, centering her entire argument on evil cultural changes supposedly sought by white liberals. Schlafly often swapped the specific word *liberal* for "women's libbers." In her opening manifesto—a short pamphlet entitled, "What's Wrong With 'Equal Rights' for Women?" —Schlafly poked fun at the "New 'women's liberation' organizations" that were "popping up, agitating and demonstrating, serving demands on public officials, getting wide press coverage always, and purporting to speak for some 100,000,000 American women. It's time," she said, "to set the record straight." More important than any of her specific arguments was how she painted her opposition. "The women's libbers are radicals who are waging a total assault on the family, on marriage, and on children," she wrote. "The women's libbers don't understand that most women want to be wife, mother and homemaker—and are happy in that role. The women's libbers actively resent the mother who stays at home with her children and likes it that way." Further, "women's libbers are promoting free sex instead of the 'slavery' of marriage. They are promoting Federal 'day-care centers' for babies instead of homes. They are promoting abortions instead of families." Her rousing call: "Women's libbers do *not* speak for the majority of American women."[50]

The antilib language was part and parcel of the movement, a key demonstration of how writers on the right had congealed their siege politics around the single term, "liberal." Schlafly set about educating conservative women around the country on how to convince state legislators to oppose the ERA. In Schlafly's home state of Illinois, STOP ERA hired a plane to fly over a pro-ERA rally, trailing a sign that read: "Illinois women oppose ERA—libbers go home."[51]

Schlafly's positive polarization worked. After Schlafly began her campaign, only three more states ratified the amendment. Fierce battles took place in every remaining state. All future ratification votes were close, sometimes with First Lady Rosalyn Carter having to make personal appeals to get the final supporting votes. But by 1982 the amendment still didn't have the votes, and some states were repealing their previous support. The *New York Times* wrote, "The 'backlash' against feminism looks more like a tidal wave."[52] Phyllis Schlafly had killed the ERA and churned up a tidal wave, powered by the language of antiliberalism.

————

Out of all this politics of negativity, Nixon at least made an effort to develop a positive solidarity, one group to unite the many whose support he sought. It was a real problem, unifying supporters of George Wallace, who sometimes appeared on the racist fringe, with those who thought the federal government had grown too powerful, with historic Republicans in wealthier parts of the country, with social conservatives who feared the breakdown of "traditional" values. Was there a positive label that could embrace the lot? Nixon tried a few, borrowing the "silent center" from the great Illinois liberal Senator Paul Douglas. But that didn't catch on. He then tried the "quiet Americans," a "new majority," the "forgotten Americans," "the forgotten majority," "the backbone of America," "the nonshouters," and "the nondemonstrators," but none of those stuck. Sometimes he tried several at once: "A great many *quiet Americans* have become committed to answers to social problems that preserve personal freedom. As this *silent center* has become part of *the new alignment*, it has transformed it from a minority into a majority."[53]

But no single name caught on until a few days after Agnew's 1969 Halloween speech. Less than a week after Agnew lambasted the "political hustlers . . . who would tell us our values are lies," Nixon lionized "the great—silent—majority of my fellow Americans," asking for their support in opposing those who opposed the Vietnam War. "The more support I can have from the American people," he said, the sooner he could negotiate peace. After all, it wasn't North Vietnam that could "defeat or humiliate" the United States, "only Americans can do that," Nixon said, assuming his audience knew full well who *those* Americans were.[54]

After so many attempts to name his people, the "silent majority" finally succeeded. Fifty thousand telegrams and thirty thousand letters poured into the White House demonstrating membership in Nixon's "silent majority." Nixon kept a barrel of the letters in the Oval Office to remind him of the love.

From late 1969 onward, the "silent majority" became Republican code for Americans who resented an overly activist federal government, who believed that whatever modicum of success they had achieved was solely the result of their own hard work and who didn't think too much about the large structural factors at play, those who felt the country was leaving behind what had at one time been normative American values in favor of moral relativism, those who thought civil rights had gone too far and that guaranteeing equal rights was enough, those who hated opposition to the Vietnam War more than the war itself, those who pushed back against any claims that white liberals might still have some semblance of leadership within the nation. The "silent majority" put a positive spin on the antiliberal politics of resentment.

Once Nixon anointed it, others joined in. "As a member of the silent majority," wrote James McDavid Jr., a white man from an affluent Charlotte, North Carolina, suburb in 1970, "I have never asked what anyone in government or this country could do for me, but rather have kept my mouth shut, paid my taxes, and basically asked to be left alone." McDavid was writing to his congressman explaining why he was outraged over a plan to force school desegregation through a neighborhood busing plan. McDavid saw the plan not in racial terms, at least not explicitly, but instead as the hand of an overreaching government taking away his freedom: "I think it is time the law abiding, tax paying white middle class started looking to the federal government for something besides oppression."[55] McDavid had followed the Phillips code perfectly and then put the label "silent majority" on it all.

Throughout 1970s, the phrase began to appear in venues far afield from politics. Six months after Nixon uttered the phrase, it was well known enough to be part of advertising culture. "Break away from the silent majority," read an ad from Bell & Howell, a camera company that that had developed a handheld video recorder that could pick up sound.[56] One of the first biographies of Phyllis Schlafly was subtitled *The Sweetheart of the Silent Majority*.

Close observers might have noticed that those on the right were simultaneously putting forward two opposing arguments against liberalism. Agnew complained that liberals were taking their demands for individual rights too far, sacrificing community standards. He was for preserving communal rights and limiting individual rights. Nixon, meanwhile, saw liberals as willing to sacrifice individual rights in the name of the collective good, and he positioned himself as the defender of individual rights. At the very least, these distinctions demonstrate the amorphousness of the specter of the liberal as imagined by those on the right. Liberals were, evidently, too much in favor of both individual rights and collective equality. Either way, they were a threat.

But were those making these arguments correct? Were the needs of the "silent majority" in fact being ignored by liberals? Where did all the anger come from? Was anger at liberals real, manufactured, or both?

On the one hand, it is hard to say the white working classes were being ignored. For most Americans the economy was strong throughout the 1960s and into the 1970s. Hiring was up in the late 1960s. The great economic slowdown would not emerge in full until about 1973, and, as Phyllis Schlafly had argued, both political parties favored policies that right-wing conservatives dismissed as "liberal," including jobs programs and expansion of the social safety net.

On the other hand, there was a sense, not wholly unwarranted, that the focus of American liberal democracy had shifted toward helping Black Americans and other historically marginalized people rather than the white working and middle classes, who, liberals argued, had already been helped by government programs during the New Deal and the GI Bill of Rights after World War II. But race only played a part in the perceived slight, and perhaps even just a peripheral part. In the late 1960s, many working-class and middle-class white Americans began to believe that the country was moving in the wrong direction, that crime was on the rise, that morality was slipping, that the work ethic they had been raised to see as the road out of poverty seemed under threat, that premarital chastity was gone, that the ideas of postponed gratification, gratitude for parental sacrifice, and more all seemed to be under siege. This perception was at least one origin of resentment—widespread social change that seemed to be endorsed by white liberals.

One possible way to understand this viewpoint is to see it as a reaction to liberals' transition away from the "quantitative liberalism" of the New Deal, which focused on bread-and-butter jobs-related issues, to postwar "qualitative liberalism," which focused on higher education, government-backed retirement plans, health care for the neediest people, and access for minoritized people to the middle class. It was savvy politics by Nixon to approve the country's first federal affirmation action plan, knowing it would tear apart a potential coalition between Black activists and white working-class labor unions, which held seniority sacrosanct. Affirmative action would help sunder the New Deal coalition, and Nixon and his party would benefit.

Professional elections watchers—the press, professors, political analysts—began to recognize the power of this white working-class resentment. After the 1968 presidential election, when George Wallace took 13.5 percent of the vote, the media began to see what Kevin Phillips had already identified. In October 1969, *Newsweek* devoted an entire issue to "The Troubled American: A Special Report on the White Majority." The issue was full of startling facts demonstrating not quite the persistence of racism in America (although that certainly existed) but white exhaustion with civil rights and the sacrifices white people believed that they were being asked to make on its behalf. A whopping 98 percent of white Americans polled expressed hostility toward forced busing for schoolchildren to achieve greater racial equality in schools, and 90 percent were against forced integration in their neighborhoods. Eighty-five percent of white people thought Black militants were being coddled by the justice system, 65 percent thought that unemployed Black people were more likely than unemployed white people to get government aid, and 66 percent thought police should be given more power.

While racist sentiments were rampant, they weren't the sole or even perhaps primary source of anger. That anger derived from a sense of hopelessness in the American project and a perception that the benefits of government—signified by the qualitative liberalism of the postwar era—were no longer going to people like them. And not only were the promises of the "affluent society" passing them by; but the elites, with their fancy Park Avenue duplexes and hordes of servants, seemed to approve of this transition. "Values that we held so dearly are being shot to hell," said one person interviewed by *Newsweek*. "Everything is being attacked—what you believed in, what you learned in school, in church, from your parents. So the middle class is sort of losing heart. They had their eye on where they were going and suddenly it's all shifting sands."[57]

Nearly every major news outlet—the *New Republic*, *Harper's*, *Atlantic*, even *National Review*—sought to understand the festering anger. Pete Hamill's article in *New York* magazine (entitled "The Revolt of the White Lower Middle Class") discussed how "the working-class white man spends much of his time complaining almost desperately about the way he has become a victim."[58] In *Harper's*, a few months later, Peter Schrag wrote, "Stability is what counts, stability in job and home and neighborhood, stability in church and friends." Racism was an afterthought: "The colored (no one says black; few even say Negro)—represent change and instability, kids who cause trouble in school, who get treatment that your kids never got, that you never got." This generation of middle-class white Americans felt as though they had barely succeeded and were clinging on to their status. "He cannot imagine any major change for the better; but he can imagine change for the worse," Schrag wrote. And that's why middle-class white people were susceptible to hating white liberals, especially if they were portrayed as wealthy elitists. As Schrag concluded, it was the white middle class "who has been asked to carry the burden of social reform, to integrate his schools and his neighborhood, has been asked by comfortable people to pay the social debts due to the poor and the black." And who were the comfortable people? "It just so happens" that a lot of these resentful people are turning to reactionary politics, Schrag wrote, "and that the liberals are indifferent."[59]

One interesting component of nearly all these pieces was the suggestion that these "forgotten Americans" could have gone to either political party. It was not foretold they would become Republicans. They might have been sympathetic to George Wallace in 1968, but only because he voiced their frustrations and spoke plainly, not because his politics were theirs. And some leftists, such as Michael Harrington, thought they could be brought to the left by pointing out the hypocrisies of middle-class liberals. Schrag, for his part, knew many white working-class people who in 1968 were going to vote for Robert Kennedy, the paragon of the left who voiced their frustrations, but when he was killed, shifted their support to Wallace. "A huge constituency may be coming up for grabs, and there is considerable evidence that its political mobility is more sensitive than anyone can imagine," wrote Schrag. "A man who can change from a progressive democrat into a bigot overnight deserves attention."[60]

This was the sensibility that Kevin Phillips and Richard Nixon and all the antiliberal activists of the late 1960s and early 1970s were tapping into. Yes, economic policy proposals had turned away from the continued development of the white middle classes in the 1960s, but that was largely because quantitative liberalism had already cured that. When economic policy shifted to address those who had been left behind, it created a sense of being forgotten. And this sensibility was compounded by the social and cultural upheavals emerging from the youth rebellion, the more radical aspects of the civil rights movement, the women's liberation movement, and more, all seemingly threatening the economic and social stability of the white middle classes. That these fears would be manipulated in the political arena is hardly a surprise. The masterstroke of Republicans, though, was not in putting forward proposals that would alleviate working-class stress, but instead in identifying an enemy upon whom they could vent their frustrations—white liberals—and then turning them into elitists who didn't share the working classes' need for stability. Republicans' key insight in the latter half of the 1960s was that the political critique that came from Barry Goldwater was not enough to win elections. And so they added a cultural critique against liberals to exacerbate, shape, and harness the power of the politics of resentment. In doing so, they shifted the image of white liberals. Now white liberals were completely unserious, completely out of touch, effete, and naive. They were Leonard Bernstein hosting parties for the Black Panthers.

But this strategy also shifted the image of American conservatives. In a somewhat remarkable turn of events, the working classes and the business elite were no longer battling each other for political superiority. Instead, the two sides now found common cause through their shared opposition to the white liberal elite. Now, as journalist

Chris Lehmann put it, "owner and worker stood together in defense of the besieged values of Americanism."[61] Or, as Nixon told White House staffers in 1970, "emphasize anti-crime, anti-demonstrations, anti-drugs, anti-obscenity. We must get with the mood of the country which is fed up with the liberals."[62]

―――――――

"You know something? If you liberals go on getting your way, we're all gonna hear one big, loud flush—that's the sound of the U. S. of A. going down the toilet!"

So said one of the most iconic fictional characters of the era, Archie Bunker.[63] In 1968, the left-leaning television showrunner Norman Lear conceptualized a show that made people laugh but that also put on display the numerous divisions opening up in America, the effects of the 1960s rights movements and of Agnew's positive polarization. The show, *All in the Family*, wouldn't air until 1971. Lear played Bunker for jokes, but the last name was the tell. As portrayed by Carroll O'Connor, Archie often came across as somehow sympathetic, a regular guy ill equipped to deal with all the changes taking place—his was a bunker mentality. Life was hard for Archie, sort of, but life had always been hard for a working-class guy. The key difference now was, rather than blaming his union or the Nazis or the communists, Archie had been invited to center all his frustrations on white liberals. The creative tension in the show was that Archie's kids were all liberals, and there were sympathetic Black characters and many do-gooders trying to improve the world, and even his "dingbat" wife Edith sometimes favored kindness over resentment. No matter. To Archie, they were all liberals posing threats to a fictional past.

The embodiment of the white liberal came in the form of Archie's son-in-law, Mike Stivic, a graduate student whose wife worked while he got his higher education. Mike was more commonly known on the show by Archie's nickname for him, "Meathead." When he wasn't "Meathead," Archie referred to Mike as "Mister Liberal," as when

Archie tried to justify referring to Black people as "black beauties," by saying, "Now that's where I got you, mister liberal, because there's a black guy who works down at the building with me, he's got a bumper sticker on his car that says, 'Black is Beautiful,' huh, so what's the matter with black beauties?"[64]

Like many Americans in the 1960s, Archie was threatened by change, by potentially losing the life he felt he'd had to scratch and claw to achieve. The spirit of both fear and longing was reflected in the show's signature song, written by Lear and sung by Archie and Edith, called "Those Were the Days," which had lines suggesting that in the 1940s and 1950s, "Guys like us we had it made" and "didn't need no welfare state." Family life and gender norms were stable and "ev'rybody pulled his weight." But then something changed and "I don't know just what went wrong."[65]

Over the eight years the show ran, the answer to what went wrong became clear, at least to Archie. White liberals had put into peril the entire American project. Liberals had missed their mark. How could they be surprised that their righteous misplacements had fomented a culture of resentment? Archie's somewhat remarkable ahistorical call for a return to the days of Herbert Hoover suggests his understanding of the situation might be a bit off the mark—Hoover was president during the Great Depression. But even though he looked back incorrectly, Archie did manage to look forward correctly: on the show, he was a staunch supporter of Richard Nixon, and of Ronald Reagan in 1976, even predicting Reagan's presidential victory in 1980. Following Kevin Phillips's script, the right had succeeded in using the supposed threat of "liberals" as a *provocateur* of resentment."[66] By the mid-1970s, it was undeniable that the winner of the New Left's call for "participatory democracy" was the Republican Party, with its open mocking of white liberals as out-of-touch elitist snobs propelling them to victory.

From the 1970s onward, real-life liberals would struggle to pave a way forward. What was a white liberal to do now that their image had been so soiled?

SIX

CEDING THE 1960S, LOSING LIBERALISM

In 1982, the graffiti-artist-cum-gallery-spectacle Jean-Michel Basquiat, aged twenty-one, had just broken into the mainstream. Within the previous year, he had sold his first individual painting, had his first solo art show in New York, and become friends with Andy Warhol, gallerist Larry Gagosian, and a young up-and-coming singer named Madonna, who would within the year become his girlfriend. It was, suddenly for Basquiat, a world of riches, of first-class airplane tickets, of hard-to-get invitations, of being a star, and, as he soon learned, of vultures. Collectors who knew little about art were buying his pieces as status symbols, to show off to their wealthy friends. Those who didn't know a thing about art were swarming, requesting paintings he didn't care to make. He was becoming a symbol, a hot Black street artist with something to say but who was being tamed by the allure of money and fame, an artifact of radical chic.

Basquiat was never great at managing his emotions, and at the time all he felt was rage. In response, he crafted a scathing painting in red, white, and blue. A triptych of sorts, on the right the painting shows the power of the almighty dollar in America, a character personified with dead eyes, casual swim trunks, dollar signs as a shirt, and a cowboy hat, ready to inflict casual and thoughtless damage.

On the left side appears an artist, fraught, literally handcuffed by the system, arms up, helplessly trying to protect his value, labeled, simply, "gold." The word "ASBESTOS," repeated three times, falls from a ceiling grate above the artist. The artist is Black, making an un-subtle case against systemic racism and racialized exploitation. It could also very well be Basquiat himself. The artist in the image is labeled "SAMSON," a play on Basquiat's first graffiti partnership with his friend Al Diaz, a partnership they called SAMO, standing for "Same old shit." But there's a third figure in the painting, standing in the middle and harder to immediately understand. He raises a fist, Black Power style, with the words "NOT FOR SALE" written across his chest, suggesting allyship with the chained artist. But despite the sympathetic gestures, he nevertheless wears a top hat that could be interpreted as either Abraham Lincoln freeing the enslaved or a nineteenth-century businessman subjugating the workers. Either way, he has ghoulish, consuming eyes. But his hard-to-read middling position does nothing to alter the outcome. The themes of exploita-tion, of good intentions bastardized by greed, and of money being used to systematize and mold a certain way of living, thus killing art, all hang heavily over the image. The figure on the right is gleefully consumptive. The artist on the left is anguished and dying. The one in the middle is confused but rapacious.

Modeled on Pablo Picasso's *Guernica*, the atrocity here begins to make sense when we read the words written over the head of the middle figure, with which Basquiat titled the painting: *Obnoxious Liberals*. The liberals' middling positions and weak gestures of allyship do nothing to alter the outcome. Once again, it's all performative.[1]

What were self-proclaiming liberals to do? Despite their decades of good intentions, their spirit of expanding individual freedoms to as many people as possible through an activist state and a progressive tax policy, liberals nonetheless seemed to continually make enemies, even for things they hadn't done. The stereotypes they acquired over the decades had overtaken the reality of their good intentions. Was there a tradition worth saving? How could it be articulated successfully? Who would dare such an act when so much was stacked against them?

In the 1970s and 1980s, liberals mostly ran from the words *liberal* and *liberalism*. Some tried to perform a salvage job by assuming (rightly or wrongly) some responsibility for the radicalisms of the 1960s and then reimagining a liberalism that could work as a fighting creed in a postindustrial society. But most just ran. Because of that, *liberalism* from the mid-1960s onward remained a precarious label, dangerous to possess and always in need of defining. And without adequate defenders, the loss of a useful word to describe their tradition left progressives and the middle without a foundation to call on. And without that anchoring term, the right would help turn the factions of the left against themselves, narrowing the spectrum of political possibilities even more and toward the rightward frame.

————————

In the face of the onslaught, yesterday's liberals quickly abandoned the term. Exhibit A must certainly be the 1968 election. Lyndon B. Johnson, the last president to call himself a liberal, eagerly proclaimed his presidency a high point of American liberalism (even if he sometimes privately rebuked "liberals" as people to his ideological left). Under the banner of what he called "the Great Society," Johnson imagined the next New Deal. He expanded government services like no other president save Franklin D. Roosevelt. In his effort to end poverty, Johnson signed into law the Economic Opportunity Act of 1964, created a job corps for 100,000 men, set up national and state work-study programs, and developed a Community Action program to help enact local measures to tackle poverty. In healthcare, he developed Medicare and Medicaid, expanding nationalized medical services to the elderly and the impoverished. He engaged in educational reform, including pushing to create Head Start to offer preschool to children whose parents couldn't afford it. He developed the National Endowment for the Humanities, the National Endowment for the Arts, vehicle emissions regulations, the Consumer Product Safety Commission, and more.

And to describe this tremendous expansion of the welfare state he used with great frequency (and less great precision) the word *liberal*. To signify the proposed connection between the New Deal and the Great Society, LBJ honored FDR on what would have been Roosevelt's eighty-second birthday, saying, "His liberal compassion toward his fellowman, together with his conservative respect for the institutions of our economy and society, guided this Nation past the shoals of radicalism and reaction."[2] He heaped praise on another liberal light of the 1960s, Robert Kennedy, saying in 1964, "The United States needs a young, dynamic, compassionate, fighting liberal representing New York in the United States Senate—Bob Kennedy."[3] He told college students in 1966, "We are a great and liberal and progressive democracy."[4] At the lighting of the National Christmas Tree in 1966, he affirmed his commitment to liberalism, saying, "We have made more progress in human rights in the past six years than we have made in all the previous 100 years. And, if the goal of true equality is still far down the road, the barriers before that goal are falling every day."[5]

Because of Johnson's widespread use of the term, the word *liberal* became increasingly attached (with considerable help from those on the right and the left) not to Johnson's ambitious projects but more readily to the two most damning aspects of Johnson's presidency: the war in Vietnam and the administrative and bureaucratic apparatus of the Great Society. Thus, in the aftermath of Johnson's presidency, the words *liberal* and *liberalism* would take on yet another connotation. .Great Society liberalism was, according to its critics, not only the path toward socialism, not only elitist and dismissive of ordinary Americans, and not only too weak and fearful to achieve its declared goals, but also responsible for creating a sprawling bureaucracy that was so big it no longer worked to enhance the public good.

And so when, in March 1968, Johnson decided not to run for reelection, a handful of onetime liberals sought to replace him. Yet not a single one of them proclaimed themself a liberal despite what had often been a lifetime of gleefully claiming the label.

All the big-name Democratic contenders—Robert Kennedy, Eugene McCarthy, Hubert Humphry—had interesting things to say about modern liberalism. Kennedy had perhaps the most interesting take. The most religious of the Kennedy brothers, Bobby Kennedy had been no liberal in the 1950s, working, for instance, as a Senate staff member for Joseph McCarthy and as counsel for an investigation into corruption in American labor unions. He moved in a more progressive direction after working as attorney general under his brother and specifically after working with the Black freedom movement and seeing the Southern white opposition to it, an experience that challenged his religious understanding of humanity. He went on to favor both labor rights and civil rights when he became a senator in 1964. When he ran for president in 1968, Kennedy tried to prevent the fracturing of the Democratic coalition that Kevin Phillips saw, seeking to create bonds between the disaffected white working class and Black voters. He was unique in diagnosing the ills of the Democratic Party as a struggle to maintain a coalition premised on the fight for racial justice while paying heed to growing anxieties of the working classes. He was not afraid to tell middle- and upper-class white people they'd have to pay more in taxes to alleviate poverty, and he consciously didn't present "poverty" as a race-defined construct. He spoke empathetically not only to the starving children of Mississippi and the conditions that led "black citizens to riot in Watts" but also to the anger of young people "about the war that they are sent to fight" and to the working classes seeking desperately to "close the gaps . . . between rich and poor."[6] He said, "I think there has to be a new kind of coalition to keep the Democratic party going, and to keep the country together. . . . We have to write off the unions and the South now, and replace them with Negroes, blue-collar whites, and the kids."[7]

We can never know what the outcome of his appeal would have been because an assassin's bullet cut short any chance he could realize his vision. One thing we can say, though, is that he did not label his program "liberalism" or refer to himself as a "liberal." This avoidance of such terms was a far cry from his brother John's "If by 'liberal' they mean . . ." speech just eight years prior or LBJ's description of Robert Kennedy as a "fighting liberal" in 1964.

Hubert H. Humphrey, for his part, knew of the word's onetime power. In a 1959 campaign speech, Humphrey said that Democrats could win in the 1960s by being true to their principles. "We are the liberal party in American political life," he asserted, "and we must remain the liberal party: not only to win, but to best serve America's future." He defined "liberalism" as a forward-looking, caring philosophy that hopes to make "democracy more effective—to bring closer to full realization the inspiring dreams of justice and equal economic opportunity for all."[8] Up until the mid-1960s, he was proud to call himself a liberal, supporting government efforts to fight for racial justice, the labor movement, and even full employment.

By 1968, all that talk was gone. As Johnson's vice president, Humphrey (to his own frustration) had to defend the Vietnam War. As a result, he felt as though he had lost all credential to speak on behalf of any sort of left-leaning liberalism, so he didn't. "All I had ever been as a liberal spokesman seemed lost," he wrote forlornly in 1976. "All that I had accomplished in significant programs was ignored. I felt robbed of my personal history."[9] The alignment of LBJ's Great Society and the debacle in Vietnam forced Humphrey to run from the label he had only just recently celebrated.

More than this shift, however, Humphrey the politician knew the costs of being labeled a liberal in 1968. He put forward no speeches advocating an attempt to "stay liberal"; there were no slogans, no mottos, no nothing. "I take some solace in feeling that 1968 was simply not the year when the American people wanted liberal leadership so much as they wanted respite from anxiety and frustration," he later wrote.[10]

Perhaps the most dramatic abandonment of the term *liberal*, though, came from Eugene McCarthy, as he had most recently flown the liberal flag, and quite high, too. In 1964, McCarthy had authored a book titled *A Liberal Answer to the Conservative Challenge*, with the promotional blurb on the cover proclaiming, "A liberal Senator vigorously denies that liberalism is outmoded, and states its aims in terms of present-day problems."[11] By 1968, though, he avoided the word like the plague. McCarthy never connected with the working classes and always had a hard time articulating his vision for the future aside from ending the war in Vietnam. For our story, however, the greater point is that McCarthy abandoned the call for a liberal resurgence. His campaign did not use the word, nor did any of the speeches nominating him at the convention. Aware of the pigeonholing nature of the word, of all its layered meanings, he didn't hesitate to critique the power of the entrenched labor leaders in Michigan as "an example of liberalism gone wrong." But for the most part the man who had promised "a liberal answer to the conservative challenge" now quietly abstained.[12]

––––––––––––

All three of the Democratic candidates in 1968 were accomplished politicians, and all knew how to read the signs. There was, however, one Democrat who did use the word *liberal* in the late 1960s, but he used its elitist connotations as a battering ram instead of a coalescing force.

Mario Procaccino was a New York "machine" politician of famously diminutive stature, loud shirts, and a pencil-thin mustache. Italian-born, Procaccino moved to the Bronx at the age of nine and later went to DeWitt Clinton High School, then City College, then Fordham Law School. He was New York City all the way. After law school, he became a Democratic Party grunt through Tammany Hall and worked in his Bronx ward until, in 1965, he ran for the inglorious job of city comptroller. He was the Democrats' Italian American candidate running alongside a Jewish candidate for mayor (Abe Beame) and an Irish Catholic candidate for city council president (Frank O'Connor). Beame lost; Procaccino and O'Connor won.

Four years later, in 1969, Procaccino ran for mayor. In the primary he defeated the likes of former mayor Robert Wagner and even novelist Norman Mailer by moving to the right and embracing Republican president Nixon's call for law and order. As with Nixon and the "silent majority," Procaccino's candidacy resonated with the outer borough white working-class voters who had been the heart of the Democratic Party for nearly four decades but who were now slipping away amid the right-wing assault on liberalism.

After securing the Democratic nomination, Procaccino faced off against two candidates, and this was when he began to recognize the value of using the word *liberal* as an epithet. The Republican nominee was John Marchi, another law-and-order outer borough New Yorker of Italian ancestry. The third candidate was the incumbent mayor, John V. Lindsay, an upper-class gentleman of English-Dutch ancestry who had just been tossed out of the Republican Party and was instead running as the candidate of the tiny Liberal Party, a midcentury creation of anticommunist leftists. In the end, the two "ethnic" candidates split the law-and-order vote and Lindsay remarkably was reelected, undoubtedly helped by Procaccino's ham-handedness.[13]

Procaccino did leave one lasting gift, though. In targeting Lindsay, the six-foot five-inch darling of the Upper West Side whose wealth and entitlement allowed him to personally avoid many of the transformations going on in New York City, Procaccino coined the term "limousine liberal." The "limousine liberal," as Procaccino imagined it, was a wealthy, out-of-touch member of the elite proclaiming sympathies for the poor without understanding their plight. "Limousine liberals" were the ones embracing Tom Wolfe's "radical chic." Procaccino constantly attacked the "rich super-assimilated people who live on Fifth Avenue . . . and have no feeling for the small middle class shopkeeper, home owner, etc." People like Lindsay, Procaccino said, "preach the politics of confrontation and condone violent upheaval in society because they are not touched by it and are protected by their courtiers, doormen, and private police guards."[14] Lindsay was nothing more than "a swinger in the city," an upper-class libertine far removed from the moral convictions of working-class people who lived in the outer boroughs, Procaccino contended. In Procaccino's coinage, "limousine liberals" like Lindsay were well bred, well educated at elite institutions, and well paid, interested in the plight of the impoverished without demonstrating concern for the working and middle classes. With "limousine liberals," white liberals had been given yet another disparaging name by whatever remained of the white working classes within the Democratic Party.

The phrase caught on. And, although Lindsay's wealth made him the ideal type, the epithet quickly extended beyond Lindsay. Conservative speechwriter William Safire defined a "limousine liberal" as "one who takes up hunger as a cause but has never felt a pang; who will talk at length about the public school system but sends his children to private schools."[15] The epithet was used against wealthy liberals in almost any instance throughout the 1970s, including when Senator Edward "Ted" Kennedy did in fact send his kids to private schools while speaking of the need for integrated public schools. Historian Steve Fraser has argued that the phrase "limousine liberal" managed "to mobilize an enduring politics of resentment directed against most of the major reforms of the last seventy-five years" and sits at "the heart of an aggrieved sense felt by millions that they have been passed over—their material needs ignored, their cultural preferences treated with contempt—by a cluster of elites that run the country."[16]

That it was a Democrat who coined the damning phrase suggests the depths to which the image of the white liberal had fallen in the aftermath of the Great Society. The Democrats were turning on themselves.

If politicians avoided "liberal" except as a term of abuse, intellectuals, who just a few years prior had been reliable defenders (even creators) of something they called "the liberal tradition," also rejected it and, more important, now devoted countless pages to undermining its historic legitimacy. The key text here was Theodore Lowi's 1969 book *The End of Liberalism*. If Kevin Phillips's 1969 book defined how Republicans should position their attacks on white liberals, Lowi's book demonstrated to the left that liberalism was killing democracy and deserved the abuse people were heaping upon it. Lowi was a well-known political scientist who, in 1964, had even coedited a book with Robert Kennedy. No fiery leftist, no conservative Republican, he was middle-of-the-road. But Lowi began his 1969 book with a blistering argument: that the dominance of liberalism from the 1930s to the 1960s had expanded the role of government so much that its reach had become nearly interminable, and this had now become a threat to democracy. There was, he pointed out, special irony in that fact that, in a country designed to limit the power of the ruling class, the most well-meaning political philosophy in the country's history—liberalism—had extended federal powers so far as to replace one leviathan with another. After a flourishing few pages showing the government's reach throughout American life beginning in the New Deal and continuing through the Great Society, Lowi wrote, "It should thus be clear that the issues with which the book deals are remote from the mere question of more government or less government. We already have more."[17]

The problem, argued Lowi, was that the notion that government was entitled to solve all our problems led to massive corruption and interest-party rule—meaning the people no longer ruled and democracy had been defeated. As he saw things, any interest group could bring a problem to the government and have bureaucratic solutions and federal dollars thrown at it. But these issues were bound to be outside the expertise of any existing government body. So under the banner of kindhearted liberalism, Congress or the president simply created new bureaucracies to adjudicate the problem. But the new bureaucracies needed leaders, and those with the required knowledge to lead them often had a stake, which meant people with private interests were overseeing public outcomes. This, warned Lowi, parceled

out "to private parties the power to make public policy."[18] In one
example, Lowi showed how farming interests had won the power
to regulate themselves, leading to a farm policy that didn't serve any
kind of "public interest" but instead enriched the best-organized farm
groups. Lowi named this conundrum "interest-group liberalism."[19]
In the late 1970s, economists would relabel it "regulatory capture."
Well-meaning, problem-solving liberalism had been taken over and
corrupted by human greed.

In Lowi's view, this was how low American liberalism had sunk:
its good intentions were destroying democracy because it misjudged
people's capacities for greed. In the midst of existential crises about
race, the American Dream, the fate of democracy, and the role of the
United States in world affairs, all we got was interest-group politics
whereby rich people enriched themselves with public dollars. It was
no longer a moral or political philosophy, just a bureaucratic process.
All liberalism had created was a marketplace for haggling.

Lowi marketed his book as a political science primer, but it was
mostly a jeremiad. The government envisioned by America's founders had turned into "a gigantic prehistoric beast, all power and no
efficacy . . . power with purpose but without definition, finesse, discrimination, ending in disappointment," he lamented.[20] Lowi named
the period between 1932 and 1969 the "Second Republic of the United
States," demonstrating its distance from the founding generation.
With the Great Society, he argued, "the United States had a crisis
of public authority and died."[21] Lowi had a flair for the dramatic.

As a solution, Lowi called on Congress to take stronger control and the judicial branch to become more impartial. Anything to
reduce the power of the bureaucracies. But throughout the 1970s,
most people focused only on the questions he raised. Had liberalism
inadvertently killed democracy? Was this the inevitable outcome of
the philosophy envisioned by FDR and John Dewey? Throughout the
first half of the 1970s, the book was much discussed, and in 1978 Lowi
was named the nation's most influential political scientist in a poll
of the American Political Science Association's members.[22] In 1979,

Lowi brought out a second edition of *The End of Liberalism*, arguing that his 1969 thesis had been proven more correct in the intervening decade. In a country turning inward throughout the 1970s, one that had, to a large degree, lost hope in large-scale social projects and in government's ability to benefit those most in need, Lowi placed the blame squarely on liberalism.

And all this was before "acid, amnesty, and abortion," yet another phrase tossed at white liberals as a term of disparagement supposedly describing all the things they supported. And, as with "limousine liberal," the similarly famous alliterative phrase came from one Democrat tarnishing another.

In 1972, when George McGovern won the Democratic Party's presidential nomination, he had strong credentials as a liberal candidate harking back to liberalism's heyday. After cutting his teeth as a New Deal Democrat, by 1972 he was the most labor-friendly candidate since perhaps Roosevelt himself. McGovern campaigned against the Vietnam War and even offered, vaguely, a financial "peace dividend" that would alleviate the economic burdens of the war on the white working classes. He was a former Protestant pastor able to speak to religious conservatives and cite Bible verses to justify his beliefs. But his distinguished biography—he even flew thirty-five bombing missions over Europe during the Second World War— belied a lack of personal charisma. He was almost *too* good so as to be unrelatable. Norman Mailer said McGovern reminded him of a not-of-this-world squeaky-clean astronaut: "It was in that sense he gave off of Christian endeavor, of total commitment of strength, of loneliness and endless stamina, of the tireless ability to bear interruption of his mood, and all of that same astronaut impersonality." Mailer called him "St. George."[23]

But in 1972 against Richard Nixon, McGovern didn't stand a chance. For he was running at what was perhaps the peak time in history for making liberals pay for the supposed excesses of the 1960s. Instead of being seen as a good if moralizing candidate from South Dakota (hardly a People's Republic), McGovern instead became the candidate of "acid, amnesty, and abortion."

The phrase, used widely by the Nixon campaign throughout 1972, was actually coined by a conservative Democrat who would—surprise, surprise—eventually be nominated as McGovern's running mate, Senator Tom Eagleton. The story goes that newspaper columnist Robert Novak was seeking quotations for a piece he was writing about whether McGovern would be able to connect with the white working classes that Nixon was working so hard to win over, and Eagleton, who, at the time, supported Maine senator Ed Muskie for president, gave Novak the juicy line: "The people don't know McGovern is for amnesty, abortion and the legalization of pot [marijuana]," adding that, once "middle America—Catholic middle America, in particular"—once they find out what he's for, "he's dead."[24] The line, given in anonymity, was quickly picked up by McGovern's opponents, first within the Democratic Party and then by Nixon. Somewhere along the line, "legalization of pot" was replaced by the more alliterative "acid," replacing a milder drug enjoyed by many people with the more dangerous hallucinogenic LSD used by far fewer, thus ramping up the perceived threat. McGovern was thereafter tarnished as the candidate of "acid, amnesty, and abortion."[25]

The story is filled with ironies. For one thing, the alliterative line and then Eagleton himself were the two key reasons McGovern was completely uncompetitive in the presidential race. Eagleton was dropped from the ticket eighteen days after his nomination once it emerged that he had received electroshock therapy for "nervous exhaustion," demonstrating that McGovern had been a poor judge of character or, at best, a poor manager of his campaign. And the alliterative line made McGovern and his party out as radicals. While it was always going to be difficult to beat an incumbent, especially one who was not afraid to bend the rules, these two Eagleton-based events destroyed the political career of George McGovern.

Another irony was that the line wasn't even close to accurate. McGovern did not favor legalizing any drugs, much less acid, and Eagleton's marijuana line was actually a cruel reminder that McGovern's teenage daughter had, in 1968, been arrested for marijuana possession. McGovern did favor amnesty for Vietnam draft resisters, but that was a normal stance in 1972, supported even by Nixon. And McGovern's stance on abortion was that the issue was a matter better left to the states, a position far more conservative than the yet-to-be-decided *Roe v. Wade* decision of 1973 that would be overturned by a conservative-led US Supreme Court in 2022 in favor of just such a position. McGovern was clearly no radical.

But by the early 1970s, liberalism and those who upheld it were being forced to accept all the supposed extremes of the 1960s—sex, drugs, political protests—and McGovern of all people had to bear the brunt, even though he was, essentially, a New Deal liberal.[26] Once the right saw how powerful this critique was, as one historian has written, "'acid, amnesty, and abortion' became a symbolic battle cry that was, in one form or another, to dominate Republican politics for many years."[27] Often shortened to be "the three As," not only were liberals demonized for a supposedly errant political philosophy, they were to eat the failures of the 1960s, too.

————————

Those to the left of liberalism were little help. Instead of seeking common ground to stage an attack on the emergent conservatism—a common enough tactic throughout the twentieth century—they felt liberalism's rhetorical demise was just deserts.

In a thoughtful column from 1973, for instance, left-wing stalwart Michael Harrington blamed the Democratic Party's foibles on liberalism's inherent conservatism. In "Out Beyond Liberalism," Harrington suggested that Nixon was right to attack "limousine liberals of the sixties" for throwing "money at problems to create a permissive, drop-out, addicted and welfare-dependent America."

Clearly Harrington was not immune to the image crafted by those on the right. But Harrington pushed the argument in the other direction, too, claiming that "the sixties failed" not because they did too much but "because they did so little." Liberals at their peak didn't put forward creative plans for full employment, nor for major ideas regarding income redistribution. Plans to improve cities were absent while subsidies were provided "to the rich in suburbia." And no one really mentioned anymore "free medical service for all."[28]

Harrington acknowledged that his own plans for these issues had "socialist inspiration," but his hopes lay with what might arise from the embers of liberalism, a new version more aligned with the left than the center, one he suggested was somehow "on the left wing of realism." He saw the demographic transformations taking place within the Democratic Party, with the party's focus increasingly on students, minoritized peoples, and suburbanites, warning against each group's "tendencies toward a self-righteous elitism." Still, he hoped to help "bring out best potentials" from the new Democratic voters. "We think," he concluded, "that liberals must now discuss going beyond liberalism."[29]

To where, though?

———————

With friends like these, who needs enemies? And so it might be surprising that some liberals actually did continue to defend liberalism. But some did. The word had been magnetic in the past, a perfect descriptor of the place between socialism and laissez-faire, between mass democracy and authoritarianism. Why not see if some of that magic could be saved? Was there room for liberalism in a postindustrial world? And, more important, what did it look like?

Daniel Patrick Moynihan was the chief philosopher of liberalism's postindustrial vision, although his vision would struggle to gain adherents. So associated with New York it's startling to learn he was born in Oklahoma, Moynihan moved with his parents from there to Hell's Kitchen when he was six, and he called it home for most of the rest of his life. Part of working-class Irish Catholic life, Moynihan went to City College for a year before joining the war effort in 1944. He went on to get a doctorate from Tufts University and bounced back and forth between academia and public life for the rest of his life.

Moynihan's interests in labor and in unearthing the causes of poverty led him to be a student of New Deal liberalism, looking for ways to update its ideals. He had, he said, always embraced "the activist national liberalism of the New Deal" and was "unabashedly a product of that tradition."[30] This liberalism led him to become a primary architect of Lyndon Johnson's War on Poverty and a commentator on the economic effects of racial segregation, the realities of which led him away from overly idealistic progressivism.

His experience with trying to develop social policy for the Great Society turned out to be chastening. In the early 1960s, Moynihan later wrote, "American liberalism had lost a sense of limits. We would transform the Mekong Delta, resurrect Detroit, enlighten South Asia and defend it too." The problem was that "the presidential advisers of the Kennedy and Johnson era had underestimated the difficulties of social change . . . a naiveté born of noble purpose. The limits of policy were less and less emphasized while the potential for matters to get worse rather than better was increasingly ignored."[31]

Beyond losing a sense of limits, Moynihan asserted that the "qualitative liberalism" of the postwar era strove toward impossible ends. Government, he wrote in 1968, "cannot provide values to people who have none, or have lost those they had."[32] A fan of Theodore Lowi's analysis, Moynihan strongly believed that liberalism needed course correction.[33] "Look at what American liberalism has done!" he said after watching the 1976 Massachusetts Democratic primary results come in with racist George Wallace, of all people, winning the Boston area.[34] Reminding liberals of liberalism's limits was a key to restoking the tradition.

Moynihan had solid liberal credentials, too. He was a national board member of the left-leaning Americans for Democratic Action (ADA) while nonetheless speaking out against the antiwar left, which he saw as the work of bored middle-class youth, and the Black Power movement, which he saw as detrimentally separatist. Meanwhile, alongside his work in the ADA, he worked in the Nixon White House as assistant to the president for domestic policy and executive secretary of the Council of Urban Affairs, eventually even joining Nixon's cabinet. But as with the left, so with the right: in the Nixon administration, Moynihan was constantly critical of the direction he saw the Republican Party going, which he viewed as veering into mean-spirited libertarianism through a politics of resentment.

In the late 1970s, watching the two sides pull apart, stabbing the centrist tradition from their respective corners, Moynihan sought to forge an alliance between liberals and conservatives. He failed, but not without trying. He labeled his effort "intelligent liberalism."

He coined the phrase in 1976, while running for senator against the libertarian incumbent, James Buckley (William F. Buckley Jr.'s brother). Moynihan developed a rhetorical two-step process for redefining liberalism. Step one: own up to liberalism's past mistakes. "The dilemma for liberals," admitted Moynihan in his 1976 stump speech, "is that we faced unprecedented government problems which however had come about under the auspices of impeccably liberal governments." The government *had* grown bloated. Expenses *were* up. Garbage was not being picked up on time. With the end of the postwar economic boom and widespread deindustrialization, Democrats had played down the plight of the white working classes. In the midst of economic decline, there was, he said, "a crisis of government, a crisis of the economy, and a crisis of social organization." What Moynihan promised "was to sort out our situation and to be as honest about it as we dared."[35]

Moynihan claimed that the liberal tradition had fallen prey to "usurpers who have made off with [liberalism's] banner and corrupted its language." Their "so-called liberalism" was premised on the notion "that the American political system is sick and that only radical surgery can save it, if indeed it can be saved at all."[36] This thoughtless left wing had laid claim to the liberal tradition, and true liberals had allowed it to happen. Now liberals like him needed to accept at least some blame for the "corruption of liberalism" while fighting to get their liberalism back. When Moynihan was asked after winning the primary over left-wing candidate Bella Abzug if he was eager to make peace with "the liberals," Moynihan responded, "*We* were the liberals in the race."[37] The mantle had to be reclaimed from the image foisted on it by the right.

On the one hand, it was a remarkable balancing act. Moynihan was simultaneously taking the blame for the mistakes of the 1960s while also saying those mistakes weren't the fault of *true* liberals. But what was potentially even more damning was taking the blame at all, even when it might be hard to pin the blame on liberalism for the Middle Eastern oil crisis, deindustrialization, the rise of foreign economic competition, or the increasingly radical demands coming from minoritized peoples. Similarly, liberals would be hard pressed to take blame for the bloated government of 1976, which was the eighth straight year of having a Republican in the White House.

Still, Moynihan knew the tarnish needed polishing. His gamble was to accept some of the stereotypes of liberals that had emerged, apologize, reclaim the tradition, and start again.

Step two in Moynihan's effort was to propose policies that moved liberalism to the political center. Moynihan claimed that the dreamy liberals of the 1960s had removed individual responsibility from liberalism's code, making failure not an individual problem but a systemic one. Moynihan thus demanded that government programs be redesigned to ensure greater accountability—to offer a hand up, not a handout, in the parlance of the time. "The viability of liberal thought," Moynihan said, "rested on the ability of the country which adopted it to be largely self-regulating, self-maintaining, and self-improving." But with the Great Society, the government had institutionalized programs tied to providing services rather than income, and doing so ironically created a permanent class of workers dependent on the perpetuation of poverty while also robbing the poor of incentives to move on. "The American welfare system is one of the proudest achievements of a generous and compassionate people," he wrote. "But it must not be allowed to become the economic system of a permanent sub-culture. Men need jobs, families need fathers, communities need independence."[38] Government should therefore act only as an "umpire," directing people in "socially useful ways." If governments imposed too many roadblocks, then creativity would break down, inequalities would be exacerbated, and freedom denied. We would, he said, have "public affluence and private squalor," or vice versa. "We do not need more government in America," he said, suggesting that "the real task is making it work."[39]

After the 1976 election, Moynihan told the *New Republic* he "ran as a liberal willing to be critical of what liberals had done." Postwar liberals, he said, had "gone soft." They had thrown government money at problems instead of figuring out root causes. They had built social safety nets that ignored individual responsibility. Now, Moynihan's "intelligent liberalism" would be premised on creating an economic floor that no American could fall below, an infrastructure-based public works program to help alleviate institutionalized poverty, and basic regulations for everyone to follow. Pointing to the fact that his version of liberalism was more tempered than that of the Great Society, Moynihan said, "Does it seem bearish? Despairing? Illiberal? It did not to my audiences. It seemed true."[40]

In 1976, Moynihan's "intelligent liberalism" won New York State by 585,961 votes. "I won because I was able to persuade the voters that there was still [a] sound and responsible tradition of liberalism in the center of Democratic politics worthy of their support," he told an audience of union workers in 1978. He welcomed the workers in, too, referring to "we, the forces of the liberal center."[41]

With speeches like this, Moynihan did perhaps more than anyone to try to resuscitate the label "liberal" and the philosophy of "liberalism" in the 1970s. Moynihan authored dozens of articles and nineteen books, and he has more than a thousand boxes in the Library of Congress, many of which reflect on his reformulation of what it means to be a white liberal in the 1970s. Moynihan's liberalism was patriotic and internationalist. It favored universal solutions over interest groups. It sought to create programs to give people work rather than systems in which they would become entrenched. And it was weary of making promises it could not keep. Liberalism still had a leg to stand on in the modern world.

Or so Moynihan thought.

———————

Moynihan was not alone in trying to resuscitate a liberal tradition. Immediately after McGovern's disastrous loss in 1972 to Richard Nixon (who took forty-nine of the fifty states in electoral votes, the lone holdout being Massachusetts), a handful of centrist Democrats tried to take the party back from what they saw as the failed "New Politics" coalition of university students, minoritized peoples, and suburbanites. This eclectic bunch of politicos included Bayard Rustin, Midge Decter, Jeane J. Kirkpatrick, Nathan Glazer, Daniel Bell, Zbigniew Brzezinski, A. Philip Randolph, Michael Novak, and James Roosevelt (Franklin and Eleanor's son), who together established something called the Coalition for a Democratic Majority. "For too long now," they announced in ads in the *New York Times* and the *Washington Post*, "the voices of common-sense liberals have been barely audible in the blare of the New Politics." New Politics, they said, "has derided the organized labor movement, . . . sneered at the greatness of America," and "dismissed as morally unworthy the long-range values and daily concerns of tens of millions of ordinary people." They wanted "the American people to know that there is another, more responsible tradition of progress in America." They sought to end discrimination, embrace a "pluralistic political process in which no single group or class enjoys a special moral status," be aware of the "tens of millions of Americans who are genuinely and correctly concerned about public safety and respect for law," and acknowledge that "involvement in international affairs continues to be necessary to the establishment of a stable and viable international order."[42]

The group fell flat. Their principles were simply co-opted by the right. "We tried to wrest the Democratic Party back from the left, and we failed," said Midge Decter.[43] Like many in the group, Decter eventually became a Republican. Jeane Kirkpatrick went on to work in the Reagan administration. Their "common sense liberalism" couldn't attract much of an audience.

And this was typical for those seeking to reclaim the "liberal" label throughout the 1970s. Aside from Moynihan and a few small organizations like the Coalition for a Democratic Majority, most Democrats simply ran from the label. Morris K. "Mo" Udall, a Democratic representative from Arizona, for example, ran for president in 1976 by trying to attract wealthy suburbanites, "wine and cheese liberals," as his opponents called them. (They, meanwhile, claimed to be after the "lunch pail Democrats.") But Udall avoided the word *liberal*, preferring to describe himself as a "progressive." "Liberal," he acknowledged, had become "a worry word" that caused otherwise sympathetic voters to "[tune] you out before you start." The right-wing definition had carried the day. Despite Udall's attempts, conservative columnist George Will joked that Udall had, with "exquisitely awful timing . . . established himself as the liberal candidate at a moment when liberalism seems stale."[44] Udall ended up splitting the left-wing vote with California governor Jerry Brown, opening the path in 1976 for the centrist Jimmy Carter to secure the Democratic presidential nomination.

And what did Jimmy Carter do with the liberalism as refashioned by Moynihan and hoped for by the Coalition for a Democratic Majority? Carter, too, avoided the "liberal" label. Indeed, he not only distanced himself from it but defined himself in opposition to it. He often referred to the left wing of the Democratic Party as "liberals" and himself as the moderate. He allowed the press to run with a narrative about "the liberals" in his party going after him, especially when "the liberals" tried to organize a "Stop-Carter" movement after Carter's surprise victory in the New Hampshire primary. But to no avail. As he had learned during his gubernatorial elections in Georgia, the way Democrats could win in a post-Nixon, postliberal era was to triangulate between "liberals" as imagined by the right and the growing libertarianism of the Republican Party. "Deftly avoiding liberalism had won him both a governorship and the presidency," wrote one historian.[45]

Another candidate who might have been likely to defend liberalism in the 1970s and 1980s also casually demurred. In 1980, Ted Kennedy campaigned to Carter's left in the Democratic primary. Seen with good reason as the embodiment of his brother John's version of active liberalism, Ted Kennedy considered Carter's centrism a betrayal of his brother's tradition. Even worse, he thought Carter's sober persona and general pessimism "violated the spirit of America."[46] Despite some early promise, Ted Kennedy never gained traction as a candidate. He was ill prepared to run, not having solid answers to many key questions. And he certainly had nothing to say about the legacy or future of liberalism.

———————

The general abandonment of the term *liberal* in the 1970s had important consequences. Without staunch defenders, during the 1970s, journalists and other casual users began to affix a single meaning to the term. It no longer referred to a political philosophy of any substantive kind. Instead, it became a general term referring to anything to the left of whatever they were talking about. This was a long-standing journalistic and linguistic practice, but often in the 1950s and 1960s it invited confusion with the profound tradition of liberalism. By the 1970s, there was no more confusion. When Jimmy Carter ran as a centrist Democrat, for instance, the *New York Times* published an article headlined "Carter Target of Liberals after New Hampshire

Gain." The reporter couldn't name a single person claiming to be a "liberal" but nonetheless referred to something called "the liberal establishment—an amorphous but powerful group of lawyers, politicians, lobbyists and journalists." Still, no one was actually named. Indeed, the only people in the article who used the word were those warning against it. As one strategist put it, when people use the word *liberal* "they press a trigger," explaining that "to the Democrats that Carter won in New Hampshire—the kind of Democrats Richard Nixon took away from us in 1968 and 1972—'liberal' means busing, big spending, elitism, which are all the things they want us to see."[47] The word had been successfully co-opted.

The casual solidification of the term's meaning as anything dismissively progressive cemented a popular understanding of the word in ways Richard Nixon could only have dreamed of. It also allowed the entire political spectrum to shift to the right. When Carter ran for reelection in 1980, he had to fend off in the Democratic primary what newspapers called a "liberal" candidate to his left in Ted Kennedy (who never referred to himself as such); and when Carter ran against Republican nominee Ronald Reagan in the general election later that year, newspapers suggested that Carter was the liberal candidate to the left of Reagan. Carter, like Kennedy, also claimed no such tradition. In his 1978 State of the Union address, Carter committed fratricide when he said, "Government cannot solve our problems. It can't set the goals. It cannot define our vision. Government cannot eliminate poverty, or provide a bountiful economy, or reduce inflation, or save our cities, or cure illiteracy, or provide energy."[48] As president, Carter deregulated industries, balanced budgets, and ended restrictions on banks. In 1980, Arthur Schlesinger Jr. wrote, "On [economic] matters he is not a Democrat," and "to take Carter's view of government is to deny the heritage of the modern Democratic party," and "to deny that heritage is to disarm us all in face of the great national problems."[49] But in the game of 1980s politics, Carter was nonetheless smeared with the label "liberal."

As liberalism lost any meaning that actual liberals could control, as liberals and liberalism were forced to own the failures of the 1960s, those on the right could dismiss even centrists like Carter as "liberals." Those who might have been onetime liberals now ran to the center, afraid to be marked with the label. And with no one defending the fortress, long-accepted public policies, once heralded as triumphs of liberalism, were easily reinterpreted as falsehoods from a debunked tradition.

In the 1980s and 1990s, the unboundedness of the liberal tradition not only would allow for the overturning of many onetime "liberal" initiatives but would also invite several people to try to push it back to an earlier meaning, a meaning that supposedly predated FDR but which nonetheless took on the moniker "neoliberal."

SEVEN

NEOLIBERAL (NEO-LIBERAL?) AMERICA

Michel Foucault was a French intellectual straight out of central casting. Bald and lean, sporting academic glasses and showing a penchant for black or gray turtlenecks, Foucault the philosopher dazzled nearly everyone he met. He spoke the language of theory, which meant most people didn't understand half of what he said but everyone assumed he was brilliant. He was even purported to write in a way that would be difficult for translators to translate, ensuring that those who spread his ideas would be acolytes.[1]

Foucault made as the grand subject of his life's work nothing so modest as the conditions for human freedom, or rather, the institutions and ideas that have, throughout history, curtailed freedom so that, even without thinking about it, people simply fall in line with the dominant order, giving up freedoms as we go. Foucault wondered: What are the hidden rules of society? How do those structures and norms get formed, and at what cost to us? Foucault was especially interested in how power operated outside politics, in how discipline and punishment were meted out, in how societies determine what is criminal behavior and what isn't, in how norms are developed and enforced. His work on how wardens control prisoners was designed

to make correctional facilities look like schools and offices and ware-
houses, the metaphor a bit obvious but effective nonetheless. His
work on academic disciplines demonstrated that something we call
"knowledge" has boundaries that shift (he called academic departments "dubious disciplines"). His studies in the history of sexuality
showed not only that the body dictated how humans act in the
world (evolutionary biology) but also how society came to define
what was "normal" sexual behavior, at great cost to those who lived
outside those norms. Power relations were hidden everywhere, he
taught, forcing us to get in line or suffer consequences, acts of mostly
unconscious acquiescence.[2]

   Because of his fascination with power, governments were easy
pickings for Foucault. Politics are little more than battles over power.
He defined "governmentality" expansively, as how "one conducts the
conduct of men," signifying the entire edifice of institutions that
shape conduct through consent, not discipline. He fit governments
in here.[3] Why do we choose to give up what we do? What are the
trade-offs? Are the promises on offer worth it? And in this vein, in
the late 1970s Foucault, at the peak of his game and the height of
his fame, grew interested in twentieth-century liberalism. True to his
grand inquest into all things that curtail freedom, Foucault argued
that despite its pretense of *liber* (freedom), liberalism in the 1970s
had become simply yet another mask for power and control. In a
series of lectures in 1978 and 1979, Foucault argued that "natural laws"
and "inalienable rights" and other rationales underpinning liberalism
were little more than fictions. Moreover, the very workings of liberal
government obviously curtailed some freedoms. "Liberalism must
produce freedom," he wrote in 1979, "but this very act entails the
establishment of limitations, controls, forms of coercion, and obligations relying on threats."[4] One might say that in a truly liberal society,
"my freedom ends when my fist hits your jaw" (thus causing harm
to another), but Foucault pointed out that taxes, speed limits, the
use of certain words, and the ways in which we define "normal" were
all curtailments of freedom long before anyone's fist hits anyone's

face. Like nearly all other institutions in society, then, liberalism was
a sleight of hand that allowed power to operate stealthily. And as
liberalism expanded its purview throughout the 1960s and 1970s, it
had been found out, leading to what Foucault called the "crises of
governmentality."[5] All the institutions of power premised on expanding *liber* seemed to be crumbling, exposed as the ruses they were.

Foucault's critique of liberalism earned him some strange bedfel-
lows. Several economically minded thinkers in Austria and the United
States, such as F. A. Hayek, Milton Friedman, and Gary Becker, began to echo Foucault—or rather, as Foucault quickly discovered, he
began to echo them. This school of economists, many of whom were
Austrian or had transplanted themselves to the University of Chicago
(forming "the Austrian School," "the Chicago School," or what some
observers dismissively called "the Chicago boys"), had been making a
similar critique of liberalism for decades.[6] These thinkers also claimed
to want to retake *liber* from the New Deal/Great Society liberals.
They also attacked the various infrastructures that had been built in
the name of "liberalism" through the twentieth century, arguing that
New Deal liberalism and everything after it had constrained freedom
rather than expanded it. These thinkers sought instead to unleash raw
capitalism to determine what prospered and what didn't—a shadowy
throwback to the market-based version of liberalism from the nineteenth century but without much consideration for the "generosity
of spirit" aspect of the definition.

Foucault was sympathetic with their diagnosis of liberalism if not,
ultimately, their prescriptions. Their thinking, Foucault wrote, "arose
in a very precise context as a critique to the irrationality peculiar
to excessive government, and as a return to a technology of frugal
government," something he sought and understood.[7] In his view,
the bureaucracies had grown too big, limiting people's abilities to
define freedom for themselves. And as Foucault also recognized, the
Chicago school also wanted "to extend the rationality of the market,
the schemas of analysis it offers and the decision-making criteria
it suggests, to domains which are not exclusively or not primarily

economic: the family and the birth rate, for example, or delinquency and penal policy."[8] These were all arenas that fascinated Foucault, too. He wondered: Could prioritizing the economic aspect of humanity, something he called "*homo œconomicus*," lead to greater flourishing? Was it a way to achieve more *liber?*

In the 1970s, Foucault read the Chicago school voraciously and wrote hundreds of pages unpacking their ideas. He never did endorse their project, though.[9] As was his typical practice, he lent a sympathetic ear to better understand, leading some commentators to misinterpret his sympathies. But he was clear: the Chicago school simply sought to exchange one illegitimate rationale for power with another. And, to boot, in Foucault's mind, it would never work: the prioritization of *homo œconomicus* relied on the workings of a functioning civil society in order to establish trust, but *homo œconomicus* brought people together only for instrumental reasons (to move capital), thus altering the premises of civil society, which, to Foucault, was based on "the active bonds of compassion, benevolence, love for one's fellows, and sense of community."[10] These were all concepts foreign to *homo œconomicus. Homo œconomicus* thus relied on trust, but its consequences were destined to prioritize the individual over civil society, thereby destroying its own infrastructure. So, Foucault concluded, the Chicago school and the unleashing of capitalism would never democratize *liber.* Instead, they would simply enrich the few while altering moral codes away from "compassion, benevolence, love for one's fellow." Foucault understood the critique of the Chicago school but dismissed its solution as wrongheaded.

But even if he never endorsed their ideas, he did help give them a name that would last. Throughout the 1960s and 1970s, the Chicago school had been lumbering over a term for their kind of thinking. They still thought of themselves as "liberals" in the pre–New Deal understanding of the word, sometimes calling themselves "classical liberals," even if their proposals were far afield from those proposed by the Gladstonian Liberals in Britain. In Chile, the Chicago school worked with the newly empowered military regime to develop an economics after socialism, which Milton Friedman called "liberalism" but which Chileans sometimes called *neoliberalismo*. To Foucault, that sounded about right: these thinkers wanted in fact a new liberalism premised on using the power of the state to more easily move capital—and thus he, too, dubbed them "the neoliberals." It would take a decade to catch on, but the name stuck.

The word *neoliberalism* was hardly used in the English language before about 1980, with its use skyrocketing in the 1990s and 2000s, as scholars rediscovered Foucault's work on the topic and were trying to put a name to what seemed to be a dominant ideology coursing through the world.[11] The term in fact traces its earliest origins to 1910s and 1920s Austria, where it was briefly used to critique the small intellectual circle around the laissez-faire economist Ludwig von Mises. These critics hated his free-market advocacy and suggested with the German term *Neoliberalismus* that von Mises was simply abandoning any efforts at state control over the economy and advocating a return to nineteenth-century free-market liberalism. Von Mises recognized the term as a pejorative and ignored it.[12] The term more or less lay fallow after that—with the exception of an idiosyncratic use by economists Louis Rougier and Alexander Rüstow in 1938 at a conference hosted by the American thinker Walter Lippmann.[13] It had a Spanish-language moment as *neoliberalismo* in Chile, when Augusto Pinochet brought in economists from the University of Chicago to help convert Chile's economy to free-market principles, although most of the Chicago school insisted on calling the system simply "liberalism."

Foucault paid little attention to the earlier uses of the word, although he certainly knew about them. His definition was relatively simple and fairly broad: with British economist John Maynard Keynes as the "common enemy" and with twentieth-century New Deal liberalism a unifying target, Foucault conflated von Mises,

Hayek, Rougier, and Rüstow and all those who shared "the same objects of repulsion, namely, the state-controlled economy, planning, and state interventionism."[14] He also noted that some of these economists pushed their theories beyond the world of economics and developed an entire framework for how to live and govern, leading to a "radical alteration of the values, coordinates, and reality principles that govern . . . in liberal orders," as political theorist Wendy Brown put it.[15] Americans like Milton Friedman and Gary Becker had taken an economic model and made it the foundation of life.

After Foucault, the history of the term unfolded in familiar fashion: as a word, "neoliberalism" came to mean prioritizing *homo œconomicus*, with deregulation a primary goal, government intervention in the economy desirable only to insulate the movement of capital around the globe, and lower taxes as formative policy demands. It also came to signify a worldview by which economic values like efficiency and austerity pushed into domains well beyond the economic, helping decide how to run schools, public transport, and even culture. Its ideas shaped the development of the world for the next half century, from roughly 1979 to today.[16] And it was generally a bad word from the start, one that prioritized economic gains over the good of civil society. A slightly respectable genealogy emerging from bona fide economists had morphed into a worldview that seemed destined to destroy civil society. No one would claim to be a neoliberal.[17]

———————

On the other hand: "We are the neoliberals!" Or so proclaimed Charlie Peters in 1979 in a drunken celebration of his newly formed "club" of like-minded American politicos.[18] It would turn out that Michel Foucault was not the only one trying to resuscitate the word *liberal* in the 1980s.

In Charlie Peters's "Neo-Liberal's Manifesto," which first appeared in the *Washington Post* in 1982, Peters apologized for the label, which he called, "a terrible name for an interesting, if embryonic, movement," a movement of young Democrats trying to rescue the party from the 1960s' version of liberalism.[19] His "neo-liberalism" (almost always with a hyphen) had nothing to do with Austrian economists, the Chicago school, or Michel Foucault. Peters was, it seems, blissfully unaware of the parallel history of the term. (In fairness, Foucault's lectures weren't published for nearly twenty-five years.) Instead, it was the name Peters gave to a group of young, energetic Democratic politicians trying to wrestle their party away from the heirs of Lyndon Johnson and the Great Society. Sure, these young "neo-liberals" wanted to prioritize economic growth and the development of a new kind of economy— toward high technology, away from industrial manufacturing—but they didn't want to reorder all of society toward *homo œconomicus* nor prioritize economic thinking over everything else. Their simple notion was that liberal dreams could only be realized with a solid economic foundation, and the Democratic Party had for too long been married to industrial labor unions and excessive social spending directed by a handful of special-interest groups. As things would turn out, their ideas would last longer than their name.

Peters was the early ringleader, or, as an *Esquire* article from 1982 called him, "the party's ex officio cattle prod."[20] Peters was a West Virginia Democrat who had helped John F. Kennedy develop the Peace Corps and then helped lead the organization for most of the 1960s. But as expansive Great Society liberalism's shortcomings grew increasingly apparent in the late 1960s, Peters left the Peace Corps to start a monthly magazine "with a point of view," the *Washington Monthly*. Peters's point of view was that "there were a lot of things wrong with a lot of the big-government solutions we tried [in the 1960s]. But there was *never* anything wrong with the ends we were seeking—justice, fair play, and liberal ideals."[21] He sought not to abandon New Deal liberalism in favor of a free-market approach; instead, he sought to reorder the priorities of the Democratic Party.[22] Although it took a decade or so, his ideas would eventually form the foundation of the Democratic Party for the following fifty years.

Throughout the 1970s, Peters organized weekly breakfast meetings with Bill Bradley, the professional basketball player–turned–New Jersey Senator, Colorado's Senator Gary Hart, Massachusetts's Senator Paul Tsongas, Montana's Senator Max Baucus, Tennessee's Senator Al Gore Jr., Missouri's Representative Richard Gephardt, and Massachusetts Governor Michael Dukakis—in short, the majority of the up-and-coming Democratic Party. "We're not the people who went through and voted on the Great Society, or even Nixon's regulatory program," said another self-proclaimed "neo-liberal," Representative Tim Wirth of Colorado. "We didn't have any stake in those programs, and we're able to view them with a little more skepticism."[23]

In the 1980s, the gatherings turned into "Wednesday night bridge club" meetings led by Gephardt where they eyed a young governor named Bill Clinton from Arkansas. Joseph Biden Jr. from Delaware sometimes attended. They floated ideas including embracing balanced budgets, a negative income tax, the importance of supporting new technologies, and mandatory national service for all Americans. They did not like bureaucracies, antibusiness stances, nor high taxes, especially on businesses and the middle classes. In short, they recognized the importance of the good economy to the success of liberalism after World War II. "What Roosevelt was talking about was economic liberalism," said Susan Thomases, a New York political strategist who helped Bill Bradley get elected. "Johnson added to it social liberalism, and that had a very high price tag." Her "neo-liberals" wanted to return to "Roosevelt liberalism or even more to classical liberalism, where there is a heavier emphasis on economic rather than on social issues."[24] They sought a retreat from the belief in the perfectibility of man and the notion that government should be in the business of defining "the good life." One of their young guns would, a decade later, go on to say, "It's the economy, stupid."[25] In the 1980s, it seemed all liberal dreams had to flow from that.

The neoliberals found eager friends, especially in the context of a series of elections that were bona fide disasters for the Democratic

Party, which was still tarred as the party of rampant 1960s liberalism. "Why can't liberals start raising hell about a government so big, so complex, so expansive, and so unresponsive that it's dragging down every good program we've worked for?" asked Maine's Democratic senator Edmund S. Muskie, in 1975. Muskie advocated fiscally oriented efficiencies: "Our challenge this decade is to restore the faith of Americans in the basic competence and purposes of government. . . . Well-managed, cost-effective, equitable, and responsible government is in itself a social good."[26]

A defining moment came in 1980, when thirty-nine-year-old Massachusetts Senator Paul Tsongas shocked the national convention of Americans for Democratic Action by telling that stalwart liberal group, founded in the aftermath of World War II, that their version of Great Society liberalism was irrelevant. They were simply, he said, "passe." Tsongas told the crowd, "Liberalism must extricate itself from the 1960s . . . and we must have the answers that seem relevant and appropriate to the generation of potential liberals." He later added fuel to the fire: "If the basis of liberalism is just 1960's rhetoric, then the last meeting of liberals will inevitably be held in an old-folks home." The speech was also a direct rebuke to the insurgent presidential campaign of his fellow Massachusetts senator, Ted Kennedy, a symbol of old-school 1960s liberalism. David Broder's *Boston Globe* column on Tsongas's speech was titled "End of Kennedy-Style Liberalism?" Tsongas told Broder, "Either we're going to leave the future to conservatives, with all their Cold War baggage, or we're going to begin to find a new rationale and definition of liberalism."[27] The liberal tradition was at its nadir, symbolizing the politics of bureaucracy, high taxes, special interests, welfare for the poor, and elitism—the common reasons so many people hated white liberals throughout the 1970s.

Tsongas followed up with a 1981 book, *The Road from Here: Liberalism and Realities in the 1980s*. It was, he wrote, a book of "compassionate realism" that said the liberalism of the 1960s and 1970s was bound to fail in the 1980s.[28] A year later, Peters hammered the theme home in his 1982 "Neo-Liberal's Manifesto." The manifesto began by admitting the 1970s were awful times for the liberal dream and that the reasons for it were not only economic but also bureaucratic: "declining productivity, the closed factories and potholed roads that betrayed decaying plant and infrastructure; inefficient and unaccountable public agencies that were eroding confidence in government; a military with too many weapons that didn't work and too few people from the upper classes in its ranks; and a politics of selfishness symbolized by an explosion of political action committees devoted to the interests of single groups."[29] Peters was tired of the bureaucracies that created gridlock for entrepreneurs and single-interest groups that didn't care about the good of the commonweal.

The detritus ran both ways, though—to bleeding-heart liberals and to corporate tycoons. The "Neo-Liberal's Manifesto" advocated curbing ridiculously high wages for company executives as well as for union bosses. It sought not an end to regulation but just limits, including retaining vigorous regulation on matters of health and safety for workers and consumers. These "neo-liberals" didn't want a "mindless Reaganite attack on the bureaucracy." Instead, they wanted to bring back the New Deal's Works Project Administration "to rebuild the nation's infrastructure, to give people jobs, to give the poor money to spend." Clearly convinced by Theodore Lowi's analysis of twentieth-century liberalism, the "Neo-Liberal's Manifesto" pointed a finger at interest groups as a key component of the problem. Seeing the National Rifle Association as the most powerful lobbyist in the country, the manifesto colorfully declared, "Today everyone is imitating the National Rifle Association. That's the way to have a successful lobby. It's also the way to ruin America." But perhaps most radically, the manifesto pushed to give workers shares in companies as part of their pay packages. "We're trying to free ourselves from the old liberal prejudices such as being prolabor or antibusiness, while retaining the liberal tradition of compassion and caring," said Peters.[30] The "neo-liberals" wanted the middle class back. They were trying to save liberalism from itself, or at least that's how they saw things.

In the early 1980s, then, the "neo-liberal" agenda as Peters saw it promised business-friendly policies, sure. But also a lot more: patriotism, losing liberalism's reputation of being beholden to special interests. Most especially, though, the "neo-liberals" sought to defang the accusation of liberal snobbery. "The snobbery that is most damaging to liberalism is the liberal intellectuals' contempt for religious, patriotic, and family values," the manifesto read. "Instead of scorning people who value family, country, and religion, neo-liberals believe in reaching out to them to make clear that our programs are rooted in the same values." As an example of a missed opportunity, Peters discussed how school prayer should not have been outlawed but instead replaced by "a few minutes of silent mediation." But liberals had insisted on draconian measures, removing it completely. "It is this contempt for the 'hicks' that is the least appealing trait of the liberal intellectuals," Peters wrote. "[Liberals] don't really believe in democracy," he alleged. "Neo-liberals do—we think a lot of those hicks are Huck Finns, with the common sense and good will to make the right choices if they are well informed."[31]

As part of their program to win back the silent majority, these 1980s "neo-liberals" saw the future of the American economy not in refurbishing industrial manufacturing through high tariffs and steep protectionism but instead by supporting the burgeoning high-tech industry. They sought to create conditions where there were "more Route 128s and Silicon Valleys" (Route 128 being a high-tech cluster around Boston, similar to California's Silicon Valley).[32] The paradigmatic neo-liberal hero was no longer the line worker in a factory but instead "the risk-taking entrepreneur who creates new jobs and better products," a *New York Times* reporter observed. Neo-liberals harped on about technology so much that many people in the press began calling them the "Atari Democrats," referencing the hugely popular video game console that had recently come on the market. Throughout the 1980s, the phrase "Atari Democrat" was used interchangeably with "neo-liberal."[33]

"Neo-liberals" had their own economic gods. Columnist and future dean of the Massachusetts Institute of Technology's Sloan School of Management Lester Thurow served as a dynamic guide, especially via his 1980 book *The Zero-Sum Society: Distribution and the Possibilities for Economic Change*, which argued that government protection of certain industries forestalled the growth of other, more dynamic industries. But if government shouldn't prop up dying industries, Thurow argued, it should redistribute wealth in ways that encouraged growth, either through higher taxes on the rich or an expanded program for public-sector employment.[34]

But the most famous economist to emerge from the ranks of the neo-liberals was Robert Reich. In his midthirties in the early 1980s, Reich taught public policy at Harvard University but became known for developing policy ideas on how Democrats could stimulate the economy and steer government resources into high tech while also preserving a redistributive state. "The Democratic Party desperately needs new ideas," said Mort Kondracke, editor of the *New Republic*, and Reich is "an idea man and a good one."[35] Reich advocated a trade policy that would assist American businesses against foreign competition, tax breaks for innovation and the middle class, and, most important, a change of focus in industrial policy. "I'm advocating a speeding up of the industrial evolution that's taking place," Reich said. "Unless we make this kind of economic adjustment efficiently and equitably, demands for protectionism will increase," which would only protect dying industries and rob developing ones.[36]

The challenge of developing new sectors of the economy presented a huge problem for any Democratic politician, though: the shift in focus left organized labor out in the cold. "If you switch from steel to semiconductors," said one labor activist, "you go from union to nonunion and I don't see how you can get Lane Kirkland [president of the AFL-CIO] to sign onto that bargain."[37] In addition, because the new technology often required advanced training, including typically a college degree, the 1980s neo-liberals were, in practice, working to shift the base of the Democratic Party away from the working classes and toward the middle and upper middle classes.

In 1984, this shift was, to an extent, the tactic of Gary Hart, a Democratic presidential hopeful. Hart was a flawed candidate who was smart but lacked charisma or a sense of humor (something he tried to joke about). But in the early 1980s, he was a solid part of the neo-liberal camp.[38] Yet when journalists tried to hang the neo-liberal label on him, he rejected it—as he did all labels. He said "neo-liberal" was a "dumb label" and that he was "too independent, too Jeffersonian" to have any label at all: "I don't like having others defining my ideology."[39]

He wouldn't have to worry for long. Hart narrowly lost the 1984 nomination to party stalwart Walter Mondale, who went on to get trounced by Ronald Reagan, who garnered the electoral votes of forty-nine states to Mondale's one (his home state of Minnesota). It was the Democrats' second forty-nine–to–one debacle in four presidential elections (the first being Richard Nixon's win over George McGovern in 1972, discussed in chapter 6).

As soon as Hart's appeal to just the upper middle classes demonstrated the electoral shortcomings of "neo-liberalism" as a label, the term essentially vanished from the Democratic lexicon. Michael Kinsley of the *New Republic* dismissed the "rather vacuous blow-dried side to the neolib business," suggesting that its youthful intrepid spirit was also filled with faulty idealism and empty-headed promises.[40]

Or perhaps it was just bad marketing. Despite the label's decline, the ideas central to the neo-liberal agenda did not fade. In 1985, a group of neo-liberals formed the Democratic Leadership Council (DLC) and rechristened themselves "New Democrats." Strategist Al From recalled that they wanted to become "the party of upward mobility," believing that "social and economic progress in America is built on the talents and efforts of all Americans, not just the wealthy elites."[41] In 1988, after yet another embarrassing performance for Democrats in a presidential election, From commissioned academics William Galston and Elaine Kamarck to decode what was wrong with the party. Galston and Kamarck thought it was obvious. It was their "unacceptably liberal" positions on policy issues and the sense they were beholden to special-interest groups, most especially Black voters and labor unions; in short, the neo-liberals were right. "Too many Americans have come to see the party as inattentive to their economic interests, indifferent if not hostile to their moral sentiments and ineffective in defense of their national security," read Galston and Kamarck's report. The New Democrats of the late 1980s and early 1990s would need to win back the white middle class, and to do that, they'd need to alter their policies, gamble their historic constituency, and fight back against any accusation that they were too "liberal."[42]

When it came to policy ideas, the New Democrats were perhaps less adventuresome than they had been as "neo-liberals" (there were, for instance, few calls for required national service or workers sharing profits with bosses), but their tempered proposals eventually met with electoral success. In 1992, Bill Clinton led the DLC just before he was elected president by promising to cut taxes for the middle class, offering industrial workers "training and retraining" to "achieve a high-skill, high wage economy," and pushing for research and development investments in "emerging technologies."[43] One of Clinton's political strategists, James Carville, posted a sign at Clinton headquarters that hammered home Clinton's core message: "It's the economy, stupid." Al Gore was also a neo-liberal and then a New Democrat before being tapped to be Clinton's vice president. Robert Reich served as Clinton's secretary of labor from 1993 to 1997. Joe Biden was also an early member. "Neo-liberal" may have been a wonky name that Peters had to apologize for, but the ideas central to it would effectively run the Democratic Party for the next fifty years—although to do so, they'd have to sacrifice the "liberal" label.

One could be forgiven for seeing parallels between the two neo-liberalisms that emerged almost simultaneously starting in the late

1970s—one from Foucault's analysis of the Chicago school and one from Charlie Peters and the New Democrats. Both prioritized economic growth. Both hated excessive government intrusion. Both were attempts, in rhetoric at least, to expand individual freedoms. But the Democratic "neo-liberals" were more welcoming to social welfare programs, national allegiance, and government intervention to assist people. The New Democrats imagined government to have an important role in sustaining the commonweal. They also generally, for a time, openly embraced the label "neo-liberal."

Perhaps predictably, they were also attacked immediately—their new liberalism was imagined to be just more of the same. With Ronald Reagan safely in power throughout the 1980s, Republicans generally ignored the neo-liberals. "Government is not the solution to our problem," said Ronald Reagan in his 1981 inaugural address. "Government *is* the problem." More than this, many Americans began to adopt a language of economic "choice" and of "market determinism." Charlie Peters's "neo-liberals" were easily used as affirmation that "Reaganomics" was the correct course and that even some Democrats knew it.

The strongest indictments against the early 1980s neo-liberals, however, came from the labor left and people of color. For instance, Mike Davis, the organic socialist intellectual, tore apart the Democratic neo-liberals for sacrificing the goals of the Great Society and the civil rights movement. They had, Davis wrote, "scant loyalty to labor or minorities."[44] In the era of business-minded ascendency, with the economic crisis of the 1970s leaving the working class adrift, "Democratic neoliberalism . . . asserts that the first function of the state is to provide welfare to the well-to-do and preserve a dynamic frontier of entrepreneurial, professional and rentier opportunity."[45] Dismissing the assertation of the "neo-liberals" that they were simply advocating "a transition from an old smokestack capitalism to a new silicon-chip entrepreneurialism," Davis argued that they had, in fact, "abandoned perennial commitments to full employment and national healthcare, and, for the first time in a modern Democratic convention, [in 1984] refrained from calling for substantial new social spend-ing."[46] Davis specifically attacked Gary Hart, Paul Tsongas, New York mayor Ed Koch, Richard Gebhardt, California representative Tony Chelho, and others for trying to move the Democratic Party "away from Blacks and labor, and toward the upwardly mobile middle classes" by favoring "flat rate tax reform, victim's rights, the curb-ing of entitlements, urban enterprise zones, and so on."[47] He called the neo-liberals "the white yuppie establishment-in-formation."[48] And he worried, not without reason, that their friendly overtures to business would strike a damning blow against those who, like him, opposed the unadulterated spread of capitalism.

Jesse Jackson, meanwhile, spearheaded the Black complaint against the neo-liberals. In the three-way race for the Democratic presidential nomination in 1984, Walter Mondale had the lion's share of establishment Democrats, including the labor left. Gary Hart had the young and highly educated white middle- and upper-middle-class voters—the neo-liberals. And Jackson polled well in the South, where Black voters made up a majority of the Democratic base. Jackson's fear was that both Hart and Mondale were moving the party to the center, leaving behind commitments to civil rights and social programs.

Jackson started talking down the neo-liberal agenda. Mondale and Hart responded in kind. By 1991, Jackson was snubbed from DLC conventions, with DLC members saying that Jackson rep-resented "an old style of politics." Jackson in turn called the DLC "the Democrats for the Leisure Class."[49] By the early 1990s, Jackson admitted that the DLC controlled the Democratic Party, and he worried that they had left Black people behind. Once again, supposed liberals had been little more than halfway friends to people of color.

———————

Nothing made Jesse Jackson's argument more obvious than Bill Clin-ton's "Sister Souljah moment."

Sister Souljah is a singer and Black political activist who, in 1992, appeared on a Sunday morning TV show in the immediate aftermath of the deadly Los Angeles riots. Interviewers wanted to know why Black people were so mad and if it was wise for them to attack white people in general when white people still held so much power in American life. Forgoing any historical explanation, Souljah doubled down: "Yeah, it was wise. I mean, if black people kill black people every day, why not have a week and kill white people?"[50] The line was picked up by the press, and Sister Souljah was forced to wear the mantle of "angry Black woman."

A month later, she appeared as a panelist at a meeting of Jesse Jackson's Rainbow Coalition. And the day after that, Democratic presidential candidate Bill Clinton spoke to the coalition himself. He took the opportunity to pillory Sister Souljah. "Her comments before and after Los Angeles were filled with the kind of hatred that you [the Rainbow Coalition] do not honor," Clinton said. Clinton even brought up a lyric from one of Sister Souljah's songs: "If there are any good white people, I haven't met them."[51]

Clinton's comments became front-page news, with the *Washington Post* story titled, "Clinton Stuns Rainbow Coalition."[52] Jackson was furious, saying Sister Souljah "represents the feelings and hopes of a whole generation of people," even if he himself had distanced himself from her more violent outbursts.[53] For Clinton, though, Black people were not his intended audience. His remarks were politically calculated to win over middle-class white voters. Clinton had to prove he was a moderate, not a "liberal," to win in 1992. Along with all its other baggage, "liberal" had been pinned as a free-spending advocate of the welfare state with "entitlement" benefits earmarked for Black and Brown Americans. Clinton did not want to be seen as that kind of liberal. As the prominent civil rights activist and former US assistant attorney general Roger Wilkins recognized, Clinton "came there to show suburban whites that he can stand up to blacks. It was contrived."[54]

And it worked. An Arkansas native, Clinton had already sewn up the endorsement of several prominent Black leaders in the South, and he kept those endorsements despite his comments. And many middle-class white voters appreciated the notion that he would not be beholden to what they perceived to be the liberal wing of his party. As Al From recalled, after the Sister Souljah speech, "it was clear that Clinton was not just another Democratic nominee pandering to the party's interest groups."[55] He was not just another liberal.

Countless politicians have subsequently sought their own "Sister Souljah moment." Republican George W. Bush gently attacked the religious right when he outlined his version of "compassionate conservatism."[56] Barack Obama distanced himself from his pastor Jeremiah Wright, saying some of Wright's statements were "a bunch of rants that aren't grounded in truth."[57] Moderation and independence are the go-to methods for avoiding supposedly extreme labels like "liberal." Attack someone on the far end of your party's political spectrum, tar them as liberal, and proceed as a moderate—that was the lesson.

It was only in the early and mid-1990s that Foucault's definition of "neoliberal" as an economically centered social order reentered the conversation—this time as a wholly negative term. It started with a group of British political theorists who lived through the Margaret Thatcher years of efficiency and austerity and had grown increasingly fascinated with Foucault's thought on politics and power. In 1991, Colin Gordon, a researcher out of Oxford, published an essay on Foucault's concept of "governmental rationality" that centered on Foucault's 1978–79 lectures on "neoliberalism."[58] Gordon was responding to British New Left social theorist Stuart Hall, who had critiqued Thatcher's politics as "neo-liberal," by which he meant embracing "self-interest, competitive individualism, anti-statism."[59]

Gordon wanted to add intellectual heft to the term. Following Foucault, Gordon argued that neoliberalism was more than an antistatist political sensibility, it was a form of rule. Gordon's piece reignited interest in Foucault's analysis, and the word *neoliberal* gained descriptive power to identify a growing body of political thought that surrounded Thatcherism in Great Britain and Reaganism in the United States.

Aware of Gordon's analysis, in 1991 and 1992, a group of London-based theorists including Andrew Barry, Peter Miller, Thomas Osborne, and Nikolas Rose began fleshing out Foucault's meaning of the term *neoliberalism* in relation to the economic changes of the 1980s and 1990s.[60] They organized a conference on "Foucault and Politics" and eventually a book, *Foucault and Political Reason: Liberalism, Neo-Liberalism, and Rationalities of Government*. (In this instance, the hyphen in the title was simply in keeping with British spelling style, rather than an effort to conform with Charlie Peters's deliberate usage.) "Despite the enormous influence of Michel Foucault in gender studies, social theory, and cultural studies," read the jacket copy, "his work has been relatively neglected in the study of politics."[61] Now, through Foucault, these theorists were able to show how something called neoliberalism "involves less a retreat from governmental 'intervention' than a re-inscription of the techniques and forms of expertise required for the exercise of government."[62]

By the late 1990s, Foucault's understanding of neoliberalism had taken off within academia. In 1999, Susan George gave a speech entitled "A Short History of Neoliberalism: Twenty Years of Elite Economics and Emerging Opportunities for Structural Change."[63] She relied on Foucault's definition of "neoliberalism" (as a mode of governmentality not only focused on easing flows of capital but also on ascribing value based on economic measures) without even citing Foucault but identifying the same starting point—Austrian economists in the 1940s. In 2001, the German academic Thomas Lemke published a prominent article on Foucault's use of *neoliberal*.[64] In 2004, Paul Treanor published an influential article entitled "Neoliberalism: Origins, Theory, Definition."[65] Foucault's definition was cemented in 2005 with the publication of David Harvey's *A Brief History of Neoliberalism.*[66] And in 2004, Foucault's lectures on neo-liberalism were finally published in French; they would be translated to English in 2008.[67]

Still, even within academia, *neoliberalism* was hardly omnipresent early in the first decade of the twenty-first century, especially outside the disciplines that traded in theory. "I've been asking colleagues in several departments and disciplines whether they've ever come across the term 'neoliberalism,'" wrote prominent English professor and *New York Times* columnist Stanley Fish in a 2009 blog post. Only "a small number acknowledged having heard the word; a very much smaller number ventured a tentative definition."[68] Still, Fish knew it was almost always "invoked as an accusation," signifying a social and political order that put economics before humanity. More than two dozen readers commented on the post, some of whom thought Fish was insane. "I do not know what Universities you polled but Neo-liberalism is an every day subject in every single one of my courses," wrote one. "Thanks for shedding light to the non intellectual world on a term that everybody has been using for years."[69]

Ever since about 2005, the word *neoliberal* has been safely un-derstood in the Foucauldian mold defined as, in David Harvey's words, "a theory of political economic practices that proposes that human well-being can best be advanced by liberating individual en-trepreneurial freedoms and skills within an institutional framework characterized by strong private property rights, free markets, and free trade" and, moreover, that "the social good will be maximized by maximizing the reach and frequency of market transactions, and it seeks to bring all human action into the domain of the market."[70] Historians then traced this version of neoliberalism backward, to F. A. Hayek and Milton Friedman, to Augusto Pinochet's Chile in the 1970s, to Margaret Thatcher's economic programs beginning in 1979, to Reaganomics in the United States in the 1980s, and onward. Histo-rian Gary Gerstle has argued that the ideas central to this version of neoliberalism had become so accepted by 1979 that they constituted

a "political order," which Gerstle defined as "a constellation of ideologies, policies, and constituencies that shape American politics
in ways that endure beyond the two-, four-, and six-year election
cycles."[71] Whatever it was called, starting in the 1980s, "market ideas
moved out of economics departments to become the new standard
currency of the social sciences," wrote historian Daniel Rodgers.[72]
This was the neoliberal order.

The victory of market fundamentalism over New Deal liberalism
beginning in the 1980s occurred not necessarily because it had the
best ideas but primarily because it had excellent timing and a severely
weakened enemy in "liberalism." In the 1970s, the economic boom
that had sustained liberal dreams in the postwar era came crashing
down. Although there were weaknesses in several economic sectors
in the late 1960s and early 1970s, the decline became widely recognized in the United States in 1973, with the Middle Eastern oil
embargo and a subsequent recession. Interest rates soared, with the
prime rate rising from 2.25 percent in 1950 to more than 20 percent
by 1980. Inflation rose to 14 percent. With money more expensive to
borrow, investments declined, which led to layoffs. Unemployment
rose from 3.5 percent in 1969 to 10.8 percent in 1982.[73] Economists
came up with a new term to identify a stagnating economy during
a time of high inflation: "stagflation."

Stagflation is famously difficult to fight. Monetary tools can lower
or raise inflation, but they usually bring recession or growth, respec-
tively. Meanwhile, government spending can put more money into
the economy through investments and purchasing, but that causes
inflation. Government intervention seemed fruitless in the face of
stagflation. Neoliberalism in the Thatcher and Reagan mold at least
proposed an answer: unleash the power of business. Because "liberalism" had been a scapegoat for so many critics for so long, it was
powerless to stop the assault.

There was an irony in the rise of neoliberalism. In the neoliberal order of the Chicago school, the economic forces that dictated one's material life became even more distant than ever before, as decisions one can't control led to all sorts of personal turmoil. A factory looking for cheap labor moves abroad. Bankers maximizing profits destabilize the housing industry. And as the economic world grows increasingly perilous, people look for security. The definition of *liberalism* that was predominant in 1980s America did not provide it. Absent that heritage, Americans were left with two alternatives: individualism, which would force people to accept the blame for their station, or the hope that free-market capitalism would eventually work for them. The Republican Party offered both. Deploying the language of individualism allowed the blame for society's ills to fall on people considered unworthy. It was Horatio Alger all over again. A lot of the right-wing self-help books of this era preached the gospel of individualism. The works of Larry Elder and Laura Schlesinger are fine examples, arguing for individual solutions to large problems because the large problems are so large and diffuse, and because the language of collective action is so impoverished, it's the only language that made any sense. Meanwhile, the state was deployed primarily to ease the movement of capital around the world, destabilizing local economies all the more.

If you want to know "what's the matter with Kansas," it isn't entirely that Kansans are getting duped by cultural issues. It's that, because liberalism only offered an ill-defined and supposedly bankrupted tradition, free-market capitalism was the only game in town. The triumph of what we today call neoliberalism happened in large part if not exclusively because of the widespread disdain for what was understood to be American liberalism in the 1980s and 1990s. It would be yet another irony that, from the 2000s through the 2010s and 2020s, the populist revolt against neoliberalism, from both the right and the left, would, through a slight alteration of terms, target someone they called "the liberal elite." Poor liberals could never win.

These frustrations might have been put best by the Bay Area punk band the Dead Kennedys, a name so offensive the band's producers begged them to change it, which of course only led them to hold on to it more tightly. In 1979, they wrote a paean to the general frustration with self-righteous white liberals, "Holiday in Cambodia." The song advises a young, wealthy white kid, probably a "neo-liberal" New Democrat, who has "been to school for a year or two" and knows they've "seen it all." But the kid is in their "daddy's car . . . playing ethnicky jazz to parade your snazz on your five-grand stereo" bragging about how they know "the slums got so much soul." The kid wanted everyone to "to act like you, kiss ass while you bitch, so you can get rich, but your boss gets richer off you." But the kid's self-righteousness and know-it-all behavior led them to advocate on behalf of causes they knew little about. Their critique of capitalism might have led them to speak kindly on behalf of American anticolonial adventures. What the kid needed was a dose of reality. The kid needed a holiday in Cambodia, which was then in the midst of genocide under the communist dictator Pol Pot. In Cambodia, "you'll work harder with a gun in your back for a bowl of rice a day," all before "your head is skewered on a stake." The song aired the general frustration with the white liberal establishment, a politics of fuck-youism that would continue to grow in the 1990s and 2000s, leading liberals to be defined to the point of absurdity.[74]

EIGHT

FIRST AS TRAGEDY, THEN AS FARCE

Owning the Libs

Among those who in early summer 1988 were frustrated with George H. W. Bush's ham-handed campaign for president of the United States, perhaps most annoyed was President Ronald Reagan. Bush was Reagan's heir apparent, the sitting vice president. But Bush lacked charisma, and the American people could tell he had a soft touch. The press called it "the wimp factor." And when Bush tried to rectify this characterization by attacking, he came across as shrill and mean, not as playful and dismissive, a trick Reagan had mastered. In May 1988, Bush was slipping dangerously in the polls, and against someone Reagan perceived as an easy target: Michael Dukakis, the diminutive Massachusetts Democrat. Reagan believed he himself could mop up Dukakis by lifting little more than his little finger. The method was out there, tried and true: paint Dukakis as an out-of-touch member of "the liberal elite" who would bring back the radical 1960s. Dukakis was the Harvard-educated governor of Massachusetts—that practically screamed "liberal"! Frustrated though he was, Reagan tried to remain presidential and stay on the sidelines. Bush was his own man.

But after polls showed Bush with a double-digit deficit in early June 1988, Bush's advisors, including several former Reagan men, pushed a new line of attack. Their proposal was indeed to go negative, to make Dukakis look like a "liberal at odds with the most basic American values."[1] It didn't matter that Dukakis had balanced budgets in his home state (a neo-liberal initiative) or that he had inherited from a previous Republican governor laws that could be portrayed as soft on crime. One poll showed that only 19 percent of voters thought Dukakis' was "too liberal."[2] Perceptions would have to change, the advisors advised.

What followed was what one Bush biographer has called "one of the most slashing attack campaigns in presidential history."[3] A June 9 speech at the Texas Republican State Convention in Houston set the tone. In front of the friendliest audience Bush could imagine, he attacked Dukakis for what Bush called his "old-style Sixties liberalism" that included raising taxes, bloating the government, being soft on crime, and making the US weak in foreign policy. The political red meat played well and, for the next five months, Bush's campaign was almost entirely negative. In case they slipped from the message, one of Bush's campaign advisors, Lee Atwater, carried in his pocket a three-by-five-inch notecard highlighting key talking points: paint Dukakis as "High-tax, high spending, To the left" of previous administrations, and little more than a "McGovern/Kennedy/Jackson liberal."[4]

Energized by the new tactic, Reagan finally engaged. From June onward, Reagan traveled to Bush campaign events at least twice a week. In Miami, Reagan called Dukakis "a true liberal who, instead of controlling government spending, raises taxes." Reagan urged Americans not to "return to those worn-out policies that bring high taxes, low-growth and a loss of direction and purpose."[5] Reagan's Dukakis was pledging to return to the days of Black Power, Vietnam, and overbearing government. It was "acid, amnesty, and abortion" all over again. In Reagan's vision, that was the essence of liberalism.

Harping on liberals was old hat for Reagan. He had famously transitioned from being a New Deal prounion liberal in the 1940s and 1950s (a politics he later described as that of a "near hopeless hemophiliac liberal") to being a conservative in the early 1960s, in part by reading William F. Buckley's *National Review* ("I'd be lost without *National Review*," Reagan wrote Buckley in 1962).[6] In his famous 1964 speech "A Time for Choosing," which put Reagan on the political map as a Goldwater conservative and was later called "the manifesto of the modern conservative movement," Reagan's most famous line was, "The trouble with our liberal friends is not that they're ignorant; it's just that they know so much that isn't so."[7] Almost always affable, Reagan would bemoan the foolish wrong-headedness of American liberals before casting them as downers whose own policies made them sad.

Reagan served as California governor from 1967 to 1975 and then stayed in the limelight from 1975 to 1980 as a newspaper and radio commentator. He developed a common theme: hammer the libs. In a *60 Minutes* interview in December 1975, Reagan claimed that "if fascism ever comes to America, it will come in the form of liberalism," adding, "And what is fascism? Fascism is private ownership, private enterprise, but total government control and regulation. Well, isn't this the liberal philosophy?"[8] The following year he said even more bluntly, "Fascism was really the basis for the New Deal."[9] This remark glossed over the fact that it was self-proclaiming New Deal liberals like FDR who organized the actual fight against fascism. But that didn't matter. Liberals in the conservative imagination were, in the 1960s and 1970s at least, little more than elite quasi communists. Reagan also knew that if you repeat something often enough, people will start to believe you.

During his two terms as president, Reagan seemed to think that the image of the liberal he had perpetuated had served its purpose. The opposition was running from the label. His attacks no longer needed to be deployed.

Until 1988.

The campaign of 1988 featured all the hallmarks of a newfound, more expansive attack on white liberals, suggesting they were not only quasi communists and aloof elitists but also soft on crime, supported only by minoritized people, and generally foolish blowhards. Reagan urged voters to look at the Democratic platform, not what they were saying: "You'll never hear that 'L' word—liberal—from them," the president said in one of his weekly radio addresses in July 1988. "They've put on political trench coats and dark glasses and slipped their platform into a plain brown wrapper." Reagan continued, "Our liberal opposition seems to think so much is bad in America."[10] Not only were liberals radicals, they were no fun, either.

At the Republican National Convention in August, Bush aired a video segment called "Close Encounters of the Liberal Kind." As became obvious to the *Christian Science Monitor*, "Republicans plan to grind down Mr. Dukakis's popularity with a relentless barrage of conservative-vs.-liberal contrasts. . . . The tactical goal is to leave no doubt in the minds of voters that Dukakis is an unabashed liberal."[11] My, had the tables turned since FDR envisioned this binary only favoring his side.

Reagan's convention speech was itself unabashed. In his twenty-five-minute address, Reagan said the word *liberal* or *liberalism* twenty-two times, mentioning Bush's name only six times. "Yes, the choice this year is between the policies of liberalism or the policies of America's political mainstream," Reagan said. "It's time . . . to use the dreaded 'L' word, to say the policies of our opposition and the congressional leadership of his party are liberal, liberal, liberal."[12]

Dukakis was no dummy. He knew a trap when he saw one: reject the "liberal" label and lose the tradition of FDR and JFK or own the label and accept all the baggage from the previous half century. There had been no plausible replacement term just yet. So Dukakis simply avoided the word as much as possible. During the Democratic National Convention, he said, "This election is not about ideology, it's about competence. And it's not about meaningless labels."[13] Without a language to defend, though, Dukakis was pilloried for being an elitist who had gone to Harvard Law School (Bush made the dubious claim that his own Yale pedigree was not as elite, since only the "Harvard boutique to me has the connotation of liberalism and elitism").[14] Dukakis's biggest gaffe on this front was riding in a tank while wearing a helmet that made him look smaller than he really was. Bush used the footage and overlaid it with a list of military spending bills Dukakis had vetoed to suggest that not only was Dukakis a wimp, he was a phony—some of the classic tropes utilized against white liberals. The ad failed to mention that Dukakis had deferred Harvard Law School for two years so he could serve in the US Army.

People begged Dukakis to push back. Marc Pearl, national director of Americans for Democratic Action, wished Dukakis would say, "If being a liberal means being a champion of worker rights, being a champion of family rights, being a champion of children's rights, and government acting as a catalyst to help people, then dammit, I'm a liberal."[15]

Bigger guns came out, too. In a column entitled "Wake Up Liberals, Your Time Has Come!" Arthur Schlesinger Jr. alleged that the American people were tired of the New Right's coalition "of economic conservatives and evangelical zealots—one wing devoted to getting government off our backs, the other to putting government in our beds." Americans, Schlesinger surmised, were ready for more liberalism, not less—although only of his kind. "I know that it remains fashionable to say that liberalism is too discredited by its record in recent years even to contemplate a comeback," Schlesinger wrote, before attempting to redefine the word. "In fact, there has not been a liberal administration in Washington since the Great Society vanished into the Vietnam quagmire in 1966." Schlesinger's examples of good liberalism went back to John F. Kennedy and the "vital center" Schlesinger had written speeches about. He even disavowed some of the inclusive gains of the 1960s, writing, "Liberal leadership will have to rise above those worthy special interests—labor, women, blacks, old folks and the rest—that have become their electoral refuge and regain a commanding national vision of the problems and prospects of the republic." Making sure his point was clear, Schlesinger even attempted to dismiss "the youth rebellion of the late 1960s" as "a weird and improbable memory, a strange interlude of national hallucination." Perhaps Schlesinger had missed the fact that the Republican Party had, for two decades, used that very image as the primary example of what happens when liberals take charge? Or perhaps (as his later writings might suggest), Schlesinger believed that the attempts at inclusion really did threaten the American project.[16]

Alongside Schlesinger, Leonard Bernstein made a reappearance. "I want to redefine that word liberal," Bernstein wrote in a 1988 *New York Times* op-ed piece called, "I'm a Liberal, and I'm Proud of It." Bernstein wanted "not to run from it, nor cower defensively at its insulting abuse, but proudly to clarify it." It had been wrongly maligned. "Liberal is a word soiled by the greedy, reactionary, backward-looking impulse toward tyranny," Bernstein wrote. But, to Bernstein, liberals should be proud. "Who fought to free the slaves? Liberals. Who succeeded in abolishing the poll tax? Liberals. Who fought for women's rights, civil rights, free public education? Liberals. Who stood guard and still stands guard against sweatshops, child labor, racism, bigotry? Lovers of freedom and enemies of tyranny: Liberals."[17]

Bernstein's letter did not go unnoticed, nor, like liberalism, would Bernstein be allowed to escape his own history (or at least its maligned image). Two days after Bernstein's op-ed, William F. Buckley Jr. replied with a column entitled, "Please, Lenny, Just Stick to Your Music." Buckley didn't meaningfully debate liberalism, instead reminding readers, "The most agitated Bernstein has been throughout his public lifetime was in January 1970" when "he threw a big cocktail party for the Black Panthers." Buckley then retold the story of "radical chic," concluding, "one of the reasons the 'L' word is discredited is that it was handled by such as Leonard Bernstein over the years."[18] (Never one to let something go, Bernstein wrote to Buckley, "Yawn. Yet another utterly predictable, indecently patronizing hate-piece."[19])

In early fall 1988, Dukakis finally addressed "the 'L' word," although he ended up making things worse for himself. Dukakis claimed to be "a liberal in the tradition of Franklin Roosevelt and Harry Truman and John Kennedy" but then left out specific policies that signified what he liked about those leaders. This omission gave Bush an open invitation to respond, which he did with supreme sarcasm: "Miracle of miracles. Headlines. Read all about it. My opponent finally . . . called himself the big 'L,' called himself a liberal." Bush keenly asked what kind of liberal Dukakis was; was he FDR or Walter Mondale? "The Governor of Massachusetts should debate himself," Bush said. "It could be entertaining. The Old Left or the New Left. He can go out there and debate each other." Then, Bush said, the question would finally be asked, "Will the real liberal please stand up? And God knows what would happen."[20]

But Bush's team didn't wait for a debate. Immediately after Dukakis declared he was a liberal, the Bush campaign aired a commercial ignoring Roosevelt, Truman, and Kennedy and instead asking, "Why would we want to go back to the tax-and-spend policies of eight years ago?" while showing pictures of a different Democratic triptych: George McGovern, Jimmy Carter, and Walter Mondale.[21] The liberal tradition had been redefined.

Lest anyone miss the racial politics attached to the conservative version of white liberals, the Bush campaign simultaneously featured an advertisement highlighting a Black criminal named William R. "Willie" Horton, who, while on furlough from a Massachusetts prison, raped a woman in Maryland. The ad was clearly race-baiting politics about what the return of "the L-word" would bring: crime, violence, racial uprising, and social disarray. The ad didn't bother to tell viewers that the furlough policy was put in place by Dukakis's Republican predecessor because, of course, that would have sullied the argument about what liberals had done to America: instigated racialized chaos through a politics of expensive victimhood.

With no one interested in debating the historic meanings of liberalism, in November Bush trounced Dukakis by more than eight percentage points in the popular vote and by a landslide in the Electoral College, 426 to 111 votes. In 1988 (and ever since), tarring your opponent as a liberal, defined as a weak-kneed, tax-and-spend radical, was a largely winning strategy.

Although it wasn't obvious at the time, 1988 would turn out to be a pivotal year in reshaping the conservative assault on white liberals and eventually pushing it to ridiculous extremes. In that year, Bush's antiliberal campaign met up with two other forces also using the specter of "1960s liberalism" as constitutive glue: the religious right and the emerging conservative media. Together, these three forces would cement the image of the white liberal in the conservative imagination for decades, making the return of the liberal a fruitless crusade.

For the religious right, it didn't take long to home in on "secular liberals" as its primary target. Where once Catholics and Jews stood as a demonic specter, from the 1980s onward the enemy was the white liberal.

Although the so-called Moral Majority began in 1979 as an evangelical Protestant lobbying group, the political and cultural direction of evangelicalism was still up in the air through the late 1970s. Indeed, it had been plagued by factionalism since its inception. In the first decades of the twentieth century, when fundamentalism first emerged in the United States, evangelical Christians fought over increasingly thorny understandings of the Bible, most especially the extent of biblical literalism and accounts of the last days. In the aftermath of the Scopes "monkey trial" of 1925, when big-city newspapers mocked antievolution fundamentalism as the backward beliefs of rednecks, conservative Christianity went relatively quiet for the next fifty years, generally taking pride in being isolated from the American mainstream. When it reemerged in the public eye in the

1970s, it had a singular claim: secular liberals had pushed an atheistic agenda onto America and were damning the country to hell. They needed to fight back.

At first, the political manifestations of this notion were hard to envision. Evangelicals initially placed their hopes in Southern Baptist President Jimmy Carter, but he disappointed them when he seemed to condone the legitimacy of homosexual relationships. The movement took its modern shape in 1980, when evangelical leader Jerry Falwell published a hard-hitting jeremiad called *Listen America!* that set the tone of the evangelical movement for the next four decades.

Like all good jeremiads, Falwell's book was written in the spirit of "the end is near, the time is now." Falwell saw moral decline and creeping socialism everywhere in 1980s America. "America has been great because her people have been good," he wrote.[22] But things had changed, he claimed, alleging that "sin has permeated our land."[23] Pornographers, abortionists, feminists, homosexuals, and secular humanists had been given free rein to adulterate American culture, he contended. How had these miscreants come to acceptance in the United States when the "people have been good"? Liberals. Yes, "liberal forces . . . have made significant inroads" into Christian America, Falwell preached. This was no time to parse scripture. Now was the time to wage war, to take the country back, he exhorted. Americans "are sick and tired of the way amoral liberals are trying to corrupt our nation."[24]

As Falwell's popularity grew, so did the vitriol against secular liberals. The point was to terrify. In his standard "Moral Majority jeremiad," Falwell often included a story about a student of his who opened a church in Long Island, New York. When the young pastor went grocery shopping with his family, an employee told him, "Listen, don't let this little girl walk around this store. Blond, blue-eyed, four year, three year, four-year-old girls are going at a very high price at the kiddy porn and the prostitution market. And your child will disappear instantly. You hold that child." Without pausing to investigate the veracity of the story and instead relying on a nationwide panic about child safety to attest to its truth, Falwell simply repeated the story hundreds of times. Liberals were, he argued, waging "a global war against the little children."[25]

Gauntlet thrown, nearly every force in the emerging religious right picked it up, echoing the theme that a liberal secular elite had seized power from everyday citizens and was using the government to enact its amoral atheistic vision. Sam Francis, a conservative intellectual advising the likes of the televangelist minister Pat Robertson (before moving in increasingly white nationalist directions), argued in an influential 1982 essay, "Liberalism flourishes almost entirely because it reflects the material and psychological interests of a privileged, power-holding, and power-seeking sector of American society."[26] Francis alleged that liberals were attacking core American values by portraying "the small town, the family, class, religious, ethnic, and community ties as backward, repressive, and exploitative; the values of work, thrift, discipline, sacrifice, and postponement of gratification (on which, as values, the moral legitimacy of the older elites rested) as outmoded, absolutist, puritanical, superstitious, and not infrequently hypocritical."[27]

If liberals were as omnipresent as Falwell and Francis imagined, and if they were hell-bent on making those who opposed them seem "backward, repressive, and exploitative," then the arenas to defend were numerous: schools, the family, businesses, and more. The war would be long. "We've got a long way to go, there is much to be done," said Falwell. "But we have bottomed out of those dark ages, the two decades of the sixties and the seventies."[28]

Tim LaHaye, a prolific writer best known for his coauthorship of the *Left Behind* series, took the lead in trying to expose all the arenas liberals had supposedly ruined, producing books with titles like *The Battle for the Public Schools* (1983) and *The Battle for the Family* (1984). He was clear on the terms of the fight: "What we have is a minority of liberal secularists leading our country astray and we have to come back as the conscience of the nation." LaHaye leaned on the religious right's imagery of the dreaded "liberal secularists" as a way of conflating "liberals" with nonbelievers, thus sidelining any person of faith who might be on the political left. "We are the victims of a secularist society," he added.[29] LaHaye took special joy in taking on John Dewey in the realm of public education. It was Dewey's "liberal education philosophy" that opened the door for schools "to be anti-God, antimoral, antifamily, anti-free enterprise and anti-American," LaHaye wrote. It was all, he thought, "educrat propaganda."[30] LaHaye argued that liberals used the idea of "neutrality" to eliminate religious perspectives from the public realm, including targeting public schools where they could brainwash generations of young people. LaHaye's entire *Left Behind* series, an international bestselling franchise that spawned numerous spin-offs, was little more than an apocalyptic call to arms against secular liberalism: join us now or be left behind in a blistering hellscape.

James Robison, a prominent televangelist, was among the many evangelicals to attack homosexuality, seeing it as a liberal allowance. "I'm sick and tired of hearing about all the radicals and the perverts and the liberals and the leftists and the Communists coming out of the closet," he said, thus feminizing his opposition. "It's time for God's people to come out of the closet."[31]

The notion that liberals were behind every evil built momentum throughout the 1980s and 1990s. During Pat Robertson's failed presidential bid in 1988, he railed against "the Eastern liberal establishment" that controlled not only American foreign policy but also the country's finances, again utilizing the conflation of liberalism with Jews that Spiro Agnew had developed.[32] Robertson said the root problem in America was a "moral decay" that expensive liberal policies would not solve. Spending money on AIDS research, for instance, wasn't going to make AIDS go away. Instead, all you had to do was tell "male homosexuals or intravenous drug users" to "stop" and then, if they didn't, let them suffer their fate. Despite their varying origins, it was not a far leap from Robertson's impulse to frame issues in terms of individual "merit" to that of the neoliberal order.

In 1992, it was Patrick Buchanan's turn to make much the same argument. Most famously, in a speech at the Republican National Convention, Buchanan sought to unite the religious right with the Republican Party through a collective hatred of liberals. He referred to the Democratic National Convention as "20,000 radicals and liberals . . . dressed up as moderates and centrists," which he called "the greatest single exhibition of cross-dressing in American political history." But, he said, these liberals actually sought to open the door for all sorts of pluralism—feminism, equality of the races, kindly social programs, gay rights. That is, he saw the broadening of human rights at the heart of liberalism as nothing short of moral rot. Again, this was war, and the religious right needed to "take back our cities, and take back our culture, and take back our country."[33] Siege mentality politics are effective when you portray the enemy as everywhere, and a loose definition of liberals allowed them to be omnipresent.

Historian Jason Bivins has shown how the modern religious right has remained unified primarily by positioning itself against a supposed liberal elite. As Bivins writes, the religious right has "mobilized under the perception that liberalism *has* become all-encompassing and that it *is* hostile to public expressions of religion," whether it is or not.[34] It was never any single issue—abortion rights, taxation on religious schools, preserving racial purity, opposition to queer rights—that brought together the religious right. Instead, as James Dobson, a prominent member of the Moral Majority, put it, it was the cultivation of the "perceived threat" of liberalism that allowed them to unify.[35]

The third conservative force against liberalism to emerge in the 1980s and 1990s was the right-wing media, most especially Rush Limbaugh from 1988 to 1996 and Fox News from 1996 onward. And it was here that the attacks on white liberals would evolve (and devolve), casting them no longer as quasi socialists, aloof elitists, or secular humanists but instead as "libtards" and terrorists. Politicians and politically minded evangelicals would follow. The politics of crafting and then attacking a particular image of liberals has sewn together the right for much of the time between the 1980s and today.

Right-wing radio traces its beginnings to the origins of radio, but in the late 1980s and 1990s it gained listeners by the millions by taking on an entirely new, much more strident tone.[36] This change in tone was in part attributable to an increased focus on the supposed "liberal bias" in the media. In 1987, Brent Bozell III, a longtime conservative advocate and William F. Buckley Jr.'s nephew, formed an outfit called the Media Research Center to "document, expose, and neutralize the liberal media."[37] In 1988, longtime conservative activist William Rusher, a publisher of *National Review*, published *The Coming Battle for the Media*, attacking the mainstream media for its "steady diet of tendentious 'news' stories carefully designed to serve the political purposes of American liberalism."[38] These were simple continuations of complaints aired by Richard Nixon and Spiro Agnew two decades prior.

But it was Rush Limbaugh who most shaped the tone of right-wing media starting in the 1980s. Trained as radio DJ and not in politics, Limbaugh generally failed on the airwaves until he embraced talk radio, and even then it took a while. He started his lasting radio show in 1984 in Sacramento, attracting listeners with an over-the-top personality and newfound political rage. The show went national in 1988, an event media historian Nicole Hemmer has called "a major disruption in the media landscape" because its point was to be political without any of the usual respectful tone.[39] It was supposed to be provocative, partisan, and pugnacious. Limbaugh was not polished, had no academic pedigree, and grew interested in politics only after Reagan became president—he was more akin to other shock jocks of the era like Howard Stern. But he later said that William F. Buckley Jr. "single-handedly is responsible for my learning to form and frame my beliefs and express them verbally in a concise and understandable way."[40]

In the late 1990s, Limbaugh located an untapped audience eager
to vent its rage and poke fun at the forces that seemingly dictated
their lives: white liberals. By the end of 1990, Limbaugh could claim
1.3 million listeners at any given moment and a total of 5 million people a week. Part of the attraction was his simplicity. As the *New York
Times* noted, "Limbaugh creates a black-and-white world where almost everything divides into liberal (bad) versus conservative (good)."
Limbaugh's "favorite enemies" could be summarized as "black activists, gay activists, abortion rights activists, homeless activists, animal
rights activists, militant vegetarians, environmentalists, artists with
erotic tendencies and, above all, 'the NOW [National Organization
for Women] Gang.'" Together, they constituted "the universe of liberal activists and protesters."[41]

Limbaugh took special ire in lambasting liberals for the advent of something that in the late 1980s and early 1990s came to
be called "political correctness." Although the phrase has a variety
of meanings dating back to the early twentieth century, in the late
1980s, conservatives began using the phrase to mock demands that
they try to use language that avoided offending particular groups
within American society. It became offensive to assume someone
had a husband or wife; it was better to use the term *partner*. The
descriptor *African American* became preferred over *Black* or *Negro*.
This policing of words morphed into a policing of viable topics. For
example, business-school scenarios should not automatically assume
a secretary is a woman. University campuses, filled with people who
operate in the realm of the written word, became a focal point for
debates about political correctness.

For Limbaugh, the topic became a primary example of how elite
liberals preached freedom but were really just out to enforce their
own vision: "Americans are increasingly convinced they have been
deceived by the so-called 'professionals' and 'experts'—particularly,
but not exclusively, in the media," adding to the list of deceivers "the
medical elites, the sociology elites, the education elites, the legal
elites, the sciences elites—the list goes on and on." To Limbaugh,

elitist liberals, taking orders from thought leaders on left-wing university campuses, were trying to dictate behaviors that enforced their vision of an egalitarian state. Instead of advocating freedom, liberals had become the thought police. A main "reason liberals fear me," he said, "is that I represent middle America's growing rejection of the elites."[42]

"Political correctness" was a perfect trope for Limbaugh. It had elite, top-down origins. It demanded respect for minoritized groups who, in the conservative imagination, were already getting significant preferential treatment. It demanded respect for women such that all of masculinity could be seen as under threat. Its goal, to Limbaugh, was not to democratize respect for all Americans but to silence conservatives. "The hard evidence that huge numbers of ordinary Americans have privately rejected the tenets of Liberalism," he said, "is a genuine threat to the decades-long liberal dominance of American institutions. Conservatives—who have been shut out of the debate in the arena of ideas for a generation—are finally understanding the stunning truth that they are not alone."[43]

With the tremendous success of his radio show, mainstream publishers lined up to get Limbaugh in print, expanding the conservative media sphere beyond radio or small-release right-wing publishing houses. Limbaugh's first book came out in 1992, and it was little more than a diatribe against what he called "liberal do-gooders." It opened with a not-so-humble buyer-beware caveat: "For those of you among the Liberal Elite who take a stab at reading this book, be forewarned. Everything in this book is right and you must be prepared to confront this reality. You can no longer be an honest liberal after reading this entire masterpiece."[44] The book proceeded to tell the story of how white liberals had taken over American institutions and used that power to "thwart the will of the people."[45] It ended by mocking "the arbiters of what is politically correct."[46] The book was a bestseller the entire summer of 1992. President Bush, again trailing in the polls in 1992, sought out Limbaugh and persuaded him to stay a night at the White House, an event that served both their interests.

Limbaugh followed up his first book a year later with a second. It was more of the same: "To liberals," read one representative passage, "compassion means expanding the dependency cycle and spreading the misery among that ever-growing dependency class."[47] The book had an entire chapter on "Political Correctness and the Coming of the Thought Police." It also became a bestseller.

Limbaugh then got a television show in fall 1992 that aired on 185 stations, further expanding the right-wing media sphere and its message of mocking the liberals. Like Bush and the Moral Majority, Limbaugh's goal was to hammer the libs. And as Hemmer, the historian of right-wing media, writes, from 1988 to the launch of Fox News in 1996, "conservative media was Limbaugh."[48]

Others took note. Copycats also recognized how he had used populist rhetoric and humor to reach beyond the intellectual elite, something conservative media had historically struggled to do.

In 1996, conservatives finally achieved a long-sought goal: an entire television network devoted to pushing conservative arguments. Though the tone was "Limbaughian," Fox News came into existence because of two other men who also carried significant resentment toward white liberals: Rupert Murdoch and Roger Ailes.

Murdoch was an Australian media mogul whose raison d'être was to turn media outlets into profit. From the very beginning, he was irritable. He hated paying taxes and abiding by government regulations, but he wasn't particularly partisan. Watching the rise of Rush Limbaugh, though, led him to believe there was a market for conservative news. But his goal wasn't to push a political agenda; it was to make money.[49]

Roger Ailes, the second founder of Fox News, was a purist. Ailes had classic credentials to develop a politics of grievance. Ailes had been born in a thriving industrial town in the heartland of Ohio, a sort of True Americana, where his father worked in a factory, talented enough to be promoted to management but not educated enough to actually join the corporate hierarchy. Showing the darker side of Americana, Ailes's dad took out his frustrations on his children with absenteeism and verbal and physical abuse. It was a combination of anger and alienation that Ailes remembered as he worked his way through college, eventually starting a career in media, helping develop the newly created *Mike Wallace Show.*

In early 1968 when presidential aspirant Richard Nixon appeared on the *Mike Wallace Show,* Ailes pushed the idea of himself serving as Nixon's media advisor. "What's a media advisor?" Nixon asked. "I am," said Ailes.[50] He later recalled, facetiously, "I never had a political thought until they asked me to join the Richard Nixon presidential campaign."[51] Ailes's biographer, Gabriel Sherman, said Ailes "imbibed Nixon's world view, learning how to connect to the many Americans who felt left behind by the upheavals of the 1960s," adding that "as a consultant to Nixon, he adopted a sense of political victimhood, and a paranoia about enemies that has marked his career ever since."[52] Ailes used this sensibility working as a consultant to Reagan and Bush. Along with Lee Atwater, it was Ailes who dreamed up Bush's negative campaign strategy in 1988, including the Willie Horton ad. In 1996, Murdoch tapped Ailes to lead his conservative news television channel. He would combine his sense of victimhood and paranoia with the tone of Rush Limbaugh to create Fox News.

Under the banner of being "fair and balanced," the network would propagate a conservative, mostly Republican agenda by attacking liberals everywhere. According to one early Fox executive, Ailes wanted "bombproof glass" windows installed in his executive suite because "homosexual activists are going to be down there everyday protesting. . . . And who knows what the hell they'll do."[53] (Bomb-proof glass doesn't exist.) The agenda was clear from the start. Ailes tapped a young Rush Limbaugh wannabe named Sean Hannity for a debate show. While they were looking for his sparring partner (eventually Alan Colmes, whom Fox made wear cosmetic glasses to better affect an elitist), they used the stand-in language: "Liberal to Be Determined."

Fox's on-air talent included Bill O'Reilly, who came across as a slightly more genteel Rush Limbaugh. But the gentility didn't last long. O'Reilly keenly recognized that what Murdoch and Ailes most wanted wasn't a news network telling viewers the news but instead a network that was telling viewers what to think. Playing the defense attorney for the little guy against the supposedly corrupt liberal elites, O'Reilly's show, "The Factor," quickly became the most popular show on Fox. Its initial specialty was attacking President Bill Clinton for all sorts of reasons captured under the expansive label "liberal." But soon he attacked Hollywood celebrities, some big businesses, and frequently his competitors. The constant theme was that the liberal elite was corrupt and constantly putting down the common man, Nixon's silent majority.

Fox News quickly added Matt Drudge, Michael Savage, Laura Ingraham, Glenn Beck, Mark Levin, and Monica Crowley to its roster. The theme for all of them was consistent: liberals have taken over the country, have led the nation astray, and need to be fought. Fox thought it was giving a voice to the unheard, which may have been true based on how strong the ratings were. Adam Bellow, who helped run several conservative media outlets, observed in in 1994, "I'm always being asked: 'What manipulative magic did you use to create this audience for conservative books?' But the audience has always been there. It's just that before, conservative ideas were walled off in a ghetto."[54]

This may have been true, but the messaging that arose through the likes of conservative talk radio and on Fox News was that of a siege politics of "us versus them," with "them" always being liberals.

The three-pronged conservative attack against liberals that developed in the 1980s and 1990s (political, religious, media) sustained a right-wing revival that dominated American politics into the first decades of the twenty-first century. The timing couldn't have been better for a crop of young conservatives eager to make their marks.

In the 1980s and 1990s, a generation of young Reaganites was hopeful they could usher in the millennium. In 1994, conservative columnist David Brooks called them "the New Establishment"—dozens of young conservatives working for conservative outlets and eager to keep up the fight against the supposed evils of liberalism. A year later, *New York Times* journalist James Atlas called them "the Counter Counterculture," defining it as "men and women in their 20's and 30's and early 40's who . . . made their living trying to tear down the liberal establishment, or what remains of it."[55]

Tear down they would, and in nearly identical registers.

Starting in 2002, for instance, Ann Coulter, a conservative propagandist who had been a member of the Federalist Society in law school, transitioned from being a careful legal polemicist to being an antiliberal blowhard. She saw the market for antiliberalism developing and wanted to cash in. Coulter found a home at Crown Forum, the conservative imprint of Random House developed to chase the dollars Rush Limbaugh had shown were out there. Coulter published a series of one-word-titled books that attacked all the ways liberals were supposedly destroying America.

The first, *Slander* (2002), was about the media's alleged unfair treatment of George W. Bush. To Coulter, liberals were untrustworthy liars eager to discredit any successful conservative. *Slander* was followed by *Treason* (2003), which argued that Joseph McCarthy was correct when he said liberals were little more than closeted communists.[56] Then came *Godless* (2006), which argued that all liberals reject God and hate people of faith, all while failing to recognize that they themselves were honoring liberalism as a faith ("The state religion of liberalism demands obeisance [to the National Organization for Women], tithing [to teachers' unions], reverence [for abortion], and formulaic imprecations").[57] It even dedicated a chapter to Willie Horton, "The Martyr" in her imagined liberal cosmology. Coulter also spent a chapter disavowing the findings of Charles Darwin and the theory of evolution. *Godless* was followed by *Guilty* (2009), in which Coulter made the argument that all liberals claim victimhood in order to oppress others ("Liberals live in a world in which everyone is either an oppressor or a victim," and "Even sports columns have a political agenda").[58] Then came *Demonic* (2011), which purported to explain "how the liberal mob is endangering America," and finally *Mugged* (2012), which addressed "racial demagoguery."[59] Crown Forum also published a collection of Coulter's columns in 2004 as *How to Talk to a Liberal (If You Must)*. Another collection of essays emerged in 2013, entitled *Never Trust a Liberal over 3—Especially a Republican.* The books all follow the same formula: a greatest hits of fading political tidbits cobbled together into a loose argument about how liberals have ruined the Great Pantheon of American Values. In Coulter's telling, liberals were liars and atheists who hated everyday Americans and were mocking them along the way. But common Americans couldn't gain purchase because liberals dominated publishing (except, evidently, for Crown Forum and other such imprints), idea formation, foreign policy, matters of faith, politics, and even the general ethos of the country. "These counterfeit victims are so full of their own self-righteousness, they believe they can do anything, live shamelessly, commit wanton violence, steal from their neighbors, and claim they were acting out of some bizarre sense of self-defense," Coulter wrote in *Guilty*.[60] "Everything liberals believe is in elegant opposition to basic Biblical precepts," she wrote in *Godless*. No liberal would recognize themself through her description. No liberal, for instance, would say they believe "human progress is achieved through sex and death . . . ," or that "[humans] are no different morally from the apes."[61]

Coulter may have perfected the image of the white liberal in the conservative imagination, but she was not alone. One of Coulter's onetime paramours, Dinesh D'Souza, became famous for attacking liberals, too. Interestingly, it was a learned response. His first book, from 1991, was perfectly titled to mock liberals: *Illiberal Education: The Politics of Race and Sex on Campus*. But the book didn't turn into a complete diatribe, playing more in the learned register of Buckley's *God and Man at Yale*. But D'Souza learned throughout the 1990s that the key to publishing success was simple: attack liberals. In 2002, he stepped up his assault. In *Letters to a Young Conservative*, D'Souza began with the standard binary: "Conservatives vs. Liberals" was the title of chapter 1. It began with a fairly even discussion of liberals (although he got the origins of *liber* wrong, mistaking its Latin roots for Greek, where Liber is a god associated with Dionysus[62]) before swerving into fairy-tale land: "For all its grand proclamations, today's liberalism seems to be characterized by a pathological hostility to America, to capitalism, and to traditional moral values. In short, liberalism has become the party of anti-Americanism, economic plunder, and immorality."[63] In case readers missed the point, D'Souza titled chapter 28 "Why Liberals Hate America," which ironically enough besmirched "liberals" for being peaceniks who ignored the fact that "violence helped to end the regimes of Adolf Hitler and Benito Mussolini," which, once again, was an act led in part by the first white liberal, Franklin D. Roosevelt.[64] But to educate was not his point. Over time, D'Souza's books grew increasingly conspiratorial and were disowned even by many people on the right. But throughout all his writings, "liberals" as he imagined them were consistently the problem.

Laura Ingraham was yet another commentator in this mold. Ingraham worked as a speechwriter in the Reagan administration before becoming a television host in the late 1990s, and then a radio host in 2001, where she really found her audience. In 2000, she published a book, *The Hillary Trap*, which railed against Hillary Clinton, the former First Lady who was elected to the US Senate that year, and argued that Clinton's "liberal feminism has created a culture that rewards dependency, encourages fragmentation, undermines families, and celebrates victimhood," all themes Ingraham would develop in the coming years.

Ingraham's 2003 book, *Shut Up and Sing*, was a Coulter lookalike, except for the fact that its title had four words. Ingraham began, "They think we're stupid. They think our patriotism is stupid. They think our churchgoing is stupid. They think our flag-flying is stupid. They think where we live—anywhere but near or in a few major cities—is stupid. . . . They think owning a gun is stupid. They think our abiding belief in the goodness of America and its founding principles is stupid. . . . And without a doubt, they will think this book is stupid."[65]

Stupid or not, the book certainly was not original. She railed against the liberal elites who supposedly controlled the media, who believed they were smarter than everyone else, and who practiced moral relativism, lived without God, played the victim, favored international agreements over America First, and hated Walmart. It was over-the-top and ridiculous, and it was designed to provoke. In the first two decades of the twenty-first century, the conservative image of the white liberal became increasingly predictable and increasingly focused on buttressing an image that was useful to right-wing stalwarts to stoke anger.

It's easy to recite dozens of other examples. In 2002, Sean Hannity started with *Let Freedom Ring: Winning the War of Liberty over Liberalism*, following it up in 2004 with *Deliver Us from Evil: Defeating Terrorism, Despotism, and Liberalism*. Jonah Goldberg's 2008 book *Liberal Fascism: The Secret History of the American Left* was followed up in 2012 with his *The Tyranny of Clichés: How Liberals Cheat in the War of Ideas*. Michael Savage wrote a 2005 book called *Liberalism Is a Mental Disorder*. William Voegeli wrote a 2014 book called *The Pity Party: A Mean-Spirited Diatribe against Liberal Compassion*.

Even books directed at more discerning readers sounded the alarm. Linda Chavez, a prominent Latina conservative who worked in the Reagan administration and was nominated to be secretary of labor, titled her 2002 autobiography *An Unlikely Conservative: The Transformation of an Ex-Liberal (Or, How I Became the Most Hated Hispanic in America)*.[66] Thomas Sowell, an economist and one of the few Black conservatives, published a collection of essays in 2005 titled *Black Rednecks and White Liberals*. The titular essay argued that "black ghetto" culture in twenty-first century America derived from white "redneck culture" in the antebellum South and that twenty-first century white liberals were unknowingly supporting antebellum redneck culture when they showed compassion toward modern Black culture.[67]

One important theme to nearly all these books was the way they located power in academic and cultural realms rather than in economic or political ones: it was professors mandating political correctness that was curbing your freedom; it was Hollywood's left-wing agenda shaping how people felt about issues like abortion. The religious right and Rush Limbaugh had already made this case, but these books solidified it. This relocation of power, from politics and economics to values and culture, meant that, no matter who was in office or how friendly policies were toward business interests, it always made sense to hate the liberals. It was a subtle move, one that went largely unnoticed. With power supposedly in the hands of snobby academics and out-of-touch Hollywood executives, corporate raiders were free to flex their economic muscle and go unpunished—and often even be lionized. The blame for the economic anxieties fueling much of the rise of the right wing could helpfully be placed on the tedious liberals pointing out that small-town America had been hoodwinked. It was no wonder many economic titans supported the likes of Coulter, Ingraham, and D'Souza.

———————

Whereas Rush Limbaugh developed the trolling tone of twenty-first-century right-wing antiliberalism, painting liberals as effeminate elitist thought police, and Fox News helped germinate dozens of copycats who released the tidal wave of cartoonish hatred against white liberals, the supercharging of right-wing antiliberalism for the past few decades has moved to the internet. Freed from the regulatory mechanisms overseeing television, radio, and publishing, the internet invited caustic trolling by anonymous authors eager to outdo one another with creative provocations of rage. If the image of the white liberal had become increasingly cartoonish, it was on the internet that the language of antiliberalism became increasingly violent.

Perhaps the paradigmatic invention here was the coinage of the term "libtard." The word's origins are hard to pin down, and even those who claim to have created it agree that it probably emerged simul-taneously in several places shortly after the turn of the twenty-first century. One person claiming authorial rights described it as a simple modification from the more popular troll word "fucktard." "I just replaced the 'f' word with 'lib' and used it to describe Al Gore and his cohorts," said the neologist. Another claimant said they originated it in 2003 or 2004, posting on message boards as "libtarddestroyer." In perhaps good news, this person reported being "maybe not so proud of this today."[68] The *Cambridge Dictionary* published by Cambridge University Press defines *libtard* as "an offensive word used by some people on the extreme right of politics to refer to someone who holds left-wing political beliefs."[69] The open-sourced Urban Dictionary, however, has a slew of reader-contributed definitions, including "used when a liberal is being a retard!!!"[70] The layered strike here is not only the caustic name-calling but also the use of the noun *retard*, a word conservatives say has been policed out of the discourse by oversensitive but controlling liberals.[71]

Right-wing social media accounts have also invented ridiculous imaginings of what liberals supposedly are. One account called "Libs of TikTok" is a multiplatform handle that largely reposts doctored videos of supposed "liberals" doing things conservatives might find offensive. Developed in 2021 by former Brooklyn real estate agent Chaya Raichik, the videos typically mock migrants, queer activists, and Democratic politicians. The theme is right-wing victimhood: one video of a souped-up truck doing donuts over a gay pride mural claims the nineteen-year-old driver was arrested and faced felony charges, but "imagine if it was a MAGA mural . . . he would receive a reward!"[72] Although that outcome seems unlikely, the facts of the case don't matter. The outrage does. Another social media account, "The_Typical_Liberal," is the brainchild of Grant Godwin, another right-wing provocateur and a self-proclaimed "citizen-journalist fighting for truth." Godwin more or less copied Raichik's model, relying heavily on mocking the LGBTQ+ community. Godwin, however, added a celebration of toxic masculinity, suggesting that liberals have denied men ample space to exert their masculinity. As of 2024, both accounts had more than three million followers.

They have spurred action, too. The accounts essentially serve as focus groups for conservative politicians to learn which angles and which issues will garner traction with conservative voters, to learn what will spark rage. The platforms have been praised in the right-wing atmosphere by Elon Musk, Tucker Carlson, Joe Rogan, and a large number of politicians. Raichik has been named an advisor to an Oklahoma board overseeing the selection of library books, even though she isn't a citizen of Oklahoma. After gay marriage became widely accepted in the United States and no longer a lodestone of conservative anger, social media accounts like Raichik's and Godwin's tested other potential arenas of outrage and landed on drag shows, gender-affirming health care, human trafficking, and border control. These issues subsequently became increasingly vital right-wing talking points. Together, social media accounts like these have pushed the image of "the liberal" in the right-wing imagination to, in the words of another social media provocateur, Alex Jones, "Liberal, liberal, liberal, liberal, happy, fun, la, la, la, human smuggling, fentanyl deaths, forced government euthanasia, chopping up children's genitals, la, la, la, liberal."[73] Jones has faced legal consequences for some of his most outlandish remarks, most especially having to pay nearly $1.5 billion to the families of victims of a school shooting, which he claimed was a "false flag" operation acted out by gun control advocates. But it's clear his popularity emerged from his increasingly virulent attacks on white liberals.

In the 2010s and 2020s, the American right became filled with people out to "own the libs." To "own" someone in this reference is not a throwback to the days of slavery but instead premised on a 1990s term from the world of computer hacking, used to describe conquering one's opponent completely. But the right has modified this meaning. Now, "owning the libs" largely signifies a high-octane performance for one's already adoring audience about countering the supposed evils predicated by liberals. The goal is not to engage but to enrage.

And in this way, "owning the libs" has cemented a right-wing tribal identity. The Republican Party has, since at least the 1980s, been divided between economic conservatives and social ones. Economic conservatives are against most government taxes and most regulations on business. They have been moving in an increasingly libertarian direction. Social conservatives, meanwhile, push legislation that would enhance more "traditional" family values, an effort increasingly focused on opposing rights for members of the LGBTQ+ community. In the 1980s, Reagan's good nature and the Cold War served as the glue keeping the two factions together. But with the end of both Reagan's presidency and the Cold War in 1989, conservatives needed new glue. They found it in the language of antiliberalism.

The result of all these antiliberal efforts, then, from Bush to Falwell to Limbaugh, was tribe formation. And as the tribe developed, the often humorous, sometimes violent antiliberalism that served as glue drew in even more Americans, most especially those suffering economic anxieties largely brought on by neoliberal policies. The language of antiliberalism is capacious indeed. Through the rightwing media machine, liberals have been forced to own both the 1960s and neoliberalism.

Scholars Hyrum Lewis and Verlan Lewis have shown how this tribe formation happened. Fascinated by political ideologies, the Lewises' driving questions are: Why do people become Republicans? Why do they become Democrats? And after surveying a host of policies put forward by the various parties, they found little to no grounding philosophy for either party. All Democrats don't think people are instinctively good while all Republicans think they are bad. All Democrats are not all idealists and all Republicans are not all realists. Instead, the two Lewises found that people belonged to the various parties because they liked to be part of the tribe. Policies wavered and changed. But people retained their party affiliation. As Lewis and Lewis put it in their 2023 book *The Myth of Left and Right*, "ideologies do not define tribes, tribes define ideologies; ideology is not about what (worldviews), it is about who (groups); there is no liberalism or conservatism, only liberals and conservatives; and the political spectrum does not model an essential value, but only tribes and what they stand for at a specific time and place."[74] The goal of the parties, then, is not to bring about any sort of political program but to preserve tribal identities.

Since the 1980s, the key unifying feature of the Republican Party hasn't been opposition to taxes or a desire to rout gay people—though there are people in the party who dearly hold both those positions. No, its constituent glue has been its assault on liberals. And it has worked because it offers solace to and a scapegoat for the discomforts of life in postindustrial America. It speaks to the frustrations of people disaffected by the changes of the information age or the demands of living in a multicultural society or the notion that their freedom is being denied by the supposed policing of both speech and thought. The entire point of "owning the libs" was to make people feel heard. Ingraham finished her book *Shut Up and Sing* by saying, "The elites will always fail to understand America because they fail to recognize the true source of its greatness. America is not great because of its dot-com millionaires, or its Hollywood starlets, or its brightest intellectuals. America is great because of the millions of so-called 'average' Americans who get up every day and do the best they can to build a better world for themselves and their children."[75] By fashioning an outgroup—white liberals—the Republicans were able to foster a strong tribal allegiance.

Donald Trump brilliantly encapsulated this fear in 2016. His son Donald Trump Jr. said the Trump campaign's entire goal was not to elevate any political vision but simply to "make liberals cry again," to force them to own the ramifications of the supposed nanny state and political correctness and endure another series of forty-nine–to–one losses in state electoral vote counts.[76] You can today find that slogan on any number of items for sale on Etsy—baby onesies, travel mugs, T-shirts. When Madison Cawthorn, one of Trump's favored politicians, won a North Carolina congressional district, Trump tweeted, "Cry more, lib." Trump's aim was not to lower taxes, get government off people's backs, or uphold the sanctity of life. The point was cruelty toward liberals, who, several generations of American have been told, will ruin America if not checked. "You all don't get it," said one voter named Bev, in 2020. "I live in Trump country, in the Ozarks in southern Missouri. . . . They don't give a shit what [Trump] does. He's just something to rally around and hate liberals, that's it, period. . . . The fact that people act like it's anything other than that proves to them that liberals are idiots, all the more reason for high fives all around. . . . If you keep getting caught up in . . . 'How can they still back Trump after this scandal?' then you do not understand what the underlying motivating factor of his support is. It's fuck liberals, that's pretty much it. . . . Fuck liberals is the only relevant thing."[77]

As for the image of the white liberal, Bev reported, "They consider liberals to be weak people that are inferior, almost a different species, and the fact that liberals are so weak is why they have to unite in large numbers, which they find disgusting, but it's that disgust that is a true expression of their natural superiority."[78]

In 2019, a writer named Adam Sokol took a job deleting the most offensive comments posted to a conservative news site. He realized that only one thing united supporters of Donald Trump: "Cultural conservatives, fiscal conservatives, the weirdos who talked only about chemtrails—they all had one thing in common. They wanted a president who would stick it to the liberals."[79]

Aside from Donald Trump, a huge number of Republican politicians have tried to gain traction playing in this register. "Owning the libs' is a way of asserting dignity," says Helen Andrews, a senior editor at the *American Conservative* magazine.[80] Another politics watcher, Marshall Kosloff, points to the role "owning the libs" has played in allowing the Republican Party to woo voters despite its often unpopular policy initiatives. "It basically offers the party a way of resolving the contradictions within a realigning party that increasingly is appealing to down-market white voters and certain working-class Black and Hispanic voters, but that also has a pretty plutocratic agenda at the policy level," he writes.[81] Several journalists noticed this trend in the early 2020s. In 2021, the online journal *Politico* published a piece called "How 'Owning the Libs' Became the GOP's Core Belief."[82] A year later, the *Atlantic* followed with "Owning the Libs Is the Only GOP Platform."[83]

And as the originators of right-wing antiliberalism age out, another generation is eagerly taking up the call, displaying even more anger and vitriol. Limbaugh died in 2021 after a lengthy battle with cancer, and he was heralded by many on the right as a conquering hero who taught the right how to battle. The man who took Limbaugh's airtime on many of channels was a podcaster named Dan Bongino. He already knew the formula. "My entire life right now is about owning the libs," Bongino said in 2018.[84] The *New Yorker* described him in 2022 as "rightwing radio's first post-Rush, post-Fox, post-Drudge megahost," someone who was going to take up the mantle and push it forward.[85]

"The liberals are the Man," Bongino said in August 2021. "They run big corporations. They run YouTube. They run Facebook. They run the government." The remarkable thing about this statement is that, in the late 2010s and 2020s, liberals were now, at least in the right-wing imagination, supposedly responsible for the advent of neoliberalism, whose policies and mindset first found favor in Ronald Reagan's presidency and most Republicans ever since. While it is fair to say the policies of Democratic presidents Bill Clinton and Barack Obama played into the interests of bankers and free-trade advocates, it is a remarkable slight of hand to suggest that the liberal elite must now own the ramifications of (and anger toward) the entire neoliberal order. Speaking to his audience, Bongino continued, "We're the real misfits, we're the real rebels now," echoing a line as old as William F. Buckley Jr.[86] As was now typical, Bongino spoke as though he and his audience were in an "existential showdown" with white liberals. And, as each of the previous generations had done before him, he pushed his antiliberalism even farther: "We are descending at an increasingly rapid rate into fascism. *Chaos.* You're seeing the evaporation of civil liberties in live time, the Bill of Rights being used like toilet paper, the Constitution being thrown out, the rapid spread of insane deadly ideas, like the defunding of the police and the abolition of our military." He said, without evidence, "There are people now openly silencing and attacking conservatives, trying to have them jailed, trying to have them sanctioned, bankrupted financially, fired from their jobs. This is all happening right now! And it's all happening because of the Democrat Party and the liberals."[87]

TIME FOR
SOMETHING NEW

In the late 1990s, television writer Aaron Sorkin dreamed up a show that might fulfill his wildest liberal dreams. Sorkin envisioned a brilliant president who knew a lot about economics (a Nobel Laureate sympathetic to Keynes!) and religion (a Roman Catholic with deep biblical knowledge!). This fictional president, whom Sorkin named Jedediah Bartlett, played by Martin Sheen, prioritized the white working classes and sympathized with racial minorities but curbed the things that might tear the nation apart (reparations, radical secularism, calling himself liberal). At the show's inception, Sorkin figured *The West Wing* would demonstrate what President Bill Clinton could do better, but when Republican George W. Bush became president in 2001 after being awarded the Electoral College victory by the US Supreme Court despite losing the popular vote to Clinton's vice president Al Gore, the show served as an alternate universe for liberals in hiding. *If only the case of* Gore v. Bush *had been decided differently . . .*

The fantasy lasted two presidential terms. But as fictional President Bartlett's second term came to an end in 2005, the two aspirants to replace him debated the ideologies that guided American politics. It was actually something of a historic moment for television. Called

"The Debate," the 2005 episode was televised live, once for East Coast audiences and once for the West Coast, and it went the way many Americans wished presidential debates would go: wide-open affairs operating at a high caliber with deep discussions about important issues. After Sorkin stopped day-to-day writing of the show, Laurence O'Donnell became head writer; he called the episode "my wish-fulfillment debate."[1]

And what was the wish?

In one exchange, the Republican candidate, played by Alan Alda, chided the Democrat, played by Jimmy Smits, for being an "unthinking liberal" who foolishly assumes "evil capitalists" are "screwing the workers."

Smits fired back: "I know you like to use that word 'liberal' as if it were a crime."

Alda pushed: "I know Democrats think liberal is a bad word, so bad you had to change it. What do you call yourselves now, progressives?"

To which Smits pointed out that liberals—Democrats and Republicans—once did things together, like end slavery, before wondering what happened to all the liberal Republicans:

What did liberals do that was so offensive to the [Republican] Party? I'll tell you what they did. Liberals got women the right to vote. Liberals got African Americans the right to vote. Liberals created Social Security and lifted millions of elderly people out of poverty. Liberals ended segregation. Liberals passed the Civil Rights Act, the Voting Rights Act. Liberals created Medicare. Liberals passed the Clean Air Act, the Clean Water Act. What did conservatives do? They opposed them on every one of those things. Every one.

So when you try to hurl that label at my feet, 'Liberal,' as if it were something to be ashamed of, something dirty, something to run away from, it won't work, Senator. Because I will pick up that label and I will wear it as a badge of honor.[2]

Alongside Sorkin, there have been numerous twenty-first century attempts to rehabilitate the image of liberalism and of white liberals. There are books and books and books, of course.[3] Most make the argument that Americans need to realize that liberalism was once a fighting faith, one that brought the nation out of the Great Depression, won World War II, and created the post–World War II economic boom. It had produced a proper formula that made government responsive to people's needs and staved off reactionaries right and left.

But they often neglect all the ways in which the words *liberal* and *liberalism* have been damaged. And, rather than ground the words in their historic uses, which have changed over time to meet various demands, most of the authors who are invested in rehabilitation efforts have tried to make liberalism simply the way things are supposed to be. As Adam Gopnik put it in his attempted salvage job, "Liberalism isn't a political theory applied to life. It's what we know about life applied to political theory," as natural as the sun, the moon, and the stars. Liberalism, absent any history, is the obvious answer for well-meaning people everywhere. "Wherever there is a movement for humane reform there is always a liberal around somewhere," promised Gopnik.[4] Long live liberalism and its spirit of generosity! Be gone the tarnish of history!

Almost every reviewer finds the try-hard nature of these books off-putting. As one reviewer wrote of Gopnik's book, its "aimless joyride of free-associated clichés and its stubborn refusal to look at reality may indicate more broadly how little the American establishment has learned."[5] Another review began, "A specter is haunting the straight white liberal sixtysomething American dad—the specter of his damn socialist kids."[6]

Absent any firm, historically grounded understanding of what has happened to liberals and liberalism, the books have failed to bring about a revival. They don't seem to understand what they are up against.

Journalists and academics have tried to rehabilitate the words *liberal* and *liberalism*, too. In 2009, historian Timothy Garton Ash said of President Barack Obama's first term, "Those of us who believe in the universal, enduring value of liberalism" (which Ash failed to define) were happy to see Obama start doing "liberal" things. "Perhaps in his second term," Ash hoped, "he might even dare to rescue the word." After all, he asserted, "liberalism is the American love that dare not speak its name."[7] Equating liberalism with homosexuality ("the love that dare not speak its name" was the euphemism used against gay writer Oscar Wilde at his 1895 trial for "gross indecency") seems a particularly fraught way to encourage universal support, especially after the politically astute Obama himself had announced in 2004, "There's not a liberal America and a conservative America; there's the United States of America."[8] But Ash was trying![9]

Even comedians made an effort. In 2011, a collection of New York entertainers parlayed a long-standing "Drinking Liberally" social salon into the "Laughing Liberally" comedy show. Mostly the comics took jabs at Republicans, but a reporter who stumbled upon the scene was surprised to discover people still using the word. "Perhaps you, like [me], thought that liberals had been eradicated through some kind of spraying program or inoculation," the reporter wrote. "No elected official has admitted to being one since the Carter administration [this statement, as I've shown, is wrong], and the very special word 'liberal' ranks right up there with 'care to respond to the rumors about your love child?' as guaranteed to make Sunday morning talk-show guests change the subject."[10]

Try as they might, twenty-first-century liberals have had a hard time affixing a positive meaning to the word *liberal*. This failure is important, too. Absent any positive understanding of the word and stuck with the buffooning terms imposed especially by the right, liberalism has suffered. Without a way to articulate an active defense, those seeking to defend New Deal liberalism, or qualitative liberalism, or Great Society liberalism, or even Moynihan's "intelligent liberalism," have lost their way. They don't have an effective word to say what they are for. The word they'd like to use, *liberalism*, has been too damaged. In 1995, historian and theorist Immanuel Wallerstein wrote a book called

After Liberalism, but he too struggled to articulate what he thought might come next. The best he could come up with was for liberals to figure out to "which shore you want to swim. And . . . make sure that your immediate efforts seem to be moving in that direction." Then he threw his hands up: "If you want greater precision than that, you will not find it, and you will drown while you are looking for it."[11] Ruy Teixeira, author of the influential book *The Emerging Democratic Majority*, put it similarly in 2022 when he said, "The thing about moderates today is I don't think they have a worldview. . . . 'Don't do dumb stuff' is not a worldview."[12] He has since tried to locate smart stuff to stand behind in his newsletter, "The Liberal Patriot." For all these efforts, Donald Trump still recognized the utility of the word in mobilizing the right wing. In 2024, he successfully defined his opponent as "Failed. Weak. Dangerously Liberal."[13]

For lovers of the word, there might be a few inklings of hope, but not many. In the face of rising authoritarian governments around the world, President Obama, who rarely if ever employed the word *liberal* while governing, even when pushing his signature health care act, finally claimed the mantle of liberalism in his final speech before the United Nations in 2016, saying, "There appears to be a growing contest between authoritarianism and liberalism right now," pointing to authoritarian leaders in Russia, China, Poland, Brazil, and other nations. "And I want everybody to understand, I am not neutral in that contest." He even put a little meat on the bones, giving his understanding of liberalism the beginnings of a definition: "I believe in a liberal political order—an order built not just through elections and representative government, but also through respect for human rights and civil society, and independent judiciaries and the rule of law."[14] But this reclamation effort didn't come until the last months of his presidency, when he never had to run for office again, which might be indicative of the work he felt was left to do to recuperate the word.

Still, the rise of perceived authoritarians has led some people to find solace in the word. Ever since 2016, when Donald Trump was first elected President, the number of Democrats claiming to be "liberal" increased. By the early 2020s, it defined the way in which more than 50 percent of Democrats described their politics.[15] Polling data don't tell us what these people mean when they say "liberal," but the timing suggests that, to them, the word signifies the opposite of what they think Donald Trump is: authoritarian, reckless with the rule of law, deliberately polarizing, overly business friendly.

But even such minor attempts to give the word a twenty-first-century meaning wouldn't go unchecked. We have already seen how the American right has attacked the "libs" during the first quarter of the twenty-first century. Abroad, three years after Obama's 2016 pronouncement, Russian president Vladimir Putin put forward his own analysis, saying that "the liberal idea" had "outlived its purpose," arguing that liberalism's willingness to grant people representative government and human rights necessarily included giving power to bad people, thus threatening social order. "This liberal idea presupposed that . . . migrants can kill, plunder and rape with impunity because their rights as migrants have to protected," Putin said. While this assertion is certainly untrue, Putin insisted that, by granting rights to everyone, "the liberal idea . . . has come into conflict with the interests of the overwhelming majority of the population."[16] Similarly, in 2019, China's leader, Xi Jinping, extolled the strength of an all-powerful state and "self-confidence in our system," suggesting that liberal democracy had no place in his country.[17]

Around the world as across the United States, hyperbolic attacks on liberals and liberalism have taken a toll on democracies. According to the researchers behind V-Dem, an academic tool designed to measure the health of the world's democracies, the number of nations practicing liberal democracy peaked in 2012 at forty-two, but a decade later the number had fallen to thirty-four, home of just 13 percent of the world population. And in most of the liberal democracies that still remained, "toxic polarization" was on the rise.[18]

———————

As these wrestling matches continue, some Americans who would have at one time gleefully adopted the name "liberal" have tried, and failed, to find alternatives. In 2007, Hillary Clinton, at that time a Democratic presidential candidate, brushed aside a question about whether she was a "liberal" by saying that it "was a word that originally meant that you were for freedom . . . but it has been turned on its head and made to be a word that describes big government." Not wanting to suffer the same fate as Michael Dukakis in 1988, she added, "I prefer the word progressive," calling herself a "proud modern American progressive."[19]

Others have picked up the label, too, including both moderates and those on the left, hinting at another alliance between centrists and leftists akin to the New Deal, albeit this time under the label "progressive." They tended to find common cause over the use of the federal government as a ballast to the growth of large corporations and especially large financial institutions. They generally supported labor unions. Most believed that Obama's Affordable Care Act, which required Americans to have health insurance and offered subsidies to those who needed help paying for it, was not enough, favoring instead a national health care plan. And many were champions of equal rights, and especially minority rights. In 2016 and 2017, "progressive" groups formed all over the country.

This development, perhaps predictably, prompted conservatives to attack the "progressive" label, usually by aligning it with the already tarnished *liberalism*. Charles Kesler, a Harvard-trained political scientist who edits the conservative *Claremont Review of Books*, paved the way. In his analysis of twentieth-century American political history, he argued there were "three waves of liberalism" against which conservatives needed to push back. The most recent was Lyndon

Johnson's Great Society, which Kesler called "cultural liberalism." Before that was Franklin Roosevelt's New Deal, which Kesler called "economic liberalism." But according to Kesler, the first "wave of liberalism," the one that started it all, occurred at the turn of the twentieth century, during the so-called Progressive era, which Kesler labeled "political liberalism." In Kesler's schema, Progressives were the first liberals (even if they almost never used the label). Kesler was trying to weigh down the progressive label by giving it liberal baggage. Many commentators on the right, most famously television host Glenn Beck, used Kesler's topography to rail against progressives.[20]

Either because of Kesler's smart political move or because *progressive* is often deemed further to the left than most self-proclaiming liberals, the "progressive" label has, in general, failed to gain significant traction in American life. It has signified a politics too far to the left to win the moderate voter. It has remained an outlier.

And so it turns out there is a profound impoverishment in our language in describing how we understand our world. Many Americans profess an interest in celebrating the collective nature of our nation, in the ways in which the United States has been able to fashion a lasting democracy despite having tremendous diversity, in how the government has been able to help many Americans achieve great things, albeit imperfectly. But there is no longer a viable word that describes the political philosophy that encapsulates these accomplishments. It used to be *liberalism*. But now no more. Some words work for a while to describe something, but then they get weighed down by other meanings. That's when it's time to find new words.

Are there other words out there that describe what *liberal* and *liberalism* used to mean? Is there a phrase that has come to signify the position whereby the government performs a positive good to society? Is there a language to capture (in Eleanor Roosevelt's words) a "high sense of individual responsibility for oneself and one's neighbor, a conviction that the best society is a brotherhood that enables the great numbers of its members to develop their potentialities to the utmost"?[21] Nothing has yet captured the national imagination. When in 2012 President Barack Obama tried to make a case for the importance of the commonweal, he told entrepreneurs they should respect the infrastructure put in place by federal and state governments. "Somebody invested in roads and bridges," he said. "You didn't build that."[22] But he didn't give the underlying philosophy a label. And he flubbed the delivery, too, making it seem as though he was denying entrepreneurs their accomplishments.

Meanwhile, between 2020 and 2024, President Joe Biden made tremendous efforts to move the nation's economy beyond a globalized neoliberal order. He used the government to stoke American manufacturing, doing so by favoring environmentally conscious businesses, small-to-midsized companies, and regions badly damaged by the departure of heavy industry, all while supporting unions, pushing for laws that raise wages for workers, and signing no new international trade agreements that would bring foreign goods to the United States. By many measures, the plan was hugely successful, too, even if the cost of goods went up temporarily. But lacking a term to describe and market the huge plan, voters punished Democrats in 2024. "The biggest mistake we made," Biden reflected, was that "we didn't put up signs saying 'Joe Did It.'"[23] There was no language to describe what it was he was trying to do.

Meanwhile, the August 2024 cover of *New York* magazine featured an image of Vice President Kamala Harris, the Democratic nominee for president, sitting atop a coconut. The title blazing across the cover harked back to John F. Kennedy. "Welcome to Kamalot," it read, trying to tie Harris to a moment when liberalism was a fighting faith. Yet the key to the diminished language of the twenty-first century is not the reference to JFK's Camelot myth but actually the coconut. In what became a meme all over the internet, the previous year Harris had made a case for supporting the commonweal by telling a story about her late mother Shyamala Gopalan, who used to chastise young Kamala for thinking she could do everything on her own and assuming that her actions didn't have carry-on effects. "You think you just fell out of a coconut tree?" Harris would impersonate her mother as saying. The lesson Harris learned was that "you exist in the context of all in which you live and what came before you."[24] Absent a word to describe that sentiment, we are left with a coconut.

But that doesn't mean a better word won't come along. After all, it was only in the summer of 1932 that FDR picked *liberalism* as a word of last recourse and molded it to the kind of politics he wanted. Nearly a hundred years later, after all the mudslinging and weight affixed to the term *liberal*, it's time to imagine something new.

There are currently no obvious contenders. Coining new words is hard. Making things even more difficult is the fact that any word attempting to balance individual responsibility with communal awareness, government assistance with a market orientation, will have to craft a coalition that is already angry and anxious about the consequences of neoliberalism. *Progressivism* and *socialism* seem too tainted by the past, too easily targeted by opponents. *Labor* parties (such as the Labour Party in England) are too rhetorically limiting in the United States, offering no clear space to those outside the working classes or those unfriendly to unions. *Reform* parties are too vague. Reform what? *People's* parties suffer similarly. Although it might be far-fetched to imagine, *social democracy* may have the best chance to make a run of things, as most Americans claim to be for democracy and also for limiting the ethos of extreme individualism for the sake of the common good. Plus, *social democracy* has the advantage of being generally foreign to American politics, meaning it doesn't possess too much historical baggage. It's also vague enough to encompass commitments to the preservation of regulated capitalism and the challenges diversity brings to those commitments. Plus, it has a small amount of recent pedigree. If Donald Trump was able to forge a coalition of the economically anxious with other members of the Republican base, Senators Bernie Sanders and Elizabeth Warren have also made inroads with those anxious communities, and done so, if not always directly, under the banner of social democracy. But it, too, will be a tough sell. It is rhetorically close to *socialism* while also lacking deep philosophical roots. But perhaps a social democratic future awaits?

Regardless of whether or not *social democracy* emerges as a viable descriptor, losing *liberal* will not be such a tremendous loss, and in fact might even be a win. Giving up the fight to preserve a damaged word could even help diminish the perpetual polarity between "liberal and conservative" and allow for a less antagonistic politics. And if those who uphold the ideals that *liberal* used to stand for—and there are lots of them—don't locate another term themselves, they'll either be stuck in the same rut they are in now or have one affixed to them by their opponents.

And what of white liberals?

They had a good run. From the moment they were given that moniker, they fought mightily to stave off radicalisms, to find a balance between freedom and equality, and to defend against enemies at home and abroad. Sometimes they ventured too far toward freedom or equality, sometimes they struggled to live up to their own ideals, sometimes their good intentions got in the way of effective governing. They always paid the price for any misstep. Yet they achieved a great many things. But now their image has become so sullied it's hard to imagine a way back. Those seeking to reclaim their tradition in American life have something venerable to uphold, but it will have to be done under a name other than *liberalism*.

ACKNOWLEDGMENTS

For their advice and support, I'm delighted to thank a number of people important to me. First, my agent, Andrew Stuart. It might sound a bit materialistic to start with him considering my critique of neoliberalism in chapter 7, but without Andrew this book never would have happened. He helped me conceive the book over lunch one day and has been a champion ever since. Tim Mennel at the University of Chicago Press is a keen reader, smart thinker, and good friend. He's among the best editors I've ever worked with, and his team at the University of Chicago Press has been fantastic. The Midwestern Intellectual History Group, which I am lucky enough to lead alongside Jennifer Ratner-Rosenhagen, gave valuable advice on several chapters. Comments from Ray Haberski, Andrew Hartman, Joel Isaac, John McGreevy, Michelle Nickerson, Tim Lacy, and others were vitally important at key moments in this book's development. The informal American intellectual history Zoom group that Jennifer and I assembled during the COVID-19 pandemic quarantine was also incredibly helpful, most especially specific comments from Jeff Sklansky, Caroline Winterer, and Daniel Rodgers. Do I miss quarantine? No. But I do miss this group. Dan did double duty

later when he read a complete draft of the manuscript, offering unbelievable guidance, sharpening my argument, and saving me from
myself more times than I care to admit. The Department of History
at the University of Illinois Chicago (UIC), my intellectual home
since 2007, gave generously, especially through helpful comments
during our Wednesday Brownbags. John Abbott, Cynthia Blair,
Jon Connolly, Jonathan Daly, Lilia Fernández, Gosia Fidelis, Adam
Goodman, Laura Hostetler, Lynn Hudson, Robert Johnston, Michael
Jin, Ralph Keen, Tom Kernan, Clare Kim, Rama Mantena, Marina
Mogilner, Junaid Quadri, Jeff Sklansky, and Keely Stauter-Halsted
offered incredibly thoughtful critiques. Double thanks to Tom for
reading extra chapters and helping with permissions. One of my
undergraduate students, Samuel Scruby, helped considerably with
some of the research on chapter 6. Ed Schmitt was incredibly helpful
with parts of chapter 4. None of these people bear responsibility for
any mistakes in the book. Finally, my family deserves a huge thanks.
They offered support, guidance, and levity. Life is better when you
have people to enjoy it with, and laughter rings loudly throughout
our house. Thanks to Danielle and all the kids. Lucky Seven indeed.
      Thanks, too, to Ava the dog.

NOTES

INTRODUCTION

1. William Attwood, "Word 'Liberal' Makes Its Users Stop and Think," *New York Herald Tribune*, February 14, 1949, A9. For the reader responses, see "Readers Answer the Query: 'What is a Liberal?'" *New York Herald Tribune*, February 13, 1949, A7.

2. Christopher Ellis and James A. Stimson, "Symbolic Ideology in the American Electorate," *Electoral Studies* 28 (2009): 389. Italics added.

3. The classic statement here is Thomas Frank, *What's the Matter with Kansas? How Conservatives Won the Heart of America* (New York: Picador, 2004).

4. Ellis and Stimson, "Symbolic Ideology in the American Electorate," 397.

5. Although Johnson usually tried to portray himself as a centrist between "liberal" and "conservative" poles, he often spoke kindly of liberals and liberalism, including referring to Robert F. Kennedy, his own mother, and himself as a liberal. See, for instance, Lyndon B. Johnson, "Remarks Upon Receiving an Honorary Degree at the University of Denver, August 26, 1966," American Presidency Project, accessed April 8, 2024, https://www.presidency.ucsb.edu/node/238929.

6. Ellis and Stimson, "Symbolic Ideology in the American Electorate," 399. Italics in original.

7. Matt Vespa, "Lefty Commentator Just Threw Cold Water over the Left's Future Election Hopes," Townhall, September 3, 2021, https://townhall.com/tipsheet//mattvespa/2021/09/03/lefty-political-scientist-wokeness-is-going-to-kill-democrats-in-national-elections-n2595142.

8. Bankole Thompson, "Biden Campaign Achilles' Heel Is Black Voters," *Detroit News*, January 29, 2024, https://www.detroitnews.com/search/?q=Biden+Campaign+Achilles'+Heel+Is+Black+Voters.

9. Anjimile Yvonne Chithambo, "Animal," track 5 on *The King*, 4AD Records, 2023.

10. Kim C. Domenico, "Darkened Saints and Neoliberal Innocence," *Counter-Punch*, December 8, 2023, https://www.counterpunch.org/2023/12/08/darkened -saints-and-neoliberal-innocence/.

11. Prominent among those who have made the attempt include Mark Lilla, *The Once and Future Liberal: After Identity Politics* (New York: Harper, 2017); Adam Gopnik, *A Thousand Small Sanities: The Moral Adventure of Liberalism* (New York: Basic Books, 2019); Jill Lepore, *This America: The Case for the Nation* (New York: Liveright, 2019); James Traub, *What Was Liberalism? The Past, Present, and Promise of a Noble Idea* (New York: Basic Books, 2019); Alan Wolfe, *The Future of Liberalism* (New York: Alfred A. Knopf, 2009); and Eric Alterman and Kevin Mattson, *The Cause: The Fight for American Liberalism from Franklin Roosevelt to Barack Obama* (New York: Penguin, 2012).

CHAPTER ONE

1. FDR advisor quoted in Ronald D. Rotunda, *The Politics of Language: Liberalism as Word and Symbol* (Iowa City: University of Iowa Press, 1986), 55.

2. Franklin D. Roosevelt, "Address Accepting the Presidential Nomination at the Democratic National Convention in Chicago, July 02, 1932," American Presidency Project, accessed June 12, 2024, https://www.presidency.ucsb.edu/node/275484.

3. Franklin D. Roosevelt, "Campaign Address at Columbus, Ohio, August 20, 1932," American Presidency Project, accessed June 12, 2024, https://www.presidency .ucsb.edu/node/288091.

4. Herbert Hoover, "Address at Madison Square Garden in New York City, October 31, 1932," American Presidency Project, accessed June 12, 2024, https:// www.presidency.ucsb.edu/node/208073.

5. Franklin D. Roosevelt, "Campaign Address in Seattle, Washington on Re-ciprocal Tariff Negotiations (Excerpts), September 20, 1932," American Presidency Project, accessed June 12, 2024, https://www.presidency.ucsb.edu/node/289310.

6. Franklin D. Roosevelt, "Campaign Address on Agriculture and Tariffs at Sioux City, Iowa, September 29, 1932," American Presidency Project, accessed June 12, 2024, https://www.presidency.ucsb.edu/node/289314.

7. Franklin D. Roosevelt, "Radio Address to the Business and Professional Men's League Throughout the Nation, October 06, 1932," American Presidency Project, accessed June 12, 2024, https://www.presidency.ucsb.edu/node/289316.

8. Rotunda, *Politics of Language*, 15.

9. Franklin D. Roosevelt, *Looking Forward* (1933; repr., New York: Gallery Books, 2009).

10. Rotunda, *Politics of Language*, 59.

11. Franklin D. Roosevelt, *The Continuing Struggle for Liberalism: With a Special Introduction and Explanatory Notes by President Roosevelt*, 1938 volume of *The Public Papers and Addresses of Franklin D. Roosevelt* (New York: Macmillan, 1941).

12. Helena Rosenblatt, *The Lost History of Liberalism: From Ancient Rome to the Twenty-First Century* (Princeton, NJ: Princeton University Press, 2018), 36–40.

13. The most famous of these is Louis Hartz, *The Liberal Tradition in America: An Interpretation of American Political Thought since the Revolution* (New York: Harcourt Brace Jovanovich, 1955). To Hartz's credit, he spends the first few pages of his book telling us which definition of *liberalism* he plans to use.

14. Rosenblatt, *Lost History of Liberalism*, 51. De Staël's full name was Anne-Louise-Germaine Necker; upon marrying Baron Erik de Staël-Holstein, she became Baroness de Staël-Holstein. However, she wrote under the name Madame de Staël, which is how she was best known.

15. This history is told in chapter 2 of Rosenblatt, *Lost History of Liberalism*, 41–87.

16. In addition to Rosenblatt's *Lost History of Liberalism*, see also Traub, *What Was Liberalism?* and Michael Freeden, *Liberalism: A Very Short Introduction* (New York: Oxford University Press, 2015). For the uses and abuses of Locke in the United States, see Claire Rydell Arcenas, *America's Philosopher: John Locke in American Intellectual Life* (Chicago: University of Chicago Press, 2022).

17. It is revealing that a now-classic series of European history written by Eric Hobsbawm labeled the years from 1789 to 1848 *The Age of Revolution* and those from 1848 to 1875 *The Age of Capital*.

18. Lest my language be confusing, it is clear, too, that slavery and other forms of forced labor fueled much of the economic growth of the nineteenth and twentieth centuries, and I join the ranks of historians who clearly see slavery as aligned with the Industrial Revolution and not as some ancient vestige of long-ago labor systems.

19. H. W. Brands, *American Colossus: The Triumph of Capitalism, 1865–1900* (New York: Doubleday, 2010), 6.

20. Brands, *American Colossus*, 7.

21. Brands, *American Colossus*, 7.

22. Rosenblatt, *Lost History of Liberalism*, 110.

23. For more on this split, and its trans-Atlantic parallels, see Daniel T. Rodgers, *Atlantic Crossings: Social Politics in a Progressive Age* (Cambridge, MA: Belknap Press of Harvard University Press, 1998).

24. Rosenblatt, *The Lost History of Liberalism*, 177.

25. Rotunda, *Politics of Language*, 34.

26. Michael McGerr, *A Fierce Discontent: The Rise and Fall of the Progressive Movement in America, 1870–1920* (New York: Oxford University Press, 2003), xv.

27. Herbert Croly, *The Promise of American Life* (New York: Macmillan, 1909), 409, 412.

28. Wilson quoted in in Rosenblatt, *Lost History of Liberalism*, 247.

29. Harold Stearns, *Liberalism in America: Its Origins, Its Temporary Collapse, Its Future* (New York: Boni and Liveright, 1919), 124, 226.

30. Max Eastman, "The Twilight of Liberalism," *Liberator* 1, no. 12 (February 1919): 5.

31. Will Durant, "The Future of American Socialism," *Dial* 66 (May 17, 1919): 495, and in Doug Rossinow, *Visions of Progress: The Left-Liberal Tradition in America* (Philadelphia: University of Pennsylvania Press, 2008), 99.

32. Joseph LeConte, *The Autobiography of Joseph LeConte*, ed. William Dallam Armes (New York: D. Appleton, 1903); quoted in Martin E. Marty, *Modern American Religion*, vol. 1, *The Irony of It All* (Chicago: University of Chicago Press, 1986), 34.

33. William Page Roberts, *Liberalism in Religion: And Other Sermons* (London: Smith, Elder, 1886), 56.

34. William James, *The Varieties of Religious Experience* (New York: Longmans, Green, 1902), 91.

35. For more on the relationship between *liberal* and Protestantism, see Elesha J. Coffman, *The Christian Century and the Rise of the Protestant Mainline* (New York: Oxford University Press, 2013). Coffman says she sought the origin story of the term "Liberal Protestant" but "didn't find much of an answer." Elesha Coffman, email message to author, April 12, 2024. And for the relationship between liberal Protestantism and FDR's use of the word, see Gene Zubovich, *Before the Religious Right: Liberal Protestants, Human Rights, and the Polarization of the United States* (Philadelphia: University of Pennsylvania Press, 2022), esp. chap. 1.

36. See, for instance, John McGreevy, *Catholicism: A Global History from the French Revolution to Pope Francis* (New York: W. W. Norton, 2022), 91–93.

37. See, for a fun corrective, Louis Hyman, "The New Deal Wasn't What You Think," *Atlantic*, March 6, 2019, https://www.theatlantic.com/ideas/archive/2019/03/surprising-truth-about-roosevelts-new-deal/584209/.

38. William E. Leuchtenberg, *Franklin D. Roosevelt and the New Deal, 1932–1940* (New York: Harper and Row, 1963), 165.

39. Jason Scott Smith, *A Concise History of the New Deal* (New York: Cambridge University Press, 2014), 2. Chapter 2 of Smith's book is called "Saving Capitalism, 1933–1934." For an American history of "liberalism" that argues that market forces have been the predominant factor in underscoring an overarching individualist ethos behind American liberalism, see Dorothy Ross, "Liberalism," in *Encyclopedia of American Political History: Studies of the Principal Movements and Ideas*, vol. 2, ed. Jack P. Greene (New York: Charles Scribner's Sons, 1984), 750–63; and, for the continued emphasis on the centrality of business to postwar liberalism, see Dorothy Ross, "Whatever Happened to the Social in American Social Thought? Part 1," *Modern Intellectual History* 18, no. 4 (December 2021): 1155–77; and Dorothy Ross, "Whatever Happened to the Social in American Social Thought? Part 2," *Modern Intellectual History* 19, no. 1 (March 2022): 268–96.

40. I do not mean to downplay Roosevelt's shortcomings, most especially his willingness to tolerate racial segregation. It is worth nothing, however, that recent research highlights the significant amount of economic growth for Black Americans between the 1930s and the 1960s. See Robert D. Putnam, *The Upswing: How America Came Together a Century Ago and How We Can Do It Again*, with Shaylyn Romney Garrett (New York: Simon and Schuster, 2020), chap. 6, esp. 202–14.

41. Eleanor Roosevelt quoted in Alterman and Mattson, *Cause*, 56.

42. Franklin D. Roosevelt quoted in Wendy Wall, *Inventing the "American Way": The Politics of Consensus from the New Deal to the Civil Rights Movement* (New York: Oxford University Press, 2008), 36.

43. David L. Chappell, *A Stone of Hope: Prophetic Religion and the Death of Jim Crow* (Chapel Hill: University of North Carolina Press, 2004), 15.

44. John Dewey, *Liberalism and Social Action*, in *John Dewey: The Later Works, 1925–1953*, vol. 11, *1935–1937*, ed. Jo Ann Boydston (Carbondale: Southern Illinois University Press, 1987), 41. All citations for *Liberalism and Social Action* are from this edition.

45. Dewey, *Liberalism and Social Action*, 41.

46. Dewey, *Liberalism and Social Action*, 64–65.

47. John Dewey, "Democracy Is Radical," in *John Dewey: Later Works, 1925–1953*, vol. 11, 297. The piece was first published in *Common Sense* 6 (January 1937): 10–11.

48. Quoted in Robert B. Westbrook, *John Dewey and American Democracy* (Ithaca, NY: Cornell University Press, 1991), 441n17.

49. John Dewey, *Liberalism and Social Action*, 63.

50. John Dewey, "The Meaning of Liberalism," in *John Dewey: Later Works*, vol. 11, 364. The piece was first published in *Social Frontier* 2, no. 3 (1935): 74–75.

51. Hartz, *Liberal Tradition in America*. There was, in fact, another book with a similar title that also aligned liberalism with freedom, calling liberalism "the noblest of political philosophies." See William Aylott Orton, *The Liberal Tradition: A Study of the Social and Spiritual Conditions of Freedom* (New Haven, CT: Yale University Press, 1945).

52. John Kenneth Galbraith, *The Liberal Hour* (Boston: Houghton Mifflin, 1960).

53. Arthur Schlesinger Jr., *The Vital Center: The Politics of Freedom* (1949; repr., New York: DaCapo Press, 1988), 209.

54. Schlesinger, *Vital Center*, 4.

55. Lionel Trilling, *The Liberal Imagination: Essays on Literature and Society* (1950; repr., New York: New York Review of Books, 2008), xv.

56. Historian Andrew Jewett has shown that the confidence of these academics in liberalism's righteousness led them to make their understanding of "liberalism" seem "natural" in the world. See Andrew Jewett, "Naturalizing Liberalism in the 1950s," in *Professors and Politics*, ed. Neil Gross and Solon J. Simmons (Baltimore: Johns Hopkins Press, 2014), 191–216.

57. Franklin D. Roosevelt, "Acceptance Speech for the Renomination for the Presidency, Philadelphia, Pa., June 27, 1936," American Presidency Project, accessed June 13, 2024, https://www.presidency.ucsb.edu/node/208917.

58. Richard Hofstadter, "The Pseudo-Conservative Revolt (1955)," in *The Radical Right (The New American Right Expanded and Updated)*, ed. Daniel Bell (Garden City, NY: Anchor Books, 1964), 75.

59. Arthur Schlesinger Jr., "The Future of Liberalism: The Challenge of Abundance," *Reporter*, May 3, 1956, 8, 9–10.

60. Alan P. Grimes, "The Pragmatic Course of Liberalism," *Western Political Quarterly* 9, no. 3 (September 1956): 639.

61. Alan P. Grimes, "Contemporary American Liberalism," in "Conservativism, Liberalism and National Issues," special issue, *Annal of the American Academy of Political Social Science* 344 (November 1962): 29.

62. Reinhold Niebuhr, "Liberalism: Illusions and Realities," *New Republic*, July 4, 1955, https://newrepublic.com/article/72180/liberalism-illusions-and-realities.

63. "Readers Answer the Query: 'What is a Liberal?'" *New York Herald Tribune*, February 13, 1949, A7; and "What is a Liberal?" *St. Louis Post-Dispatch*, February 20, 1949, 22.

64. Charles Frankel, "A Liberal Is a Liberal Is a—," *New York Times*, February 28, 1960, sec. 6, p. 21.

CHAPTER TWO

1. For Buckley as a "salesman" and for more on these years in Buckley's life, see Kevin M. Schultz, *Buckley and Mailer: The Difficult Friendship that Shaped the Sixties* (New York: W. W. Norton., 2015), 39–55.

2. William F. Buckley Jr. (hereafter WFB) to John Dos Passos, 26 September 1958, box 5, Dos Passos folder, William F. Buckley Jr. Papers, Manuscripts and Archives, Yale University Library, New Haven, Connecticut.

3. WFB to John Dos Passos, 15 April 1958, box 5, Dos Passos folder, WFB Papers.

4. WFB to John Dos Passos, 8 July 1958, box 5, Dos Passos folder, WFB Papers.

5. John Dos Passos to WFB, 10 July 1958, box 5, Dos Passos folder, WFB Papers.

6. Buckley's most complete biographer to date, John Judis, says that the book, "while serious in intent, was the book of a man unwilling to devote more than several months to its composition," adding, "for all its flaws, *Up from Liberalism* was the fullest statement of Buckley's political philosophy that he would ever make." John B. Judis, *William F. Buckley, Jr.: Patron Saint of the Conservatives* (New York: Simon and Schuster, 1988), 167.

7. John Dos Passos, foreword to *Up from Liberalism* by William F. Buckley Jr. (1959; repr., Briarcliff Manor, NY: Stein and Day, 1984), xviii.

8. Judis, *Buckley*, 167.

9. William F. Buckley Jr., "Reintroduction," in *Up from Liberalism*, xiii–xiv.

10. Saul D. Alinsky, *Reveille for Radicals* (Chicago: University of Chicago Press, 1946), 26.

11. On "Marxist pollution," see "Can Socialist Labor Leaders Control America?" in Clinton Davidson to WFB, 9 December 1954, box 2, Davidson folder, pp. 2–4, WFB Papers.

12. Ayn Rand, *The Fountainhead* (1943; repr., New York: Penguin, 2005), 639.

13. William F. Buckley Jr., *God and Man at Yale: The Superstitions of "Academic Freedom"* (1951; repr., Washington, DC: Regnery Publishing 1986), lx–lxi.

14. Buckley, *God and Man at Yale*, lxi.

15. "That trend of the times—towards collectivism—has never been effectively opposed in the decisive area of opinion-making," Buckley wrote in an effort to raise founding funds for the *National Review*. WFB to Robert Donner, 5 January 1955, box 2, Donner, Robert folder, p. 1, WFB Papers.

16. Judis, *Buckley*, 160.

17. Whittaker Chambers, *Witness* (1952; repr., Washington, DC: Gateway Editions, 2002), 471.

18. Chambers, *Witness*, 472.

19. Chambers, *Witness*, 473.

20. Chambers, *Witness*, 741. Italics added.

21. Chambers, *Witness*, 793.

22. A 1948 study concluded that, while "liberals and conservatives are to be found in both of the major political parties, those who call themselves liberals appear to feel more at home with Democrats, and conservatives with Republicans," suggesting there were still plenty of liberal Republicans, although they were feeling less and less at home with their party. See Erwin L. Linn, "The Influence of Liberalism and Conservatism on Voting Behavior," *Public Opinion Quarterly* 13, no. 2 (Summer 1949): 299.

23. Joseph McCarthy, speech to ASNE, April 1950, in Richard M. Fried, *A Genius for Confusion: Joseph R. McCarthy and the Politics of Deceit* (New York: Rowman and Littlefield, 2022). 127.

24. Frankel, "A Liberal Is a Liberal Is a—."

25. Eisenhower quoted in Rotunda, *Politics of Language*, 11.

26. Buckley quoted in Judis, *Buckley*, 79.

27. Buckley, *God and Man at Yale*, 195.

28. WFB to Donner.

29. "The New Deal and the Intellectuals," WFB Memo to Clinton Davidson, 23 December 1954, box 2, Davidson folder, WFB Papers.

30. Kevin Corrigan to WFB, 27 March 1955, box 1, Corrigan, Kevin folder, p. 2, WFB Papers.

31. "Can Socialist Labor Leaders Control America?" p. 5.

32. For part of his fundraising appeal for the founding of *National Review*, see WFB Memo to Davidson. Buckley also expresses here the sentiment that he came to conservatism out of a hatred of "Liberalism."

33. "Our Mission Statement," *National Review*, November 19, 1955.

34. "Our Mission Statement."

35. "Our Mission Statement."

36. Buckley quoted in Judis, *Buckley*, 135.

37. Buckley quoted in Judis, *Buckley*, 162.

38. Buckley, *Up from Liberalism*, 37.

39. Buckley, *Up from Liberalism*, 55.

40. Buckley, *Up from Liberalism*, 219.

41. Barry Goldwater, *The Conscience of a Conservative* (New York: Macfadden Books, 1960), 3.

42. Phyllis Schlafly, *A Choice Not an Echo* (self-pub., 1964), 75, 108.

43. JFK63Conspiracy, "Billy James Hargis Warns of Kennedy's 'Liberal Associates,'" January 5, 2010, YouTube video, 2:08, https://www.youtube.com/watch?v=4ssybQg1ZAY.

44. Billy James Hargis, *Distortion by Design: The Story of America's Liberal Press* (New York: Christian Crusade, 1965).

CHAPTER THREE

1. William F. Buckley Jr. and Norman Mailer, "The Role of the Right Wing: A Debate," *Playboy*, February 1963, 115–16. "The Conservative versus the Liberal" is what blared across the opening pages of the article. The debate took place in Chicago on September 22, 1962, a day before the championship boxing match between Floyd Patterson and Sonny Liston. For more on Buckley, Mailer, and the debate, see Schultz, *Buckley and Mailer*, 11–32.

2. For an exploration of liberalism that sees "totalitarianism" as the driving force behind its postwar iteration, see D. Ross, "Whatever Happened to the Social in American Social Thought? Part 1," 1155–77. For Mailer's use and vision of totalitarianism, see Sophie Joscelyne, "Norman Mailer and American Totalitarianism in the 1960s," *Modern Intellectual History* 19, no. 1 (March 2022): 241–67, https://doi.org/10.1017/S1479244320000323.

3. Norman Mailer, *Advertisements for Myself* (1959; repr., Cambridge, MA: Harvard University Press, 1992), 17.

4. Norman Mailer, letter to the editor, *Playboy*, April 1963, 8.

5. Norman Mailer, "The Debate with William Buckley—the Real Meaning of the Right Wing in America," in *The Presidential Papers* (New York: G. P. Putnam's Sons, 1963), 165.

6. Norman Mailer, *Advertisements for Myself*, 19.

7. Alinsky, *Reveille for Radicals*, 33.

8. Alinsky, *Reveille for Radicals*, 27.

9. Alinsky, *Reveille for Radicals*, 28.

10. Alinsky, *Reveille for Radicals*, 28.

11. Alinsky, *Reveille for Radicals*, 28.

12. Alinsky, *Reveille for Radicals*, 29.

13. Hannah Arendt, *The Origins of Totalitarianism*, new ed. with added prefaces (New York: Harcourt, 1985), ix.

14. On fears of too big a government and the need to modify liberal's alignment with the left, see Schlesinger, *Vital Center*, 182–88.

15. This theme is developed in David Ciepley, *Liberalism in the Shadow of Totalitarianism* (Cambridge, MA: Harvard University Press, 2006); and Rossinow, *Visions of Progress*, 195–232.

16. Saul D. Alinsky, *Rules for Radicals: A Practical Primer for Realistic Radicals* (1971; repr., New York: Vintage Books, 1989), xiii.

17. Alinsky, *Rules for Radicals*, xiii.

18. Rossinow, *Visions of Progress*, 201.

19. Eleanor Roosevelt quoted in Alterman and Mattson, *Cause*, 110.

20. Grimes, "Contemporary American Liberalism," 26.

21. D. Ross, "Whatever Happened to the Social in American Social Thought? Part 1," 1155–77.

22. William S. Burroughs, *The Letters of William S. Burroughs, 1945–59*, ed. Oliver Harris (New York: Penguin Books, 1993), 61.

23. On advertisers co-opting potentially radical artistic messages, see Thomas Frank, *The Conquest of Cool: Business Culture, Counterculture, and the Rise of Hip Consumerism* (Chicago: University of Chicago Press, 1997).

24. Editors, "A Word to Our Readers," *Dissent*, Winter 1954, https://www.dissentmagazine.org/article/a-word-to-our-readers-winter-1954.

25. Editors, "A Word to Our Readers."

26. Irving Howe, "The Shame of U.S. Liberalism," *Dissent*, Fall 1954, 309.

27. Howe, "Shame of U.S. Liberalism."

28. Reisman quoted in D. Ross, "Whatever Happened to the Social in American Social Thought? Part 2," 268–96.

29. Norman Mailer, "David Riesman Reconsidered," *Dissent*, Fall 1954, reprinted in Norman Mailer, *Advertisements for Myself* (New York: Putnam's, 1959), 190–204.

30. This description is from John D'Emilio, *Lost Prophet: The Life and Times of Bayard Rustin* (Chicago: University of Chicago Press, 2003), 214–15.

31. Richard Volney Chase, *The Democratic Vista: A Dialogue on Life and Letters in Contemporary America* (New York: Doubleday, 1958), 145.

32. Galbraith, *Liberal Hour*.

33. John F. Kennedy, "Address of John F. Kennedy upon Accepting the Liberal Party Nomination for President, New York, New York, September 14, 1960," John F. Kennedy Library and Archives, John F. Kennedy Library and Museum, accessed

June 18, 2024, https://www.jfklibrary.org/archives/other-resources/john-f-kennedy
-speeches/liberal-party-nomination-nyc-19600914.

34. Kennedy, "Address Accepting Liberal Party Nomination."

35. Robert Martinson, "State of the Campus: 1962," *Nation*, May 19, 1962, 434;
and quoted in Grimes, "Contemporary American Liberalism," 32.

36. This is the argument of Allan J. Matusow, *The Unraveling of America: A
History of Liberalism in the 1960s* (1984; repr., Athens: University of Georgia Press,
2009), 32–33.

37. This is the central argument of Ira Katznelson, *Fear Itself: The New Deal and
the Origins of Our Time* (New York: W. W. Norton, 2013).

38. Grimes, "Contemporary American Liberalism," 26.

39. C. Wright Mills, "Letter to the New Left," *New Left Review*, September
1, 1960, 18–24.

40. Mills, "Letter to the New Left," 22. Italics added.

41. A useful explanation of this, which I've borrowed from heavily, is Matusow,
Unraveling of America, 310–12.

42. Matusow, *Unraveling of America*, 311.

43. Students for a Democratic Society (SDS), *The Port Huron Statement* (1962;
repr., New York: SDS, 1964), 23.

44. SDS, *Port Huron Statement*, 5.

45. SDS, *Port Huron Statement*, 5.

46. Jack Weinberg, "The Free Speech Movement and Civil Rights" (1965), Free
Speech Movement Digital Archive, UC Berkeley, Bancroft Library, Online Archive
of California, accessed July 7, 2021, http://ark.cdlib.org/ark:/13030/kt5v19n822.

47. Potter's speech is in the SDS pamphlet *March on Washington to End the War
in Vietnam*, quoted in Matusow, *Unraveling of America*, 318–19.

48. Potter quoted in Matusow, *Unraveling of America*, 319.

49. Matusow, *Unraveling of America*, 319.

50. Rudd quoted in Alterman and Mattson, *Cause*, 214–15.

51. Hofstadter quoted in Alterman and Mattson, *Cause*, 217.

52. Alinsky, *Rules for Radicals*, xiii–xiv.

53. Garcia quoted in W. J. Rorabaugh, *American Hippies* (New York: Cambridge
University Press, 2015), 65.

CHAPTER FOUR

1. *Time* wrote, "In the U.S. today there is not another writer—white or black—
who expresses with such poignancy and abrasiveness the dark realities of the racial
ferment in North and South." "The Root of the Negro Problem," *Time* magazine,
May 17, 1963, https://time.com/archive/6626512/nation-the-root-of-the-negro
-problem/.

2. "Liberalism and the Negro: A Round-Table Discussion," with James Baldwin, Nathan Glazer, Sidney Hook, and Gunnar Myrdal, *Commentary*, March 1964, 25–42.

3. James Baldwin, *The Fire Next Time* (New York: Dial Press, 1963), 119.

4. Baldwin, *Fire Next Time*, 120.

5. For Baldwin's 1963 change in outlook, see Kevin M. Schultz, "1963: Baldwin's *annus mirabilis*," in *James Baldwin in Context*, ed. Quentin Miller (New York: Cambridge University Press, 2019), 37–46.

6. For Podhoretz's version of the origin of the piece, see Norman Podhoretz, *Making It* (1967; New York: Bantam Books, 1969), 249–53.

7. "Liberalism and the Negro," 28.

8. "Liberalism and the Negro," 29.

9. "Liberalism and the Negro," 31–32.

10. "Liberalism and the Negro," 31.

11. "Liberalism and the Negro," 38.

12. "Liberalism and the Negro," 38.

13. "Liberalism and the Negro," 40–41.

14. "Liberalism and the Negro," 38.

15. "Liberalism and the Negro," 39.

16. "Liberalism and the Negro," 39.

17. "Liberalism and the Negro," 39. Emphasis in the original.

18. The section on comedians derives largely from Ronald L. Smith, *Cosby: The Life of a Comedy Legend* (New York: SPI Books, 1993), quotation at 33.

19. See Brian Temple, *Philadelphia Quakers and the Antislavery Movement* (New York: McFarland, 2014), 131–32.

20. On Frederick Douglass and liberalism, see Nick Bromell, "The Liberal Imagination of Frederick Douglass," *American Scholar*, March 1, 2008, https://theamericanscholar.org/the-liberal-imagination-of-frederick-douglass/.

21. Gunnar Myrdal et al., *American Dilemma* (1944; repr., New York: Routledge, 1995), 1405–6n72, 1406.

22. Langston Hughes, "Liberals Need a Mascot," in *The Collected Works of Langston Hughes*, vol. 8, *The Late Simple Stories* (Columbia: University of Missouri Press, 2002), 307–8. The original column ran in 1949.

23. Gwendolyn Brooks, "The Lovers of the Poor," in *The Bean Eaters* (New York: Harper and Row, 1960), 35–37.

24. Hubert H. Humphrey, "1948 Democratic National Convention Address, Delivered 14 July 1948, Philadelphia, PA," American Rhetoric: Top 100 Speeches, accessed July 22, 2024, https://www.americanrhetoric.com/speeches/huberthumphey1948dnc.html.

25. Murray Friedman, "The White Liberal's Retreat," *Atlantic Monthly*, January 1963, 44.

26. James Baldwin, *Blues for Mister Charlie: A Play* (1964; repr., New York: Penguin Random House, 1995), 14.

27. Martin Luther King Jr., "'Give Us the Ballot,' Address Delivered at the Prayer Pilgrimage for Freedom," Washington, DC, May 17, 1957, King Papers, Martin Luther King, Jr., Research and Education Institute, Stanford University, accessed July 22, 2024, https://kinginstitute.stanford.edu/king-papers/documents/give-us-ballot-address-delivered-prayer-pilgrimage-freedom.

28. Martin Luther King Jr., "'The Rising Tide of Racial Consciousness,' Address at the Golden Anniversary Conference of the National Urban League," New York City, September 8, 1960, King Papers, Martin Luther King, Jr. Research and Education Institute, Stanford University, accessed July 22, 2024, https://kinginstitute.stanford.edu/king-papers/documents/rising-tide-racial-consciousness-address-golden-anniversary-conference.

29. King, "Rising Tide of Racial Consciousness."

30. Martin Luther King Jr., "Letter from Birmingham Jail," *Atlantic Monthly*, August 1963, 81.

31. King, "Letter from Birmingham Jail," 85.

32. This is among the arguments in Chappell, *A Stone of Hope*, esp. 46–47.

33. Martin Luther King Jr., *Why We Can't Wait* (1964, repr., Boston: Beacon Press, 2011).

34. For a running catalog of King and his frustrations with "white liberals," see the work of Jeanne Theoharis, especially her annual columns on Martin Luther King Jr. Day, "Martin Luther King Jr.'s Challenge to Liberal Allies—and Why It Resonates Today," *Washington Post*, February 8, 2021; "Martin Luther King and the 'Polite' Racism of White Liberals," *Washington Post*, January 17, 2020; and "What King Said about Northern Liberalism," *New York Times*, January 20, 2019.

35. Martin Luther King Jr., *The Autobiography of Martin Luther King, Jr.*, ed. Clayborne Carson (New York: Warner Books, 2001), chap. 28. Found online at King Papers, Martin Luther King, Jr. Research and Education Institute, Stanford University, accessed August 5, 2024, https://kinginstitute.stanford.edu/publications/autobiography-martin-luther-king-jr-chapter-28-chicago-campaign.

36. Martin Luther King Jr., *Where Do We Go from Here: Chaos or Community?* (Boston: Beacon Press, 1967).

37. Malcolm X, "God's Judgement of White America" (December 1, 1963), in *Malcolm X: The Man and His Times*, ed. John Henrik Clarke (1969; repr., Trenton, NJ: Africa World Press, 1990), 284. This was Malcolm X's first speech after John F. Kennedy's assassination. It was carefully scripted and emotionally loaded, and Malcolm X knew white reporters would be there (but not white audience members), so he knew his comments would get widely reported. Most people, however, remember the speech for Malcolm X's comments in the question-and-answer session, where he said the assassination was an example of "the chickens coming home to roost." For details, see Manning Marable, *Malcolm X: A Life of Reinvention* (New York: Viking Press, 2011), 269–73.

38. BlackPast, "(1966) Stokely Carmichael, 'Black Power,'" July 13, 2010, https://www.blackpast.org/african-american-history/speeches-african-american-history/1966-stokely-carmichael-black-power/.

39. Malcolm X famously shifted this perspective after his 1964 trip to Mecca, where, he wrote, he discovered an "authentic Islam" premised on universal respect and brotherhood. For his trip to Mecca, and for the beginnings of this transformation just before his trip, see Marable, *Malcolm X*, 301–20, esp. 310.

40. Stephen D. Lerner, "Carmichael on 'Black Power,'" *Harvard Crimson*, August 23, 1966.

41. Quotation in Matusow, *Unraveling of America*, 355, quoting Carmichael, *Black Power*, 65.

42. Eldridge Cleaver, *Soul on Ice* (1968; repr., New York: Dell, 1992), 116.

43. Robert Kennedy quoted in Arthur Schlesinger Jr., *Robert F. Kennedy and His Times* (New York: Alfred A. Knopf, 1978), 334.

44. Norman Podhoretz, "My Negro Problem—And Ours," *Commentary*, February 1963.

45. Lyndon B. Johnson, "Commencement Address at Howard University: 'To Fulfill These Rights,' June 04, 1965," American Presidency Project, accessed June 20, 2024, https://www.presidency.ucsb.edu/node/241312.

46. Lerone Bennett Jr., "The Mood of the Negro," *Ebony*, July 1, 1963, 27–38, quotations at 38.

47. Lerone Bennett Jr., *The Negro Mood and Other Essays* (Chicago: Johnson Publishing, 1964), 74–103, quotations at 80, 77–78.

48. Bennett, *Negro Mood*, 90.

49. Bennett, *Negro Mood*, 78.

50. Lorraine Hansberry, "'The Black Revolution and the White Backlash,' Forum at Town Hall Sponsored by the Association of Artists for Freedom, New York City—June 15, 1964," American RadioWorks, transcript and audio file, 7:21, http://americanradioworks.publicradio.org/features/blackspeech/lhansberry.html.

51. Chappell, *A Stone of Hope*, 4.

52. "The White Liberal, by Our Readers," *Commentary*, August 1964, https://www.commentary.org/articles/reader-letters/the-white-liberal/.

53. Clips from the 48-minute black-and-white film directed by Horace Ové can be found on the British Film Institute (BFI) website; see "Baldwin's Nigger (1969)," BFI Screenonline, accessed February 12, 2024, http://www.screenonline.org.uk/film/id/480522/index.html. For an interesting discussion of it, see "Baldwin's Nigger: A 1969 Conversation with James Baldwin and Dick Gregory," Black Like Vanilla, January 9, 2020, http://blacklikevanilla.com/baldwins-nigger-a-1969-conversation-with-james-baldwin-and-dick-gregory/.

54. Stanley Kramer, dir., *Guess Who's Coming to Dinner* (Columbia Pictures, 1967).

55. James Baldwin, "Sidney Poitier," *Look*, July 23, 1968, and reprinted in James Baldwin, *The Cross of Redemption: Uncollected Writings*, ed. and with an introduction by Randall Kenan (New York: Vintage, 2011), 226–27.

56. Bennett, *Negro Mood*, 79.

CHAPTER FIVE

1. Tom Wolfe, "Radical Chic: That Party at Lenny's," *New York* magazine, June 8, 1970, 27–28.

2. Christopher Bonanos, "The Making of Tom Wolfe's 'Radical Chic,'" *New York* magazine, May 28, 2018.

3. T. Wolfe, "Radical Chic," 28.

4. T. Wolfe, "Radical Chic," 42.

5. T. Wolfe, "Radical Chic," 31.

6. T. Wolfe, "Radical Chic," 56.

7. Raymond K. Price Jr. to Thomas Wolfe, June 11, 1970, reprinted in Bonanos, "Making of Tom Wolfe's 'Radical Chic.'"

8. T. Wolfe, "Radical Chic," 54.

9. T. Wolfe, "Radical Chic," 51.

10. To be fair, there were some, certainly the exception, like Barbara Walters, who pretended to be in on the joke from the beginning, writing to Wolfe, "Thank you for writing about me with such accuracy. Your excellent article brought the whole extraordinary evening back. Wow!" Barbara Walters to Thomas Wolfe, June 19, 1970, reprinted in Bonanos, "Making of Tom Wolfe's 'Radical Chic.'"

11. Leonard Bernstein, "Materials Relating to the Black Panther Fundraiser: Tom Wolfe Article in New York, Radical Chic: That Party at Lenny's; LB's Letter to the Editor of the Jewish Ledger; Felicia's Letter to the Editor NYT; Related Clippings and Correspondence, including Letters from Coretta Scott King, Gloria Steinem, and Jacqueline Kennedy Onassis, 1970 Jan.–June," box 84, folder 1, Leonard Bernstein manuscript collection, ML31.B49, Library of Congress Control No. 2023778824, Library of Congress Online Catalog, 203 JPEG images, accessed June 21, 2022, https://www.loc.gov/item/musbernstein.100020142/ (hereafter cited as Bernstein collection).

12. See Alex Ross, "The Legend of Lenny," *New Yorker*, December 7, 2008.

13. Garry Wills, *Nixon Agonistes: The Crisis of the Self-Made Man* (1969; repr., Boston: Houghton Mifflin, 20021969), 265.

14. Kevin P. Phillips, *The Emerging Republican Majority* (New Rochelle, NY: Arlington House, 1969), 470.

15. See, for example, the way Barry Goldwater talked about race in Goldwater, *Conscience of a Conservative*. Parts of this argument come from Dov Grohsgal and Kevin M. Kruse, "How the Republican Majority Emerged," *Atlantic*, August 6, 2019.

16. Phillips, *Emerging Republican Majority*, 42.

17. Phillips, *Emerging Republican Majority*, 470.

18. Wills, *Nixon's Agonistes*, 265.

19. Phillips quoted in Rick Perlstein, *Nixonland: The Rise of a President and the Fracturing of America* (New York: Scribner, 2008), 277.

20. Phillips quoted in Robert Mason, *Richard Nixon and the Quest for a New Majority* (Chapel Hill: University of North Carolina Press, 2005), 48.

21. Wills, *Nixon Agonistes*, 266.

22. Phillips, *Emerging Republican Majority*, 141, 142, 543.

23. Phillips, *Emerging Republican Majority*, 552.

24. Nixon quoted in Dan Carter, *The Politics of Rage: George Wallace, the Origins of the New Conservatism, and the Transformation of American Politics* (Baton Rouge: Louisiana State University Press, 1995), 380.

25. Staffer quoted in Steve Fraser, *The Limousine Liberal: How an Incendiary Image United the Right and Fractured America* (New York: Basic Books, 2016), 167.

26. Richard Nixon, "Remarks on Accepting the Presidential Nomination of the Republican National Convention," August 23, 1972.

27. There is debate about whether Nixon sent Agnew on the attack against white liberals or if, as Agnew insisted, he sensed the president's exhaustion and made the move on his own. Either way, the president approved of what Agnew did.

28. Perlstein, *Nixonland*, 302.

29. Perlstein, *Nixonland*, 303.

30. Excerpts of Agnew's speech are found in Arthur Schlesinger Jr., "The Amazing Success Story of 'Spiro *Who?*'" *New York Times*, July 26, 1970.

31. Agnew quoted in Brock Brower, "Don't Get Agnew Wrong," *Life*, May 8, 1970, 69.

32. Agnew quoted in Brower, "Don't Get Agnew Wrong," 69.

33. Agnew quoted in Schlesinger, "Amazing Success Story of 'Spiro *Who?*'"

34. Robert Mitchell, "'Nattering Nabobs of Negativism': The Improbable Rise of Spiro T. Agnew," *Washington Post*, August 8, 2018, https://www.washingtonpost.com/news/retropolis/wp/2018/08/08/nattering-nabobs-of-negativism-the-improbable-rise-of-spiro-t-agnew/.

35. Agnew quoted in Schlesinger, "Amazing Success Story of 'Spiro *Who?*'"

36. Spiro T. Agnew, "Address at Republican Dinner," October 8, 1969, *Speaking Freely* (Washington, DC: Public Affairs Press, 1970), 16–24.

37. Nicole Hemmer, *Messengers of the Right: Conservative Media and the Transformation of American Politics* (Philadelphia: University of Pennsylvania Press, 2016), 218.

38. See, for instance, George Lardner Jr. and Michael Dobbs, "New Tapes Reveal Depth of Nixon's Anti-Semitism," *Washington Post*, October 6, 1999, A31, where Nixon claims, "Most Jews are disloyal" and "you can't trust the bastards. They turn against you," to which his chief of staff H. R. "Bob" Haldeman agrees: "Their whole

orientation is against you. . . . And they are smart. They have the ability to do what they want to do—which is to hurt us." See also Frank Mankiewicz and Tom Braden, "Agnew Unintentionally Triggers Renewed Round of Anti-Semitism," *Washington Post*, December 30, 1969, A15.

39. Quoted in Hemmer, *Messengers of the Right*, 227.

40. Agnew quoted in Schlesinger, "Amazing Success Story of 'Spiro *Who?*'"

41. Schlesinger, "Amazing Success Story of 'Spiro *Who?*'"

42. Brower, "Don't Get Agnew Wrong," 66.

43. Brower, "Don't Get Agnew Wrong," 66.

44. Donald T. Critchlow, *Phyllis Schlafly and Grassroots Conservatism: A Woman's Crusade* (Princeton, NJ: Princeton University Press, 2005), 3–4.

45. Schlafly, *A Choice Not an Echo*, 75, 108.

46. Schlafly, *A Choice Not an Echo*, 6.

47. Schlafly, *A Choice Not an Echo*, 116.

48. Schlafly, *A Choice Not an Echo*, 81.

49. Critchlow, *Phyllis Schlafly and Grassroots Conservatism*, 109.

50. Phyllis Schlafly, "What's Wrong With 'Equal Rights' for Women," *Phyllis Schlafly Report* 5, no. 7 (February 1972): 1–4.

51. Critchlow, *Phyllis Schlafly and Grassroots Conservatism*, 237.

52. Critchlow, *Phyllis Schlafly and Grassroots Conservatism*, 277.

53. Nixon quoted in Perlman, *Nixonland*, 277–78, 435, italics mine.

54. Richard Nixon, "Address to the Nation on the War in Vietnam, November 03, 1969," American Presidency Project, accessed July 23, 2024, https://www.presidency.ucsb.edu/documents/address-the-nation-the-war-vietnam.

55. This McDavid quotation is the first sentence in Matthew D. Lassiter, *The Silent Majority: Suburban Politics in the Sunbelt South* (Princeton, NJ: Princeton University Press, 2006), 1.

56. Advertisement in *Life*, May 8, 1970, 66.

57. "The Troubled American: A Special Report on the White Majority," *Newsweek*, October 6, 1969, 31.

58. Pete Hamill, "The Revolt of the White Lower Middle Class," *New York*, April 14, 1969.

59. Peter Schrag, "The Forgotten American," *Harper's Magazine*, August 1, 1969, 32.

60. Schrag, "Forgotten American," 34.

61. Chris Lehmann, "The Eyes of Spiro Are upon You: The Myth of the Liberal Media," *Baffler*, April 2001.

62. Richard M. Nixon, memorandum to John Ehrlichman, September 8, 1970, in D. Carter, *Politics of Rage*, 397.

63. *All in the Family*, season 2, episode 6, "The Election Story," directed by John Rich, written by Norman Lear, Michael Ross, Bernard West, and Johnny Speight, aired October 30, 1971, on CBS.

64. *All in the Family*, season 1, episode 1, "Meet the Bunkers," directed by John Rich, written by Norman Lear and Johnny Speight, aired January 12, 1971, on CBS.

65. Carroll O'Connor and Jean Stapleton (as The Bunkers), "Those Were the Days ('All In The Family' Theme)," Atlantic Records, 1971, 45 rpm.

66. Phillips, *Emerging Republican Majority*, 42.

CHAPTER SIX

1. Jean-Michel Basquiat, *Obnoxious Liberals*, 1982, acrylic, oilstick, and spray paint on canvas, 68″ × 102″ (172.72 × 259.08 cm), Broad, Los Angeles.

2. Lyndon B. Johnson, "Remarks on the 82d Anniversary of the Birth of Franklin D. Roosevelt, January 30, 1964," American Presidency Project, accessed April 16, 2024, https://www.presidency.ucsb.edu/node/240028.

3. Lyndon B. Johnson, "Remarks in Albee Square, Brooklyn, October 15, 1964," American Presidency Project, accessed April 16, 2024, https://www.presidency.ucsb.edu/node/242274.

4. Johnson, "Remarks Upon Receiving an Honorary Degree at the University of Denver."

5. Lyndon B. Johnson, "Remarks at the Lighting of the Nation's Christmas Tree, December 15, 1966," American Presidency Project, accessed April 16, 2024, https://www.presidency.ucsb.edu/node/238242.

6. "Robert F. Kennedy Launches 1968 Presidential Campaign," March 16, 1968, CBS News Special Report, YouTube video, 38:20, https://www.youtube.com/watch?v=c9Wc9ArvpBo.

7. Robert Kennedy quoted in Alterman and Mattson, *Cause*, 229.

8. Hubert H. Humphrey, "Democrats Must Stay Liberal to Win in '60, Senator Humphrey Says," press release, February 13, 1959.

9. Hubert H. Humphrey, *The Education of a Public Man: My Life and Politics* (1976; repr., Minneapolis: University of Minnesota Press, 1991), 297.

10. Humphrey, *Education of a Public Man*, xxiv.

11. Eugene McCarthy, *A Liberal Answer to the Conservative Challenge* (New York: Macfadden-Bartell Capitol Hill Book Corp., 1964).

12. Eugene McCarthy, *The Year of the People* (New York: Doubleday, 1969), 157, 186. The book also publishes several of his most important speeches, none of which use the word *liberalism* and only one of which mentions "liberal," although not in reference to himself.

13. Richard Reeves, "How Procaccino Could Snatch Defeat from the Jaws of Victory," *New York Times*, July 20, 1969, sec. 4, p. 6.

14. Procaccino quoted in Vincent J. Cannato, *The Ungovernable City: John Lindsay and His Struggle to Save New York* (New York: Basic Books, 2002), 428.

15. Safire quoted in Cannato, *Ungovernable City*, 428.

16. Fraser, *Limousine Liberal*, 7.

17. Theodore J. Lowi, *The End of Liberalism: The Second Republic of the United States* (New York: Norton, 1979), xvi. The first edition was published in 1969 with the subtitle *Ideology, Policy, and the Crisis of Public Authority*. Page references are to the 1979 edition.

18. Lowi, *End of Liberalism*, 44.

19. Lowi, *End of Liberalism*.

20. Lowi, *End of Liberalism*, xvi.

21. Lowi, *End of Liberalism*, 271.

22. Sam Roberts, "Theodore Lowi, Zealous Scholar of Presidents and Liberalism, Dies at 85," *New York Times*, February 24, 2017.

23. Norman Mailer, *St. George and the Godfather* (New York, Signet, 1972), 25.

24. Quoted in Rowland Evans and Robert Novak, "Behind Humphrey's Surge," *Washington Post*, April 27, 1972.

25. The identification of Eagleton as the source of the quotation first came out in Robert Novak's memoir, *The Prince of Darkness: 50 Years Reporting in Washington* (New York: Crown Press, 2007), and was reported in Timothy Noah, "'Acid, Amnesty, and Abortion': The Unlikely Source of a Legendary Smear," *New Republic*, October 21, 2012, https://newrepublic.com/article/108977/acid-amnesty-and -abortion-unlikely-source-legendary-smear.

26. This is the conclusion of both William Greider, the *Washington Post* journalist most favorable to McGovern, and Bruce Miroff's *The Liberals' Moment: The McGovern Insurgency and the Identity Crisis of the Democratic Party* (Lawrence: University Press of Kansas, 2007), 123–25.

27. E. J. Dionne Jr., *Why Americans Hate Politics* (1991; repr., New York: Simon & Schuster, 2004), 228.

28. Michael Harrington, "Out Beyond Liberalism," *New York Times*, March 3, 1973, 31.

29. Harrington, "Out Beyond Liberalism."

30. Quoted in Greg Weiner, *American Burke: The Uncommon Liberalism of Daniel Patrick Moynihan* (Lawrence: University Press of Kansas, 2015), 39.

31. Daniel Patrick Moynihan, *The Politics of a Guaranteed Income: The Nixon Administration and the Family Assistance Plan* (New York: Random House, 1973), 185.

32. Daniel P. Moynihan, "Politics as the Art of the Impossible," in *Coping: Essays on the Practice of Government* (New York: Random House, 1973), 255.

33. On quoting Lowi, see Weiner, *American Burke*, 147n2.

34. Martin Schram, *Running for President 1976* (New York: Pocket Books, 1977), 32.

35. Daniel Patrick Moynihan, "The Liberals' Dilemma," *New Republic*, January 22, 1977.

36. Daniel Patrick Moynihan, "New York State and the Liberal Tradition," August 28, 1976, Daniel Patrick Moynihan Papers, part 1, box 493, Library of Congress,

Washington DC, and quoted in Patrick Andelic, "Daniel Patrick Moynihan, the 1976 New York Senate Race, and the Struggle to Define American Liberalism," *Historical Journal* 57, no. 4 (December 2014): 1111–33, at 1124, https://doi.org/10.1017/S0018246X14000223.

37. Moynihan quoted in Andelic, "Moynihan and Struggle to Define American Liberalism," 1127–28.

38. Moynihan quoted in Weiner, *American Burke*, 56.

39. Moynihan, "Liberals' Dilemma."

40. Moynihan, "Liberals' Dilemma."

41. Daniel Patrick Moynihan, "Remarks to the New York AFL-CIO," August 31, 1978, Daniel Patrick Moynihan Papers, and quoted in Weiner, *American Burke*, 146n20.

42. Coalition for a Democratic Majority, "Come Home, Democrats" (advertisement), *Washington Post*, December 7, 1972, A6.

43. Decter quoted in David Shribman, "Democrats of 'Mainstream' Regroup to Try Again," *New York Times*, May 23, 1983, A12.

44. Will quoted in Patrick Andelic, "'Wine and Cheese Liberals': Mo Udall's 1976 Presidential Campaign and the New Suburban Democrats," *Journal of Arizona History*, Autumn 2021, 390.

45. Samuel Phelps Scruby, "Ideology and Insult: Jimmy Carter, Ronald Reagan, and the Ashes of the 'Silver Age of Liberalism'" (honors thesis, University of Illinois Chicago, 2020), 14; unpublished, in author's possession.

46. Ted Kennedy quoted in Kevin Mattson, *"What the Heck Are You Up To, Mr. President?" Jimmy Carter, America's "Malaise," and the Speech That Should Have Changed the Country* (New York: Bloomsbury, 2009), 174.

47. R. W. Apple, "Carter Target of Liberals After New Hampshire Gain," *New York Times*, February 27, 1976, 65.

48. Jimmy Carter, "The State of the Union Address Delivered before a Joint Session of the Congress, January 19, 1978," American Presidency Project, accessed June 24, 2024, https://www.presidency.ucsb.edu/node/245063.

49. Arthur Schlesinger Jr., "The Great Carter Mystery: Is Incompetence the Mother of Success?" *New Republic*, April 11, 1980.

CHAPTER SEVEN

1. There are many biographies of Michel Foucault, but perhaps the best is David Macey, *The Lives of Michel Foucault*, 2nd ed. (New York: Verso, 2019). See also Johanna Oksala, *How to Read Foucault* (New York: Granta Books, 2007); and Todd May, *The Philosophy of Foucault* (New York: Routledge, 2006).

2. Philosophers often break up Foucault's writings into three chronological periods: archaeology (devoted to his exploration of the history of human thought

and the conceptual frameworks that have guided us), genealogy (devoted to his study of how one framework changes to another), and ethics (devoted to how people define codes of ethics at any given time). Reading pieces from each of these periods, however, allows one to see perpetual themes within them, as I have laid out here. For this periodization of his work, see, for instance, Gary Gutting, *Foucault: A Very Short Introduction* (New York: Oxford University Press, 2005).

3. Michel Foucault, *The Birth of Biopolitics: Lectures at the Collège de France, 1978–79*, ed. Michel Senellart, trans. Graham Burchell (New York: Palgrave Macmillan, 2008), 186.

4. Foucault, *Birth of Biopolitics*, 64.

5. Foucault, *Birth of Biopolitics*, 68–69.

6. On the nicknames for this school of economists, see David Harvey, *A Brief History of Neoliberalism* (Oxford: Oxford University Press, 2005), 8.

7. Foucault, *Birth of Biopolitics*, 322.

8. Foucault, *Birth of Biopolitics*, 323.

9. For the debate on this subject, see Daniel Zamora and Michael C. Behrent, eds., *Foucault and Neoliberalism* (Cambridge: Polity, 2015).

10. Foucault, *Birth of Biopolitics*, 302.

11. See, for example, an ngram of the uses of "neoliberalism" from 1500 to 2023: Google Books Ngram Viewer, "neoliberalism," accessed December 13, 2023, https://books.google.com/ngrams/graph?content=neoliberalism&year_start=1500&year_end=2019&corpus=en-2019&smoothing=3.

12. For these early uses, see the punchy piece by Phillip W. Magness, "The Pejorative Origins of the Term 'Neoliberalism,'" *American Institute for Economic Research* (blog), December 10, 2018, https://www.aier.org/article/the-pejorative-origins-of-the-term-neoliberalism/. The American Institute for Economic Research is a conservative think tank.

13. Some historians mistakenly see the origin of the term in 1938. See, for instance, Wendy Brown, *In the Ruins of Neoliberalism: The Rise of Antidemocratic Politics in the West* (New York: Columbia University Press, 2015), 17; and Quinn Slobodian, *Globalist: The End of Empire and the Birth of Neoliberalism* (Cambridge, MA: Harvard University Press, 2018). It is key to point out that I am focused exclusively on the use of the *term* "neoliberal," not on the ideas it implies, which has had a robust life since the end of World War II, including in Mont Pélerin, Freiburg, Chicago, Cologne, Geneva, and other cities. Most of the thinkers associated with neoliberalism, though, have rejected the label.

14. Foucault, *Birth of Biopolitics*, 79.

15. Brown, *In the Ruins of Neoliberalism*, 20.

16. For the concept of the "neoliberal order," see Gary Gerstle, *The Rise and Fall of the Neoliberal Order: America and the World in the Free Market Era* (New York: Oxford University Press, 2023), esp. 1–12, 73–96. The prioritization on *homo*

œconomicus can be found in numerous texts, perhaps most brilliantly in Brown, *In the Ruins of Neoliberalism*.

17. On the global dimensions of neoliberalism and especially the ways in which neoliberal ideas were put into place in the vacuum created by decolonization, see Slobodian, *Globalist*.

18. Peters quoted in Randall Rothenberg, "The Neoliberal Club: Politicians for the Postindustrial Age," *Esquire*, February 1982, 38.

19. Charles Peters, "A Neo-Liberal's Manifesto," *Washington Post*, September 5, 1982, https://www.washingtonpost.com/archive/opinions/1982/09/05/a-neo-liberals -manifesto/21cf41ca-e60e-404e-9a66-124592c9f70d/.

20. Rothenberg, "Neoliberal Club," 45. Rothenberg expanded the article into a book as well: Randall Rothenberg, *The Neo-Liberals: Creating the New American Politics* (New York: Simon and Schuster, 1984).

21. Rothenberg, "Neoliberal Club," 38.

22. For Peters's life, see Robert D. McFadden, "Charlie Peters, Founder of the Washington Monthly, Dies at 96," *New York Times*, November 25, 2023, A19; and Timothy R. Smith, "Charlie Peters, Washington Monthly Founder, Dies at 96," *Washington Post*, November 23, 2023, https://www.washingtonpost.com/obituaries/ 2023/11/23/charlie-peters-washington-monthly-dies/.

23. Rothenberg, "Neoliberal Club," 38.

24. Thomases quoted in Rothenberg, "Neoliberal Club," 39.

25. Coined in 1991 by Democratic strategist James Carville, the talking point was one of the three central messages of Bill Clinton's 1992 presidential campaign, with the other two being "change versus more of the same" and "don't forget health care."

26. Muskie quoted in Al From, *The New Democrats and the Return to Power* (New York: Palgrave Macmillan, 2013), 22.

27. David Broder, "End of Kennedy-Style Liberalism?" *Boston Globe*, June 25, 1980, 13.

28. Paul Tsongas, *The Road from Here: Liberalism and Realities in the 1980s* (New York: Alfred A. Knopf, 1981).

29. Peters, "Neo-Liberal's Manifesto."

30. Peters quoted in Walter Goodman, "As Neoliberals Search for Closest Fit, Hart Is Often Mentioned," *New York Times*, May 15, 1984, A24.

31. Peters, "Neo-Liberal's Manifesto."

32. Peters, "Neo-Liberal's Manifesto."

33. Leslie Wayne, "Designing a New Economics," *New York Times*, September 26, 1982, sec. 3, p. 6.

34. Lester C. Thurow, *The Zero-Sum Society: Distribution and the Possibilities for Economic Change* (New York: Basic Books, 1980).

35. Kondracke quoted in Wayne, "Designing a New Economics."

36. Reich quoted in Wayne, "Designing a New Economics."

37. Wayne, "Designing a New Economics."

38. Hart was even pictured on the cover of *Esquire* the month it ran its cover story on the neoliberals. The cover read: "The New Boys on the Hill: Washington's Neoliberals; Smart and Tough, but Can They Lead?" *Esquire*, February 1982.

39. Hart quoted in Goodman, "Neoliberals Search for Closest Fit."

40. Kinsley quoted in Goodman, "Neoliberals Search for Closest Fit."

41. From, *New Democrats and the Return to Power*, 2.

42. For Galston's politics of evasion, see Jason Zengerle, "The Vanishing Moderate Democrat," *New York Times Magazine*, updated July 1, 2022, https://www.nytimes.com/2022/06/29/magazine/moderate-democrat.html.

43. See, for instance, the 1992 campaign brochure "Fighting for the Forgotten Middle Class," in Campaign Literature Archive, Democracy in Action, accessed July 26, 2024, https://www.democracyinaction.us/1992/clintonforgotten.html.

44. Mike Davis, *Prisoners of the American Dream: Politics and Economy in the History of the U.S. Working Class* (1986; repr., London: Verso, 2018), 302.

45. Davis, *Prisoners of the American Dream*, xi–xii.

46. Davis, *Prisoners of the American Dream*, 257, 289.

47. Davis, *Prisoners of the American Dream*, 303, 300. The "Revenge of the Neoliberals" section is 301–6.

48. Davis, *Prisoners of the American Dream*, 310.

49. Lisa Myers, "Democratic Leadership Council Attempts to Redefine Democratic Party," *NBC Today Show with Katie Couric*, May 6, 1991, Internet Archive Wayback Machine, transcript of video file, https://web.archive.org/web/20110818071911/http://icue.nbcunifiles.com/icue/files/icue/site/pdf/3269.pdf.

50. David Mills, "Sister Souljah's Call to Arms: The Rapper Says the Riots Were Payback; Are You Paying Attention?" *Washington Post*, May 13, 1992, B1.

51. "Clinton Stuns Rainbow Coalition," *Washington Post*, June 14, 1992, A1.

52. "Clinton Stuns Rainbow Coalition."

53. Jackson quoted in Anthony Lewis, "Abroad at Home; Black and White," *New York Times*, June 18, 1992, A27.

54. Lewis, "Abroad at Home."

55. From, *New Democrats and the Return to Power*, 178.

56. George H. W. Bush, "Fact Sheet: Compassionate Conservatism," White House press release, April 30, 2002, https://georgewbush-whitehouse.archives.gov/news/releases/2002/04/20020430.html.

57. Nick Timiraos and Jackie Calmes, "Obama Denounces Ex-Pastor For 'Rants,'" *Wall Street Journal*, April 30, 2008, https://www.wsj.com/articles/SB120947891869752797.

58. Colin Gordon, "Governmental Rationality: An Introduction," in *The Foucault Effect: Studies in Governmentality*, ed. Graham Burchell, Colin Gordon, and Peter Miller (Hemel Hempstead, UK: Harvester Wheatsheaf, 1991), 1–52.

59. Stuart Hall, *The Hard Road to Renewal: Thatcherism and the Crisis of the Left* (London: Verso, 1988), 48.

60. See, for example, Nikolas Rose and Peter Miller, "Political Power Beyond the State: Problematics of Government," *British Journal of Sociology* 43, no. 2 (June 1992): 173–205.

61. Andrew Barry, Thomas Osborne, and Nikolas Rose, eds., *Foucault and Political Reason: Liberalism, Neo-Liberalism, and Rationalities of Government* (Abingdon, UK: Routledge, 1996).

62. Andrew Barry, Thomas Osborne, and Nikolas Rose, introduction to *Foucault and Political Reason*, 14.

63. Susan George, "A Short History of Neoliberalism: Twenty Years of Elite Economics and Emerging Opportunities for Structural Change," in *Global Finance: New Thinking on Regulating Capital Markets*, ed. W. Bello, N. Bullard, and K. Malhotra (London: Zed Books, 2000), 27–35.

64. Thomas Lemke, "'The Birth of Bio-Politics': Michel Foucault's Lecture at the Collège de France on Neo-liberal Governmentality," *Economy and Society* 30, no. 2 (2001): 190–207.

65. Paul Treanor, "Neoliberalism: Origins, Theory, Definition." The article, which is cited by nearly every theorist of neoliberalism from 2005 to 2015, has seemingly disappeared. All citations I found are to a now defunct website. It has appeared in no collected volumes, nor was it ever published in a journal.

66. Harvey, *Brief History of Neoliberalism*.

67. Foucault, *Birth of Biopolitics*.

68. Stanley Fish, "Neoliberalism and Higher Education," *Opinionator* (blog), *New York Times*, March 8, 2009, https://archive.nytimes.com/opinionator.blogs .nytimes.com/2009/03/08/neoliberalism-and-higher-education/.

69. Garrett, March 9, 2009, comment on Fish, "Neoliberalism and Higher Education," https://archive.nytimes.com/opinionator.blogs.nytimes.com/2009/03/08/neoliberalism-and-higher-education/#comment-136027.

70. David Harvey, *Brief History of Neoliberalism*, 2–3.

71. Gerstle, *Rise and Fall of the Neoliberal Order*, 2.

72. Daniel T. Rodgers, *Age of Fracture* (Cambridge, MA: Belknap Press of Harvard University Press, 2011), 10.

73. J. Bradford DeLong, *Slouching Towards Utopia: An Economic History of the Twentieth Century* (New York: Basic Books, 2022), 421–34.

74. The Dead Kennedys, "Holiday in Cambodia," track 13 on *Fresh Fruit for Rotting Vegetables*, Decay Music, 1979.

CHAPTER EIGHT

1. The decision by Bush's team, absent Bush, to change tactics is demonstrated in Peter Goldman and Tom Mathews, *The Quest for the Presidency 1988* (New York: Simon and Schuster, 1989), especially the chapter titled "Accentuate the Negative," 291–313, esp. 307–8; quotation from 304.

2. David S. Broder and Richard Morin, "Dukakis Takes Early Lead over Bush," *Washington Post*, May 27, 1988.

3. Tom Wicker, *George Herbert Walker Bush: A Penguin Life* (New York: Penguin, 2004).

4. For the story of the three-by-five note card, see Goldman and Mathews, *Quest for the Presidency 1988*, 307–8.

5. United Press International, "Reagan's Ultimate Insult: Dukakis 'a True Liberal,'" *Los Angeles Times*, June 29, 1988, https://www.latimes.com/archives/la-xpm-1988-06-29-mn-5057-story.html.

6. For "hemophiliac liberal," see Alterman and Mattson, *Cause*, 324. For "I'd be lost without . . . ," see Reagan to William F. Buckley Jr., 16 June 1962, in Kiron K. Skinner, Annelise Anderson, and Martin Anderson, eds., *Reagan: A Life in Letters* (New York: Simon and Schuster, 2004), 281.

7. Scott Walker, "The Wise Words of Ronald Reagan," *Washington Times*, October 29, 2021, https://www.washingtontimes.com/news/2021/oct/29/wise-words-ronald-reagan/.

8. Reagan quotation from Ronald and Nancy Reagan interview in the segment "Mister Right" on the popular TV newsmagazine. *60 Minutes*, season 8, episode 2, "Warning: May Be Fatal/Rubinstein/Mister Right," aired December 14, 1975, on CBS.

9. Reagan quoted in Rick Perlstein, *Invisible Bridge: The Fall of Nixon and the Rise of Reagan* (New York: Simon and Schuster, 2014), 676–77.

10. Reagan quoted in Steven V. Roberts, "President Asserts Democrats Cloak Their True Colors," *New York Times*, July 24, 1988, sec. 1, p. 1.

11. Donald L. Rheem, "GOP Platform Aims to Make Dukakis Walk the Plank," *Christian Science Monitor*, August 16, 1988, https://www.csmonitor.com/1988/0816/aform.html.

12. John M. Broder, "Reagan Launches Stern Attack on 'Liberal' Foes: Criticism of Dukakis Outweighs Praise for Bush as President's Speech Sets Tone for Convention," *Los Angeles Times*, August 15, 1988, https://www.latimes.com/archives/la-xpm-1988-08-15-mn-351-story.html.

13. Michael J. Bonin, "The Dreaded L-Word," *Harvard Crimson*, October 5, 1988, https://www.thecrimson.com/article/1988/10/5/the-dreaded-l-word-pbpbresident-reagan-criticizing/.

14. Bush quoted in Maureen Dowd, "Bush Traces How Yale Differs from Harvard," *New York Times*, June 11, 1988, sec. 1, p. 10.

15. Pearl quoted in Bonin, "Dreaded L-Word."

16. Arthur Schlesinger Jr., "Wake Up, Liberals, Your Time Has Come," *Washington Post*, May 1, 1988, https://www.washingtonpost.com/archive/opinions/1988/05/01/wake-up-liberals-your-time-has-come/fe6460fd-6c06-47c4-927b-82f6dc8a0e33/. On Schlesinger's critique of multiculturalism, see Arthur Schlesinger Jr., *The Disuniting of America: Reflections on a Multicultural Society* (New York: W. W. Norton, 1992).

17. Leonard Bernstein, "I'm a Liberal and Proud of It," *New York Times*, October 30, 1988, E25.

18. William F. Buckley Jr., "Please, Lenny, Just Stick to Your Music," *Daily News*, November 2, 1988, in box 101, folder 32, Bernstein collection.

19. "Please, Billy, a Little Respect," Leonard Bernstein to William F. Buckley Jr., 3 November 1988; Buckley to Tom Wolfe, Jan. 5, 1988 [*sic*], both in Bernstein collection.

20. Maureen Dowd, "Bush Ridicules Dukakis for Belatedly Saying That He Is a Liberal," *New York Times*, November 1, 1988, A26.

21. Dowd, "Bush Ridicules Dukakis."

22. Jerry Falwell, *Listen America!* (New York: Doubleday, 1980), 213.

23. Falwell, *Listen America!* 103.

24. A 1979 direct-mail solicitation from Jerry Falwell, quoted in Robert Wuthnow, *The Restructuring of American Religion: Society and Faith since World War II* (Princeton, NJ: Princeton University Press, 1998), 210.

25. Falwell quoted in Susan Friend Harding, *The Book of Jerry Falwell: Fundamentalist Language and Politics* (Princeton, NJ: Princeton University Press, 2000), 159.

26. Samuel Francis, "Message from MARs: The Social Politics of the New Right," in *The New Right Papers*, ed. Robert W. Whitaker (New York: St. Martin's Press, 1982), 64–83.

27. Francis, "Message from MARs."

28. Falwell quoted in Harding, *Book of Jerry Falwell*, 157.

29. LaHaye quoted in "Interview With . . . Tim LaHaye," *Modern Reformation* 4, no. 2 (Mar/Apr 1995), posted online August 14, 2007, https://www.modernreformation.org/resources/articles/interview-with-tim-lahaye.

30. LaHaye quoted in Jason C. Bivins, *The Fracture of Good Order: Christian Antiliberalism and the Challenge to American Politics* (Chapel Hill: University of North Carolina Press, 2003), 95.

31. Robison quoted in Howell Raines, "Reagan Backs Evangelicals in Their Political Activities," *New York Times*, August 23, 1980, sec. 1, p. 8.

32. Pat Robertson, "The Speech: A Strong Warning That Moral Decay Is Basic Trouble Facing the Nation," *New York Times*, January 14, 1988, A20.

33. Patrick J. Buchanan, "1992 Republican National Convention Speech, August 17, 1992," Patrick J. Buchanan (website), accessed January 9, 2024, http://buchanan.org/blog/1992-republican-national-convention-speech-148.

34. Bivins, *Fracture of Good Order*, 88.

35. Dobson quoted in Michael Cromartie, *No Longer Exiles: The Religious New Right in American Politics* (Washington, DC: Ethics and Public Policy Center, 1993), 52.

36. See Clifford J. Doerksen, *American Babel: Rogue Radio Broadcasters of the Jazz Age* (Princeton, NJ: Princeton University Press, 2005).

37. Hemmer, *Messengers of the Right*, 257.

38. Hemmer, *Messengers of the Right*, 257.

39. Hemmer, *Messengers of the Right*, 260.

40. For the rise of Rush Limbaugh, see Brian Rosenwald, *Talk Radio's America: How an Industry Took Over a Political Party That Took Over the United States* (Cambridge, MA: Harvard University Press, 2019).

41. Lewis Grossberger, "The Rush Hours," *New York Times Magazine*, December 16, 1990, sec. 6, p. 58.

42. Rush H. Limbaugh III, "Why Liberals Fear Me," *Policy Review*, Fall 1994, reposted February 18, 2021, on Heritage Foundation website, https://www.heritage.org/conservatism/commentary/why-liberals-fear-me.

43. Limbaugh, "Why Liberals Fear Me."

44. Rush H. Limbaugh III, *The Way Things Ought to Be* (New York: Pocket Books, 1992), x.

45. Limbaugh, *Way Things Ought to Be*, 180.

46. Limbaugh, *Way Things Ought to Be*, 299.

47. Rush H. Limbaugh III, *See, I Told You So* (New York: Pocket Books, 1993), 6.

48. Hemmer, *Messengers of the Right*, 265. Italics in original.

49. Gabriel Sherman, *The Loudest Voice in the Room: How the Brilliant, Bombastic Roger Ailes Built Fox News—and Divided a Country* (New York: Random House, 2014), xv.

50. Sherman, *Loudest Voice in the Room*, 33.

51. Sherman, *Loudest Voice in the Room*, xii.

52. Sherman, *Loudest Voice in the Room*, xii, xx.

53. Sherman, *Loudest Voice in the Room*, 201.

54. Hemmer, *Messengers of the Right*, 268.

55. James Atlas, "The Counter Counterculture," *New York Times Magazine*, February 12, 1995, https://www.nytimes.com/1995/02/12/magazine/the-counter-counterculture.html.

56. Ann Coulter, *Slander: Liberal Lies about the American Right* (New York: Crown Forum, 2002); Ann Coulter, *Treason: Liberal Treachery from the Cold War to the War on Terrorism* (New York: Crown Forum, 2003).

57. Ann Coulter, *Godless: The Church of Liberalism* (New York: Crown Forum, 2006), 1.

58. Ann Coulter, *Guilty: Liberal "Victims" and their Assault on America* (New York: Crown Forum, 2008), 13–14.

59. Ann Coulter, *Demonic: How the Liberal Mob Is Endangering America* (New York: Crown Forum, 2011); Ann Coulter, *Mugged: Racial Demagoguery from the Seventies to Obama* (New York: Crown Forum, 2012).

60. Coulter, *Guilty*, 264.

61. Coulter, *Godless*, 4.

62. Dinesh D'Souza, *Letters to a Young Conservative* (New York: Basic Books, 2002), 3.

63. D'Souza, *Letters*, 10.

64. D'Souza, *Letters*, 209.

65. Laura Ingraham, *Shut Up and Sing: How Elites from Hollywood, Politics, and the UN Are Subverting America* (Washington, DC: Regnery Publishing, 2003), 1.

66. Linda Chavez, *An Unlikely Conservative: The Transformation of an Ex-Liberal (Or, How I Became the Most Hated Hispanic in America)* (New York: Basic Books, 2002).

67. Thomas Sowell, *Black Rednecks and White Liberals* (New York: Encounter Books, 2005), 1–64.

68. Responses to the query "Who coined the term 'libtard'?" on Quora, accessed January 29, 2024, https://www.quora.com/Who-coined-the-term-libtard. The first respondent quoted goes by the handle Zed Clampet, and the second claims John Smith.

69. *Cambridge Advanced Learner's Dictionary and Thesaurus*, s.v. "libtard," accessed January 30, 2024, https://dictionary.cambridge.org/us/dictionary/english/libtard.

70. Urban Dictionary, s.v. "libtard," accessed January 30, 2024, https://www.urbandictionary.com/define.php?term=libtard.

71. For the story of at least one person's aversion to the political correctness surrounding the word *retarded*, see Olivia Nuzzi, "Trump Haters Turned Trump Voters," *New York* magazine, January 29–February 11, 2024, 9.

72. Chaya Raichik (@libsoftiktok), "Imagine if it was a MAGA mural . . . he would receive a reward!" X, February 13, 2024.

73. Esoteric Lifter (esoteric.lifter.memes), "Hey, man, how many sets do yuo [*sic*] have left?" TikTok, September 1, 2023, video, 0:23, https://www.tiktok.com/@esoteric.lifter.memes/video/7273832542745218347?lang=en.

74. Hyrum Lewis and Verlan Lewis, *The Myth of Left and Right: How the Political Spectrum Misleads and Harms America* (New York: Oxford University Press, 2023), 3.

75. Ingraham, *Shut Up and Sing*, 339.

76. Monica Hesse, "'Make Liberals Cry Again' Became the Battle Hymn of the Republicans under Trump," *Washington Post*, November 5, 2020, https://www.washingtonpost.com/lifestyle/style/trump-republican-liberal-tears-make-america-cry-again/2020/11/04/2342f0de-1eb0-11eb-90dd-abd0f7086a91_story.html.

77. Quoted in Kris Hartley, "Owning the Libs: Post-truth in Right-wing Political Discourse," *International Review of Public Policy* 5, no. 1 (2023): 64.

78. Grady Loy, "Exploring Mysteries Inside Trump Voters' Heads," *Asia Times*, September 19, 2020, https://asiatimes.com/2020/09/exploring-mysteries-inside-trump-voters-heads/.

79. Adam Sokol, "My Life on Troll Patrol: The Life of a Comment Moderator for a Right-Wing Website," *New York Times*, March 2, 2019, SR4.

80. Andrews quoted in Derek Robertson, "How 'Owning the Libs' Became the GOP's Core Belief," *Politico*, March 21, 2021, https://www.politico.com/news/magazine/2021/03/21/owning-the-libs-history-trump-politics-pop-culture-477203.

81. Kosloff quoted in D. Robertson, "How 'Owning the Libs' Became the GOP's Core Belief."

82. D. Robertson, "How 'Owning the Libs' Became the GOP's Core Belief."

83. Molly Jong-Fast, "Owning the Libs Is the Only GOP Platform," *Atlantic*, January 12, 2022, https://www.theatlantic.com/newsletters/archive/2022/01/owning-the-libs-is-the-only-gop-platform/676692/.

84. Bongino said it on the National Rifle Association's now-defunct television channel NRATV's *We Stand* show on October 4, 2018. It is now available to view at Media Matters for America, "NRATV's Dan Bongino: 'My Entire Life Right Now Is about Owning the Libs; That's It,'" accessed January 30, 2024, https://www.mediamatters.org/nratv/nratvs-dan-bongino-my-entire-life-right-now-about-owning-libs-thats-it.

85. Bongino quoted in Evan Osnos, "Maga-phone: Dan Bongino and the Big Business of Returning Trump to Power," *New Yorker*, January 3 and 10, 2022, 35.

86. Bongino quoted in Osnos, "Maga-phone," 35.

87. Osnos, "Maga-phone," 43.

CONCLUSION

1. Lynn Elber, "Live Debate on 'The West Wing' May Shame the Real Thing," *Seattle Times*, November 5, 2005.

2. "The Debate," *The West Wing*, season 7, episode 7, NBC Television, 2005.

3. Prominent among these might include Lilla, *Once and Future Liberal*; Gopnik, *A Thousand Small Sanities*; Lepore, *This America*; and Alterman and Mattson, *Cause*. There are also Traub, *What Was Liberalism?* A. Wolfe, *Future of Liberalism*; and David Leonhardt, *Ours Was the Shining Future: The Story of the American Dream* (New York: Random House, 2023).

4. Gopnik, *A Thousand Small Sanities*, 238, 7.

5. David Sessions, "The Emptiness of Adam Gopnik's Liberalism," *New Republic*, May 6, 2019, https://newrepublic.com/article/153781/emptiness-adam-gopniks-liberalism-review-thousand-small-sanities.

6. Malcolm Harris, "Are Your Commie Children Right? Adam Gopnik's Defense of Liberalism," *Bookforum*, April/May 2019, https://www.bookforum.com/print/2601/adam-gopnik-s-defense-of-liberalism-20827.

7. Timothy Garton Ash, "A Liberal Translation," *New York Times*, January 24, 2009, https://www.nytimes.com/2009/01/25/opinion/25gartonash-1.html.

8. Barack Obama, "Keynote Address at the 2004 Democratic National Convention, July 27, 2004," American Presidency Project, accessed July 27, 2024, https://www.presidency.ucsb.edu/node/277378.

9. Ash was not alone. See Douglas S. Massey, *Return of the "L" Word: A Liberal Vision for the New Century* (Princeton, NJ: Princeton University Press, 2005); and Robert Wexler, *Fire-Breathing Liberal: How I Learned to Survive (and Thrive) in the Contact Sport of Congress*, with David Fisher (New York: Thomas Dunne Books, 2008).

10. Neil Genzlinger, "Enter Laughing, From the Liberal Wing," *New York Times*, May 20, 2011, MB1.

11. Immanuel Wallerstein, *After Liberalism* (New York: New Press, 1995), 271.

12. Teixeira quoted in Zengerle, "Vanishing Moderate Democrat."

13. Reid J. Epstein and Nicholas Nehamas, "With Dueling Ads, Harris and Trump Both Try to Define Her as a Candidate," *New York Times*, July 30, 2024, https://www.nytimes.com/2024/07/30/us/politics/kamala-harris-ad.html.

14. Barack Obama, "Address by President Obama to the 71st Session of the United Nations General Assembly," September 20, 2016, White House press release, https://obamawhitehouse.archives.gov/the-press-office/2016/09/20/address -president-obama-71st-session-united-nations-general-assembly.

15. Lydia Saad, "Democrats' Identification as Liberal Now 54%, a New High," Gallup, January 12, 2023, https://news.gallup.com/poll/467888/democrats -identification-liberal-new-high.aspx.

16. Lionel Barber, Henry Foy, and Alex Barker, "Vladimir Putin Says Liberalism Has 'Become Obsolete,'" *Financial Times* (London), June 27, 2019, https://www.ft .com/content/670039ec-98f3-11e9-9573-ee5cbb98ed36.

17. Xi Jinping quoted in Elizabeth Economy, "Xi Jinping's New World Order: Can China Remake the International System?" *Foreign Affairs*, January/February 2022, accessed July 27, 2024, https://www.foreignaffairs.com/china/xi-jinpings-new -world-order.

18. V-Dem, "Varieties of Democracy," accessed July 27, 2024, https://v-dem .net/. For more on the fate of liberal democracies, see Damien Cave, "War Serves as Warning That Liberal Democracy Is Facing a Dire Threat," *New York Times*, March 5, 2022, A12.

19. Marc Ambinder, "Hillary Clinton Insists She's No Liberal," *Atlantic*, July 23, 2007, https://www.theatlantic.com/politics/archive/2007/07/hillary-clinton-insists -shes-no-liberal/50059/.

20. For a succinct description of this schema, see the Forbes interview with Kesler, "The Roots of Liberalism," *Forbes*, updated July 11, 2012, https://www.forbes .com/2009/06/04/obama-liberalism-conservative-opinions-columnists-charles -kesler.html. For how this schema became crucial to the modern right, see Steven M. Teles, "How the Progressives Became the Tea Party's Mortal Enemy: Networks, Movements, and the Political Currency of Ideas," in *The Progressives' Century: Political Reform, Constitutional Government, and the Modern American State*, ed. Stephen Skowronek, Stephen M. Engel, and Bruce Ackerman (New Haven, CT: Yale University Press, 2016), 453–77, also available in online edition published May 18, 2017, https://doi.org/10.12987/yale/9780300204841.003.0021. Kesler's schema has picked up support. See, for example, television host Glenn Beck's book *Liars*, which tried to warn readers of progressives' supposed "insatiable thirst for control and betterment of others; the determination to build a massive, all-controlling welfare state that holds the rest of us hostage to its preferences and whims; and the flirtation with totalitarianism masked by the guise of political correctness. Progressives regularly espouse ideas and support causes that openly involve the subjugation, murder, or mutilation of their fellow human beings, always in the name

of a better world for all." Glenn Beck, *Liars: How Progressives Exploit Our Fears for Power and Control* (New York: Threshold Editions, 2017), 3.

21. Eleanor Roosevelt quoted in Alterman and Mattson, *Cause*, 56.

22. Barack Obama quoted in "Obama to Business Owners: 'You Didn't Build That,'" Fox News, updated December 23, 2015, https://www.foxnews.com/politics/obama-to-business-owners-you-didnt-build-that.

23. Joseph Biden, interview with Robert Costa, *CBS News Sunday Morning*, CBS, August 12, 2024, https://www.youtube.com/watch?v=xcfosMHL-vA (accessed November 26, 2024).

24. Kamala Harris, "Remarks by Vice President Harris at Swearing-In Ceremony of Commissioners for the White House Initiative on Advancing Educational Equity, Excellence, and Economic Opportunity for Hispanics." The White House, May 10, 2023, https://www.whitehouse.gov/briefing-room/speeches-remarks/2023/05/10/remarks-by-vice-president-harris-at-swearing-in-ceremony-of-commissioners-for-the-white-house-initiative-on-advancing-educational-equity-excellence-and-economic-opportunity-for- hispanics/.

INDEX

Spain, 18

"Spiro Agnew Knows Best" (*Life* article), 123

Stalin, Joseph, 40, 42–43, 64

Stearns, Harold, 23

Stein, Andrew, 110

stereotypes: equality and, 103–4; liberal connotations and, 6; prejudice and, 6, 83, 92–93, 97, 99, 103, 110–13, 137, 153; racial issues and, 83, 92–93, 97, 99, 103; radicalism and, 110

Stern, Howard, 195

Stevenson, Adlai, 34, 52, 56

Stimson, James A., 2–3

Stop-Carter movement, 157

STOP ERA (Stop Taking Our Privileges ERA), 126–27

Students for a Democratic Society (SDS): left-wing politics and, 60, 74–79; Mailer on, 60; March on Washington and, 76–77; radicalism and, 60, 74–79, 110; Vietnam War and, 76–77

Sweden, 17–18

Taft, Robert, 34

Taft Hartley Act, 38, 59

talk radio, 195, 200

Tammany Hall, 142

taxes: Bernstein and, 188; Bivins and, 194; breaks, 9, 171; Buckley and, 50; Dukakis and, 184, 189–90; elites and, 209; George H. W. Bush and, 189–90; income, 22, 167; left-wing politics and, 58, 61, 71; McCarthy and, 48; Murdoch and, 198; negative connotations and, 137, 140; neoliberalism and, 161, 165–68, 171, 173, 175; owning the libs and, 208; progressives and, 22; radicalism and, 114, 122, 129; Roosevelt and, 26; Taft-Hartley Act and, 38; Trump and, 209; wealthy class and, 32

Teixeira, Ruy, 216

terror, 7, 16, 56, 195

Texas Republican State Convention, 184

Thatcher, Margaret, 177, 180

Thomases, Susan, 167

Thurow, Lester, 171

"Time for Choosing, A" (Reagan), 185

Time magazine, 28, 43, 81, 234n1

Tojo, 30

totalitarianism: Alinsky and, 63; Arendt and, 64; Beck and, 253n20; Dewey and, 28; Hartz and, 65; left-wing politics and, 58, 63–65, 70, 75, 77–78; McCarthy and, 75; progressives and, 253n20; use of term, 232n2

Tracy, Spencer, 103

Treanor, Paul, 178

Treason (Coulter), 201

Trilling, Lionel, 31, 44

"Troubled American, The" (*Newsweek*), 131

Truman, David, 77

Truman, Harry S.: Buckley and, 35, 40; communism and, 35–36; Frankel on, 34; George H. W. Bush and, 189; Kennedy and, 189; left-wing politics and, 63, 66; McCarthy and, 35–36; Soviets and, 40

Trump, Donald: authoritarianism and, 217; Black people and, 210; centrism and, 218; fear and, 209–10; labeling and, 216, 218; political correctness and, 209, 251n71; popular vote and, 217; taxes and, 209

Trump, Donald, Jr., 209

Tsongas, Paul, 167–69, 175

Tufts University, 151

Tugwell, Rex, 15

Tyranny of Clichés, The (Goldberg), 204

Udall, Morris K., 156

unemployment, 11, 20, 25, 131, 180

Unlikely Conservative, An (Chavez), 204